International Law, Security and Ethics

This book examines the different ways in which the laws governing the use of force and the conduct of warfare have become subject to intense scrutiny and contestation since the initiation of the 'war on terror'.

Since the end of the Cold War, the nature of security challenges has changed radically and this change has been recognised by the UN, governments and academics around the world. The 9/11 attacks and the subsequent launch of the 'war on terror' added a new dimension to this debate on the nature and utility of international law due to the demands from some quarters for a change in the laws governing self-defence and humanitarian intervention. This book analyses the nature of these debates and focuses on key issues that have led to the unprecedented contemporary questioning of both the utility and composition of international law on the use of force as well as the practicability of using force, including handling of 'prisoners' and 'security risks'. It also identifies the sources of division and addresses the capacities of security policy and international law to adapt to the changed international environment.

This book will be of much interest to students of international law, war and conflict studies, and IR and Security Studies in general.

Aidan Hehir is Senior Lecturer in International Relations with the Department of Politics and International Relations at the University of Westminster. He has authored/edited four books.

Natasha Kuhrt is Lecturer in War Studies on the MA International Peace and Security Programme in the Department of War Studies, King's College London, and the author of *Russian Policy towards China and Japan* (Routledge, 2007).

Andrew Mumford is Lecturer in International Security in the Department of Politics, University of Sheffield.

Contemporary Security Studies

Series Editors: James Gow and Rachel Kerr
King's College London

This series focuses on new research across the spectrum of international peace and security, in an era where each year throws up multiple examples of conflicts that present new security challenges in the world around them.

International Law, Security and Ethics

Policy challenges in the post-9/11 world

Edited by
Aidan Hehir, Natasha Kuhrt and
Andrew Mumford

Routledge
Taylor & Francis Group

LONDON AND NEW YORK

First published 2011
by Routledge
2 Park Square, Milton Park, Abingdon, Oxon, OX14 4RN

Simultaneously published in the USA and Canada
by Routledge
711 Third Avenue, New York, NY 10017

Routledge is an imprint of the Taylor & Francis Group, an informa business

First issued in paperback 2013

Typeset in Times New Roman by
Swales & Willis Ltd, Exeter, Devon

British Library Cataloguing in Publication Data
A catalogue record for this book is available from the British Library

Library of Congress Cataloging-in-Publication Data
International law, security and ethics : policy challenges in the post-911 world /
Edited by Aidan Hehir, Natasha Kuhrt and Andrew Mumford.
    p. cm.
    1. International law—Moral and ethical aspects. 2. Security, International.
    3. War (International law) 4. Terrorism—Prevention—Law and legislation.
    5. Self-defense (Law) I. Hehir, Aidan, 1977– II. Kuhrt, Natasha, 1966–
    III. Mumford, Andrew.
    KZ5588.I58 2011
    341.6—dc22
    2010048777

ISBN13: 978-0-415-60742-1 (hbk)
ISBN13: 978-0-415-72410-4 (pbk)
ISBN13: 978-0-203-81608-0 (ebk)

Contents

PART III
Self-defence   109

Contributors

Don Carrick is Project Director of the Military Ethics Education Network, Institute for Applied Ethics, University of Hull

Professor James Connelly is a Professor of Politics at the Department of Politics and International Studies, University of Hull

James Gow is Professor of International Peace and Security in the Department of War Studies, King's College London

Dr Aidan Hehir is a Senior Lecturer in International Relations with the Department of Politics and International Relations at the University of Westminster

Thomas Jones is a partner in the International Capital Markets department, Allen & Overy LLP London

Rachel Kerr is Senior Lecturer in War Studies in the Department of War Studies, King's College London

Elaine Korzak is a PhD candidate at the Department of Law, London School of Economics

Natasha Kuhrt is Lecturer in War Studies on the MA International Peace and Security Programme in the Department of War Studies, King's College London

Dr Andrew Mumford is a Lecturer in International Relations at the Department of Politics, University of Sheffield

Professor Nigel White is a Professor of International Law at the School of Law, University of Nottingham

Acknowledgements

Aidan would like to thank Sarah, Esmé, Elise and Iris for all their love, fun and support.
Natasha would like to thank James for all his love and support, and Hector and Kitty for their love, and for keeping me 'grounded'.
Andrew would like to thank Hannah for her love, support and encouragement.

1   Introduction

Policy challenges to international law, security and ethics in the post-9/11 world

Andrew Mumford and Natasha Kuhrt

The discourse surrounding the execution of the 'War on Terror' has revolved around a triumvirate of interdependent issues: security, law and ethics. Indeed, the conduct of the War on Terror has been questioned legally, challenged ethically and has yet to arguably demonstrate a significant security dividend for those states prosecuting it. These three areas are related, each having an effect on the other. This volume is an endeavour to explore the underlying tension in their co-existence. For example, is a security solution necessarily ethically reconcilable or legally justifiable? 'Extraordinary rendition' has, for instance, been utilised as a security measure to remove detained 'enemy combatants' (note the nuanced legal semantics) from conflict zones for secret interrogation in third countries. Ostensibly such a measure could be construed as a necessary step towards extracting timely intelligence, thus contributing to the wider security situation in favour of the counter-terrorists. However, the methods harnessed to fulfil this security objective – hooding, 'water-boarding', and sleep depravation – nullify any security dividend by ethically compromising and legally stretching the entire liberal democratic premise of those polities engaged in the War on Terror. Such conduct runs the risk of creating more long-standing ills than the problems it sought to overcome in the first place.

All these chapters also address to varying degrees the security, legal and ethical approaches to the 'Global War on Terror', and the lack of consensus in many areas as to how to deal with the threats we face. Even the notion of security itself is a contested concept: and the locus of security for that matter – should we focus on human security, i.e. the security of the individual? Should national security take precedence? How can mutual security be assured? All the chapters to a great extent focus on the normative, legal, ethical and political considerations of the topic. The way in which we deal with these threats in policy terms is indicative of the nature and scope of the consensus regarding key issues.

Arguably one of the most worrying developments in the policy realm since 9/11 is the way in which the manipulation of legal codes and the ignoring of ethical norms have been justified in the name of 'security'. This of course contains the underlying normative assumption that security is a state than can be achieved irrespective of legal or ethical conduct. The damage done to the reputation of the United States, and to a certain extent the United Kingdom, through their prosecution of the War on Terror and their willing authorisation of acts such as prolonged detention (Guantanamo Bay) and unilateral invasion (Iraq) in the name of neutralising security threats, may actually have increased other security threats to these countries in the long term. The potential for this has been carried through the conduit of the global media and internet which has been able to purvey images and stories of incidents such as prisoner abuse at Abu Ghraib or the heavy-handed US siege of Fallujah in 2004. These events were thus able to be interpreted, or indeed manipulated, by various socio-religious groups around the world. The era of globalisation and the instant modes of mass communication that come with it has ensured that that security measures taken by the West have the potential to be recruiting sergeants for those groups keen to exploit any legal or ethical vacuum in which they are enacted. Although not sharing the same legal or ethical code as Western liberal democracies, Al Qaeda has been effective at turning American legal and ethical discrepancies into an effective narrative that attempts to reinforce a perception in the Muslim world of American brutality and deviousness.

The 'War on Terror' challenged many seminal legal and moral norms and has had a profound impact on the trajectory of international law. While international law on the use of force has always been the source of debate, the nature of the contemporary contestation is uniquely holistic. Since the end of the Cold War, the nature of security challenges has changed radically, as has been recognised by the UN, governments and academics around the world. In that period, some aspects of international law have changed as a result – chiefly the use of enforcement powers under Chapter VII of the UN Charter by the UN Security Council. Yet, those changes were often surrounded by intense debate. And where the Security Council could not agree, security challenges remained, giving rise to major areas of contestation about the ethics, law and praxis of, first, humanitarian intervention, and, later, self-defence and other aspects of war. The debates on humanitarian intervention in the 1990s exposed significant divisions on the legal prescriptions against external interference in the affairs of sovereign states and led to calls for the wholesale reform of international law and, in some cases, the subversion of existing legal tenets. The September 11 attacks and the subsequent launch of the War on Terror added a new dimension to this debate on the nature and utility of international law due to the demands from some quarters for a change in the laws governing self-defence. The War on Terror thus constituted a merging of issues that had arisen in debates on humanitarian intervention and UN enforcement action in the 1990s with pressure for a new understanding of self-defence, which challenged the relevance of existing instruments and interpretations of international law. It was clear that existing law was often ill fitted to the new era. It has also become clear that practitioners judged a need to act, despite the tension with existing law. The imperatives of action were entwined with two frameworks of wrong and right – ethics and law, with each corner of this triangle influencing the other in debate and decision. This volume explores the nexus of these issues through a set of studies comprising new research and new thinking in a complex and, as yet, largely uncharted terrain.

This collection focuses on the different ways in which the laws governing the use of force and the conduct of warfare – in terms of both self-defence and humanitarian intervention – have therefore become subject to intense scrutiny and contestation and many sources of division remain unresolved in the sphere of contemporary security. This book analyses the nature of these debates and focuses on key issues that have led to the unprecedented contemporary questioning of both the utility and composition of international law on the use of force as well as the practicability and morality of using force. This collection identifies the sources of division and addresses the capacities of security policy, international law and moral reasoning to adapt to the changed international environment. The chapters comprise a mixture of analyses of specific issues such as counter-terrorism, self-defence, humanitarian intervention and cyber attack, as well as broader reflections on the role of international law and ethics in contemporary international relations.

In Chapter 2 Nigel White details how international law has come to accommodate counter-terrorism issues before and after the 9/11 attacks. Despite long-standing difficulties in achieving global consensus on a definition of terrorism, White argues that common ground has now been found, therefore making contemporary counter-terror initiatives more amenable to international law. Urging that the UN Security Council deal with individual instances of serious cases of terrorism, rather than taking a more blanket legislative approach, White argues that states should rely on a mixture of cooperation and lawful coercive techniques (which would not include rendition, torture, or arbitrary detention) to ensure that suspected terrorists are brought to trial, working within existing bilateral, multilateral and regional cooperation regimes. He concludes that the criminal justice paradigm should be strengthened by consolidating the raft of treaties, agreeing a definition, and by allowing both the International Criminal Court and the Security Council to play a role in the counter-terrorism treaty regime.

Andrew Mumford argues in Chapter 3 that there is a popular misconception in our understanding of Al Qaeda and analysis accordingly needs to shift away from the tactical level of terrorism to strategic level of insurgency. Acts of terror, such as 9/11, should not be the primary guide by which we define Al Qaeda. Their international aims, presence and operational scope possess traits of a global insurgency. Localised insurgencies where Islamist groups are the chief protagonists of violence should be seen as parts of the whole *jihad*. Accordingly, Al Qaeda is more potent as an entity when its dispersed hubs are acting semi-autonomously in pursuit of a shared strategic goal. In policy terms what is clear, he argues, is that Al Qaeda's conflation of terrorism as a tactic and insurgency as a strategy necessitates a hybrid response. The transcendence of state boundaries in the international *jihadi* insurgency, both operationally and ideationally, has meant that the national security of states, and broader global peace and security, now has to be interpreted interdependently. In order for the Al Qaeda threat to be adequately suppressed there is an obvious need for domestic counter-terrorism to be conjoined with a wider, transnational politico-military counter-insurgency strategy.

James Connelly and Don Carrick analyse the War on Terror in a moral dimension in Chapter 4. In essence they argue that the rule of law and the demands and constraints of morality must be restored to their rightful place in the scheme of international security. Highlighting the flawed assumption that there is an automatic equivocation between law and morality, Connelly and Carrick argue that an understanding of Just War Theory cannot be sustained if it suggests that a war or invasion can take place upon the completion of a legal check list in the absence of fully developed moral reasoning. The authors assert that simply because war is being fought in a 'time of terror', we should be wary of any sort of profound change to the rules or criteria of *jus in bello*.

Within the context of the evolving nature of the character of the body of law and the character of war in the decade since the War on Terror was initiated, James Gow and Rachel Kerr explore in Chapter 5 how four particular issues have tested the interface between law and war: the transition of self-defence to the notion of 'targeted killings'; the issue of detaining quasi-Prisoners of War and the Geneva Convention; rendition, torture and abuse; and the juridification of armed conflict. These issues demonstrate the difficulties of operating in situations such as that encountered in Iraq where lines between war fighting and policing and between combatant and non-combatant are increasingly blurred. The law, Gow and Kerr argue, which has already begun to change, will continue to evolve in relation to such changes in armed conflict and the political environment as the War on Terror continues.

In Chapter 6, Aidan Hehir analyses the nature of discretion in the behaviour of the Permanent Five members of the UN Security Council (P5). He argues that because the P5 exercise a high degree of discretion when applying international law, an inconsistent level of global response to intra-state conflicts and crises is pervasive. Hehir explores how possible reforms to the UN system could impact upon the way in which humanitarian intervention is considered and conducted, ultimately concluding that without an independent international military force and an independent mechanism empowered to determine when this force can be deployed then the perceived legitimacy of international law will steadily erode.

In Chapter 7, examining humanitarian intervention and peacebuilding, Natasha Kuhrt suggests that while Iraq and 9/11 may indeed have impacted negatively on the human security agenda which is increasingly posited as an alternative narrative to state security, there is room for optimism. This lies in the growing recognition that the third pillar of the R2P, 'responsibility to rebuild' may be a means of preventing states from sliding back into conflict. The occupation of Iraq, while contentious, did not prevent approval of a UN Peacebuilding Commission at the 2005 Summit. However, problems remain in that peacebuilding can so often be viewed as a quasi-imperialist venture and, of course, the link with a kind of preventive intervention which conflates human rights abuses and a terrorist threat is dangerous. The War on Terror has highlighted the continuing preoccupation with national security, yet there is an opportunity for greater dialogue between the human security agenda and the individual security agendas of states. By returning to the core values of the Charter and emphasising the notion of a positive peace, embodied in the peacebuilding norm, Kuhrt argues that the original consensus which established the UN Charter may be partially regained.

Chapter 8 sees James Gow note how the prospect of internationally accepted norms for pre-emptive self-defence raises severe legal, ethical and security dilemmas. Locating the premise of self-defence in international history and law, Gow goes on to assess how the 9/11 attacks radically shifted the way in which the United States could legitimise a resort to military action under the guise of the 'War on Terror'. His chapter deconstructs notions of pre-emption, prevention and immediacy in international relations and international law, as well as contextualising contemporary discussions of necessity and proportionality. Gow utilises three hypothetical scenarios of self-defence in order to illustrate the role, impact and consequences of the above issues in contemporary global security and reflect upon the nature and meaning of 'armed attack' as a catalyst to acts of self-defence.

Thomas Jones aims in Chapter 9 to radically invert traditional understandings of the legal regime regarding the use of force. In particular, Jones argues that the jurisprudence that has developed around the right of self-defence included in Article 51 of the UN Charter has created an overly restrictive and unworkable legal regime for states to defend themselves against these uses of force. Jones concludes that by putting reasonable and flexible, but still robust, legal restrictions on the use of force in self-defence, states should feel compelled to argue for the legality, and therefore the legitimacy, of their uses of force within a construct where the parameters are clear and the requirements are difficult to discount.

Computer network attacks have become an increasingly prevalent mode of security breach in the twenty-first century. In Chapter 10 Elaine Korzak analyses whether cyber attacks can be interpreted as a use of 'force' in contemporary international relations, or perceived as a modern form of armed attack. The chapter also assesses the impact of cyber attack upon humanitarian norms. Ultimately, Korzak states, international law regulating cyberspace has not kept pace with the rapid advances in information technology over the past few decades, requiring states to fundamentally assess the legal frameworks they have in place to mitigate the impact of so-called 'eWMDs'.

All these chapters suggest that using the existing body of international law may well be insufficient: the Just War Tradition is a unique area where ethics, politics, law and security are conjoined, although it has tended to be rather too state-centric. The question of legitimacy is key, in particular where law is flimsy or non-existent, or state practice is inconsistent. Ethical considerations then come to the fore. However, the current lack of consensus on even what constitutes a 'just' world order is concerning. Moreover, the increased emphasis on national security after 9/11 has tended to take precedence, which suggests not only a failure to understand the fact that the new threats know no borders, but also tends to mean a move away from collective security and a common understanding of rules and norms. Collectively, the chapters in this book hold that the very *in*security felt by the West, especially the United States, since 9/11 should not be conjoined with the antonyms of the other factors in the triumvirate: *il*legal and *un*ethical. If indeed a 'war' on terrorism can be won, progress will certainly be stultified if it comes at the price of compromising the legal and ethical principles that uphold not only our societies but the broader international order.

Part I
Framing the issue

2 Terrorism, security and international law

Nigel White*

Counter-terrorism involving actions against non-state groups such as Al-Qaeda falls outside the traditional state-to-state structures of international law. However, with the developing concern for human rights protection and the notion of individual responsibility for international crimes, international law has extended its reach to cover terrorism and counter-terrorism. Early arguments in the League of Nations era that an international court should be created to try terrorists did not succeed, and it was not until the 1960s that the United Nations (UN) turned its attention to the matter when faced with Palestinian terrorist atrocities. The Cold War approach was to try and tackle the issue in a state-based, consensual manner, reflecting the traditional values of international law. The post-Cold War era saw new trends by both governments and international organisations in the form of executive-led security/military approaches that challenge international legal paradigms, while also seeing other more consensual, multilateral instruments which take a criminal justice/human rights approach. The development of more coercive responses alongside consensual ones was accelerated by the events of 11 September 2001 (9/11).

Despite there now being a number of instruments and methods of counter-terrorism, there are still few fixed points in international law concerning terrorism reflected in the lack of agreement over the definition in the Draft Comprehensive Convention. The freedom fighter/terrorist debate signifies that, to some extent at least, international law will continue to oscillate between the security imperative requiring coercive measures to tackle the terrorist threat and concern for protecting the human rights of those rightly or wrongly suspected of terrorism. This chapter, however, does conclude that there are signs of consensus, and that there can be agreement on fundamentals and so it may be possible to develop a counter-terrorism response that comes within the rule of law.

In general it must be borne in mind that human rights laws have flexibility within them that should be able to accommodate security concerns, and that derogation is allowed from a number of human rights in genuine cases of emergency. Also if

---

* This chapter is based on evidence given to the All Party Parliamentary Inquiry into Tackling Terrorism, 22 May 2007.

terrorist acts are committed during an armed conflict, international humanitarian law has a variety of mechanisms for dealing with it. In other words, the law should be able to accommodate the security imperative of being able to effectively combat terrorism and thus protect the lives of civilians as the likely targets of terrorist attacks. Within this framework the chapter tackles a number of key issues in the area of international law and terrorism; issues which highlight the aforementioned tension between achieving security and respecting international law, including human rights. It attempts to identify whether a reconciliation of these sometimes competing objectives is possible.

Multilateralism in the Cold War

During the Cold War, international legal responses to terrorism, especially Palestinian terrorism of the 1960s and 1970s, were possible but they were limited. In that period international law relating to terrorism generally respected the principles of state sovereignty and non-intervention by specifying crimes (hijacking, seizure of ships, placing on board aircraft explosive devices, attacks on airports, on oil platforms and nuclear facilities . . .), and enforcing the law by means of a number of treaties.[1]

Treaties are consensual – states can choose whether to ratify them or not. Furthermore, the treaty crimes created were to be enforced by a 'prosecute or extradite' formula, meaning that the state holding the suspects could decide whether to prosecute them itself or extradite to states willing to prosecute. Add to this an acceptance of prosecutorial discretion by the holding state, and its sovereignty was respected. State sovereignty was also respected by these treaties because the crimes created were to be enforced by national criminal justice systems, not by any international court or body.

Thus terrorism in the Cold War period was largely responded to by a criminal justice approach as opposed to a military approach, although Israel provided the main exception to this. Israel regularly struck at terrorist targets using military force at a time and in a manner of its choosing, and was normally condemned for this. Similarly when the US responded to Libyan terrorism in 1986 by using military force, it was condemned by the General Assembly for breaching international law.

The post-1945 world order initiated by the UN Charter seemed to remove the concept of 'war' from the lexicon of international law. This meant that for the norms of the Charter to apply there had to be a 'threat or use of force', which was prohibited except for self-defence or action authorised by the Security Council. In the period 1945–89, again with the possible exception of Israel, states did not accept the idea in law of a continuing war against terrorism or terrorists in which there would be intermittent blows and counter-blows ranging across decades.

The post-Cold War period has seen a concerted effort by a number of powerful states to expand the law concerning terrorism. This has been done by supplementing, sometimes replacing the criminal law approach of the 1960s and 1970s with a collective security, occasionally military, approach. Acts of terrorism are seen not just as issues for national and international criminal justice, but as threats to the peace for the Security Council to deal with, and possibly for states to respond to using their right of self-defence.

Three specific changes will be highlighted at this stage and will be returned to later. First of all, starting with the Lockerbie bombing in the late 1980s, the Security Council's powers under Chapter VII were seen as key to circumventing, sometimes overriding, the cumbersome and often ineffective treaty machinery of the 1960s and 70s. In 1992 the Security Council imposed measures on Libya designed to force it to hand over the two suspects, in effect overriding the extradite or prosecute formula in the Montreal Convention of 1971, which covered the offence of placing on board aircraft an explosive device. The Security Council's powers have since been used more widely against states and individuals, and have also taken on a wider lawmaking aspect by requiring states to combat terrorism in a number of ways.

Secondly, the military response to 9/11 saw a concerted effort to reform the right of self-defence in relation to the invasion of Afghanistan in 2001, and less convincingly in relation to the invasion of Iraq in 2003.

Finally, the Israeli vision of a continuing war with an open-ended right of defence against terrorism seemed to be gaining credence with the invocation of the war on terror.

The international legal journey in the post-1945 period has been from the relatively limited, often ineffective responses to Palestinian terrorism of the 1960s, to the much broader legislative, military and penal responses of the post-Cold War, post-9/11 era. It is not easy to evaluate whether there is a consensus in the international community for some or all of these changes. There is a recognition that the law developed during the Cold War was too weak, but that does not mean that changes either made or contemplated have all been accepted by the international community, nor does it mean that they have increased the effectiveness of the international response. Some of the developments seem to be positively welcomed, others are met with silence. While dissent is not all that prominent in many of the new areas, it might be questioned whether silence can amount to acceptance in a climate of fear – fear of being the target of terrorism, but also fear of being seen to be on the side of the terrorists.

The 'war on terror'

On one level the phrase 'war on terror' can simply be seen as a non-technical or rhetorical one used by political leaders in the same vein as 'war on drugs' or 'war on poverty', but because terrorism involves armed violence and therefore is closer to war in a literal sense there is a temptation to view it as having a deeper, legal meaning. Indeed, this is the perception created by President Bush when he declared war on terrorism in the immediate aftermath of 9/11, namely that there is a continuing state of hostilities similar to other major conflicts or wars.[2] The picture portrayed is of a violent war or 'hot' war, in contrast to the 'Cold' War which was symbolised by confrontation without violence. The reality is that while the superpowers did not clash directly many people lost their lives in ideologically fuelled wars in Indo-China, Africa and Latin America during the Cold War, losses that eclipse those suffered during the current war on terror. Nevertheless, the period of the 'war on terror' (2001–) marks the highpoint of the military/security response to combating terrorism. Though the US and the UK, the main state-protagonists, have toned down their rhetoric with changes in government, military involvement against the Taliban and Al-Qaeda has been escalated in Afghanistan and has spread to Pakistan, targeted killings using remote-controlled drones, administrative detentions of terrorist suspects and their illegal rendition, all aspects of the war on terror in the immediate post-9/11 era, have continued to be used.

Legally speaking invoking the concept of 'war' in the 21st century is problematic and counterproductive. In the 19th century there was a developed doctrine of 'war' in international law which required formal declarations, but this was swept away in 1945 with the UN Charter prohibiting the threat or use of force by states (the *jus ad bellum*), and the Geneva Conventions of 1949 using the phrase 'armed conflict' to signify the conditions when international humanitarian law would apply to protect the wounded, prisoners of war and civilians (the *jus in bello*). While declaring war might remain necessary for a few states to satisfy internal constitutional laws, in international law the doctrine of 'war' was thought to be dead. However, the constant usage of the term in the phrase 'war on terror' could be seen as an attempt to revert to some older legal order, to signify that it is not necessary to analyse each terrorist attack and the response to it in terms of whether the response was a legitimate exercise of self-defence, instead the blows and counter-blows are simply seen as part of a continuing war. If the war on terror is seen in this light then the rules of the UN Charter regulating the use of force by states do not apply. The stage where the law against war (the *jus ad bellum*) is applicable has been passed.

Israel has made this argument since its inception in 1948 – that it is in a continual state of war against terrorism and it can pick and choose when it decides to take military action to combat those that use or threaten force against it. Such an argument has not been accepted certainly during the 20th century. But if this argument has been adopted by the US and UK since 2001 then, *de facto*, the war on terror probably stretches back to the attacks on the USS Cole in 2000, US embassies in Africa in 1998, and the World Trade Center in 1993, and may stretch on not only until Al-Qaeda has been defeated but possibly international terrorism generally, as the war keeps widening.

If the vision of a continuing war is correct then the applicable legal regime is the law of war (the *jus in bello*), which regulates the types of weapons used and the targets chosen as well as protecting civilians and non-combatants. It might be argued that the United States' detention of what it terms 'unlawful combatants' at Guantanamo Bay fits in with this vision, though the United States has adopted what at best could be called 'unorthodox' interpretations of the Geneva Conventions in terms of categorisation of detainees;[3] and at worse serious breaches of human rights law and international humanitarian law in terms of their treatment while in detention (for instance by the use of simulated drowning interrogation technique known as waterboarding).[4] Despite transgressing humanitarian law, the intention presumably is that this new type of prisoner of (the) war (on terror) can be detained indefinitely until the 'war' is over. Whether the war is the continuing conflict in Afghanistan (increasingly spilling over into Pakistan) where most of the detainees were captured or whether it is the wider war on terrorism is unclear, adding to the uncertainty of the period of detention. Though the Obama administration wishes to close Guantanamo in 2010 by trying some detainees before special military commissions (with reduced due process guarantees, and with few restrictions on admissible evidence)[5] and some before US Courts, it is likely that there will remain some prisoners who will be transferred to US prisons where they will be detained indefinitely.

The vision of a continuing war is also used as a cover for targeted killings of suspected terrorists, for example the use of a remote drone by the United States on suspected terrorists in Yemen in 2002, the greater use of such weapons by the US in Pakistan in 2008–9, and the developed Israeli policy of targeted killings in the occupied territories against terrorist leaders. If in a state of war against a terrorist enemy these can be seen as lawful targeting of enemy combatants; if in a state of peace they are extra-judicial killings that violate human rights law, particularly the right to life and the right to a fair trial.[6]

Powerful states combating terrorism may view the invocation of a continuing war not only as a useful rhetorical tool but also as a legal justification for pursuing the policies outlined above, despite there being limited evidence that the idea of a 'war on terror' is accepted in a technical international legal sense. Though a device that brings some short-term benefits in terms of giving an excuse for by-passing normal human rights standards, in the longer term its continual invocation will undermine the principles of the UN Charter and the objectives behind those rules.

One of the reasons for the development of the post-1945 *jus ad bellum* – that force is prohibited except in self-defence in response to an armed attack or if authorised by the Security Council – is to stop conflicts escalating, from widening with each blow being followed by an even more devastating counter-blow.[7] There is a clear danger of this happening if it is accepted that there is a continual state of war. Arguably it has already happened with the invasions of Afghanistan and Iraq being sparked by the attacks of 9/11. Despite this there is insufficient evidence of any clear legal belief in the majority of governments, or what international lawyers term *opinio juris*, that the fundamental rules of the UN Charter have been discarded or at best radically modified. In international relations it remains accurate to state that we are not in a global state of war, legally speaking we are in a time of peace, a peace that is ruptured by terrorism and by other acts of international violence as well as localised armed conflicts such as that found in Afghanistan since 2001. Outside of that armed conflict, this means that each terrorist attack or threat of attack must be evaluated individually in terms of whether a forceful response is justified, and each response must be proportionate to the attack or threat of attack.

Of course this does not stop states from continually trying to tackle international terrorism in other ways, by means of cooperation and enforcement in matters of criminal justice. But the 'war paradigm', as opposed to the 'criminal justice' paradigm, should be the exception not the rule. That this was the consensus before 9/11 is reflected in the widely cited 1994 General Assembly Resolution on Measures to Eliminate International Terrorism, which stated that terrorism 'may pose a threat to international peace and security'.[8] The implication is that the collective security apparatus of the Security Council, predicated on a determination of a threat to the peace or breach of the peace, is not to be seen as the automatic response to terrorism.

In contrast in the post-9/11 era, the Security Council determined that all acts of international terrorism are threats to international peace and security.[9] Making such a general determination in the absence of evaluating each terrorist act seems to be an unnecessary escalation, but it does not mean that the Council is reinforcing the 'war paradigm' as it has mainly used its non-forcible Chapter VII powers in response to terrorism, and has not yet authorised military action. Thus it can still be contended that the actions of a handful of powerful states apart, there is insufficient evidence to suggest there is a significant move away from the 1994 consensus that military force should only be used to combat terrorism when absolutely necessary. The use of the phrase 'war on terror' thus gives the wrong impression and is potentially dangerous as it suggests that the normal way of handling terrorism is by military means. It is not argued that the use of military force is never to be contemplated in response to terrorism, it has its place, but the 'war on terror' gives the impression that this should be the norm.

Another reason for not using the term 'war on terror' is that if is accepted that there is a continual state of war against terrorists, then although the *jus in bello* prohibits attacks on civilians and acts of violence that terrorise civilians committed in an armed conflict, it does permit action against military targets. In an armed conflict both sides can legitimately target the military personnel and apparatus of the other side. Thus in a continuing armed conflict or war the terrorists can legitimately attack those that have declared war on them. In general the term 'war' can signify that there is a continual state of hostilities where the aim is to defeat the enemy by military means, but in doing so those prosecuting the war must legitimately expect to suffer some attacks against their forces. It must be remembered that in times of conflict it has been argued, by NATO for example during its airstrikes on Serbia in 1999, that targets can include power stations, TV stations, railways and key bridges. An acceptance of the *jus in bello* legal regime does not seem either to reflect the reality of the fight against terrorism nor is it a desirable situation. For instance, if the war on terror had predated 9/11, then while the twin towers of the World Trade Center were clearly prohibited civilian targets, the Pentagon was not.

State terrorism

While the 'war on terror' is being waged against non-state actors, it must not be forgotten that states themselves have often engaged in terrorism, either directly through their military and police forces, or through sponsoring or harbouring terrorists. On the latter, the General Assembly has adopted rules on state liability which determine whether the unlawful acts of individuals or groups can be attributed to the state.[10] A state that sponsors terrorism can be held responsible for its support depending upon the level of that support. If it commands or controls the terrorists (as may be the case with the Sudanese government and the Janjaweed), then the acts of the terrorists themselves are attributed to the state, in other words they are acts of state. However, if the level of support falls below that (for example by harbouring terrorists on its territory, arguably the relationship between the Taliban government and Al-Qaeda before the US-led invasion of 2001) then while it is not responsible for the acts of the terrorists it remains responsible for harbouring them.

Turning to the consequences of state sponsorship – if the sponsoring state is in charge of the terrorists, then the state targeted by the terrorists can take non-forcible action against it, and can treat any attack against it by the terrorists as an attack by the sponsoring state. Under the law of self-defence, the target state can therefore take proportionate and necessary action against the terrorists and the state in control of them. Whether military action can be taken against a state that is not in control of the terrorists but does harbour them will be dealt with below, when considering whether the law of self-defence has been extended in the light of recent practice. Harbouring terrorists who launch attacks in another country is a breach of international law, both of the norm prohibiting the use of force and the norm of non-intervention.[11] Self-defence aside for the moment, those states that are victims of the breach are entitled to undertake a range of responses in line with the law of state responsibility, including demands for cessation, reparation and proportionate non-forcible countermeasures until the breach is ended.[12]

State sponsors of terrorism can also be dealt with by the Security Council if it deems that such activities constitute a threat to international peace and security. Libya was the subject of non-forcible measures in the 1990s as was Sudan, both for their support for terrorist activities. The Security Council has the power under Chapter VII to impose sanctions and to authorise military action against state sponsors of terrorism, and it is not limited by the relationship between the host state and the terrorists. Thus far it has confined itself to non-forcible measures under Article 41 of the UN Charter.

Regarding more direct forms of state terrorism; if a state's armed forces commit acts of terrorism during an armed conflict then they are governed by the provisions of international humanitarian law.[13] The whole of the Fourth Geneva Convention protects civilians and their property in times of armed conflict and occupation; while during peace time state terrorism by agents of the government (army, police, etc.) is governed by human rights law, which protects basic rights such as the right to life and freedom from torture, which even in emergencies threatening the life of the nation cannot be derogated from.[14]

Thus there are clear rules of international law governing state-sponsored terrorism and more direct form of state terrorism, to the extent that it can be argued that there is no pressing need to develop a separate law of terrorism governing state activities since there exists relatively clear rules on the use of force, on non-intervention, on humanitarian law and human rights law, which between them cover the 'terrorist' activities of states. However, there are a number of weaknesses in the legal framework outlined above in addition to the problems that pervades much of international law – that of enforcement of the norms.

The first weakness is a lack of clarity on the issue of when states can respond by military means to a terrorist threat. This will be reconsidered later.

Secondly, there is unwillingness amongst states to recognise that support for terrorism can be a state *crime*. The international community has recently moved away from the idea that states can be criminals because in simple terms they cannot be locked up, and because of the influence of the Nuremberg Tribunal that said 'crimes are committed by men, not by abstract entities'.[15] In the recent Articles on State Responsibility adopted by the General Assembly in 2001, the language is one of serious breaches of fundamental norms, when previous drafts had spoken of state crimes such as aggression and genocide.[16] In some ways this is a retrograde step, because recognising that states can commit international crimes arguably is of greater consequence than if such breaches are treated the same as normal breaches of international law. In general stigmatising some state actions such as sponsoring terrorism as an international crime is a clear way of identifying international pariahs and taking collective measures against them.

Thirdly, Security Council action is discretionary and cannot be taken against permanent members because of the veto. It is at best a flawed instrument of justice and in reality is a political organ. Reform of the Security Council is a pressing concern, but very little was achieved at the UN's World Summit in 2005, apart from a watered down version of the responsibility to protect to be exercised by the Security Council in cases of genocide and crimes against humanity.[17]

Non-state actors and terrorism

The main current focus of international concern is on the threat of international terrorism by non-state actors such as Al-Qaeda. However, even before that threat emerged in the 1990s, there existed numerous treaties starting in the 1960s directed against a range of terrorist acts, a process continued after 9/11 (hijacking, hostage taking, bombings, misuse of nuclear material, etc.). In general these conventions follow a similar pattern by requiring state parties to criminalise such behaviour and to extradite or prosecute any individual within their jurisdiction who is suspected of such a crime. The crimes are defined in a way that is familiar to domestic criminal law; for example, the Montreal Convention of 1971 states, amongst other things, that 'any person commits an offence if he unlawfully and intentionally . . . places or causes to be placed on an aircraft in service . . . a device or substance which is likely to destroy that aircraft . . .'.[18] Interestingly there is no reference to terrorism in the substance of the definition. Taking the suppression conventions on terrorist acts together, Saul comments that 'most of the physical conduct widely considered as terrorist in nature is now prohibited',[19] although he goes on to state that 'one of the few remaining *normative* gaps in the network of treaties is the failure to criminalize internationally the terrorist killings of civilians by any method'.[20]

In addition to the conventional framework, the Security Council has built on its actions against Libya starting in 1992, designed to coerce the Libyan regime into handing over the two individuals suspected of the 1988 Lockerbie bombing. From this point the Security Council has concerned itself with international terrorists, increasingly against individuals and organisations (especially Al-Qaeda and the Taliban), by listing them and requiring states to take measures against them including the freezing of their assets.[21] These, and the more general anti-terrorist lawmaking by the Security Council that started after 9/11,[22] will be reviewed more fully below.

Turning to the weaknesses of the international legal framework for dealing with non-state actors involved in terrorist activities, it can be seen that the suppression conventions rely on national systems to criminalise and prosecute individuals suspected of committing treaty crimes. The 'extradite or prosecute' formula is suspect given the general practice of prosecutorial discretion. For instance, the Lockerbie bombing of 1988, when an explosive device was placed on board a PanAm flight, destroying it over Scotland, was clearly a crime under the Montreal Convention of 1971. Under the Convention Libya, the US and the UK, all parties to the treaty, claimed jurisdiction over the offence under the treaty – the US because it was an American plane, the UK given the explosion occurred in Scotland, and Libya because the two Libyan suspects were in Libya. Libya decided to prosecute the two suspects itself and not to extradite, clearly revealing the serious weaknesses of the suppression conventions.

In order to remedy this weakness the US and UK approached the Security Council and persuaded it to take non-forcible action against Libya to force it to hand over the two suspects.[23] The sanctions regime was directed against Libya but its purpose was to intervene in the criminal justice system set up in the Montreal Convention. In effect the Security Council was trying to override the Montreal Convention, using its mandatory powers under the UN Charter,[24] in combination with the priority that states should give to obligations arising under the Charter when they conflict with other treaty obligations.[25]

There is no doubt that the suppression treaty regimes are weak; the Lockerbie cases show that. To make them effective there needs to be supervision of the obligation to extradite or prosecute so that states do not hide behind lacklustre prosecutions. Arguably until they are improved the Security Council should be allowed to override them in extreme cases where terrorism has reached the level of a threat to the peace, what has been labelled 'hyperterrorism',[26] although as shall be seen since 9/11 it has moved towards categorising all acts of terrorism as threats to international peace.

Targeted sanctions against individuals are problematic in human rights terms. The listing of individuals in the Security Council without any due process or real system of appeal is recognised to be a problem.[27] At the very least there should be a mechanism whereby an individual should have the right to challenge the listing. In December 2006 the Security Council agreed to establish a focal point where individuals listed can petition for delisting in addition to requesting their national state to take up their case at UN level.[28] Though a very rudimentary acknowledgement of some due process and natural justice at the UN level, there have been further developments in this process, for example in 2008, when the Security Council decided that a summary of reasons should be given for inclusion on the consolidated list of individuals and entities connected to the Taliban and Al-Qaeda.[29] Clearly though, the protection of the human rights of terrorist suspects at the UN level falls a long way short of the international standards established in such UN instruments as the Universal Declaration of Human Rights 1948 (UDHR), which protects the right to a fair and public hearing by an impartial tribunal in determining the rights and obligations of individuals (Article 10), the right to privacy and respect for honour and reputation (Article 12), and freedom of movement (Article 13); all rights that listing seriously impedes. Though only soft law in an orthodox sense, much of the UDHR has become customary and therefore binding on all international legal persons (including the UN),[30] and further, as part of the constitutional law of the UN, is applicable to all UN actors including the Security Council.

The lack of definition of terrorism

Lawyers will be surprised to have read this far without a definition of terrorism, but that reflects the evolution of international law in this area and others. Terrorist acts have been criminalised in the suppression conventions and the Security Council has taken a range of measures against terrorist states and non-state actors, and yet there is no universally agreed definition of terrorism. The 1994 General Assembly resolution discussed more fully below contains a definition that is often referred to, as does the 1999 Terrorist Financing Convention and there is now a definition within a 2004 Security Council resolution discussed below, but there is no binding treaty definition.

The 2000 UN-sponsored Draft Comprehensive Convention has not yet been adopted due to two main sticking points. First, mainly Islamic states want to distinguish freedom fighters from terrorists,[31] and some of those states also want to include state-terrorism within any definition. Simply put the desire is to free Palestinian fighters from being stigmatised as terrorists, while at the same time stigmatising Israel as a terrorist state for its actions in the Occupied Territories.

It must be noted though that there is nothing approaching a consensus amongst the international community to exclude those fighting for self-determination from any definition of terrorism. Seminal General Assembly resolutions supporting the 'struggle' for self-determination in the 1970s did not support the use of terrorism in pursuit of that struggle.[32] Furthermore, international humanitarian law has since 1977 recognised that international armed conflicts include 'armed conflicts in which peoples are fighting against racist regimes in the exercise of their right of self-determination', therefore subjecting National Liberation Movements fighting in armed conflicts to international humanitarian law which protects civilians from attack and from terror. In other words the weight of international law is against those who want to exclude 'freedom fighters' from any definition (and therefore prohibition) of terrorism. It is a political position pure and simple, as is the desire to include state terrorism and state-sponsored terrorism, since the 'terrorist' acts of states are already covered by humanitarian law and human rights law.

Furthermore, although progress on the Comprehensive Convention has stalled on the issue, there are plenty of definitions in circulation. Thus the problem is not a legal one. It is not impossible to legally define something as abstract as terrorism; the real problem is the lack of political will to formally adopt a definition. The Terrorist Financing Convention of 1999, for instance, prohibits the financing of 'any act intended to cause death or serious bodily injury to a civilian, or to any other person not taking an active part in the hostilities in a situation of armed conflict, when the purpose of such act, by its nature or context, is to intimidate a population, or to compel a government or an international organization to do or to abstain from doing any act'.[33] The political problem that Islamic states have with such a definition is that in trying to capture the political motives of the terrorists the definition will cover acts undertaken against civilians in self-determination struggles. The Palestinian fighters have a political motive – to coerce the occupying government and settler population into withdrawing, and in some cases are driven by the motive to destroy Israel as an independent state.

The Draft Comprehensive Convention first put forward in 2000 contains a definition that would make it an offence if a person unlawfully and intentionally causes death or serious bodily injury to any person; serious damage to public or private property; damage to property, places, facilities or systems resulting or likely to result in major economic loss. The purpose of any such conduct must be 'to intimidate a population, or to compel a government or an international organization to do or abstain from doing any act'.[34] In debates on the Draft Convention there was some indication that the Organisation of the Islamic Conference (OIC) states may be willing to drop their insistence that state terrorism be included in the definition in exchange for allowing national liberation to be excluded,[35] but in debates in October 2009 Iran (speaking for the Non Aligned Movement) condemned terrorism (including state terrorism), and excluded peoples fighting for self-determination from the term.[36]

Turning to the British response to illustrate the perspective of those conducting the war on terrorism, its position in the 1970s was not to have a general definition but to deal with specific offences (via the suppression treaties).[37] After 9/11 the UK preferred the 'pragmatic approach of the Security Council to the legalist approach of the General Assembly'.[38] After the 7/7 attacks in London in 2005 the UK then supported a comprehensive convention and a definition, but has been unwilling to compromise on a national liberation exception, and more recently has appeared to return to a practical measures approach.[39]

Two choices seem to emerge from the above disagreement – either to remove the political motive from the definition and concentrate on criminalising specific terrorist acts as has already largely been done and improving the effectiveness of the suppression conventions, or recognise that targeting civilians in order to induce fear in the population even in a self-determination struggle is terrorism.

The former has been the more successful to date, but it arguably fails to distinguish terrorism from 'ordinary' criminal acts. Criminalising terrorism arises out of a desire to stigmatise, deter and punish the deliberate and random targeting of civilians that characterises many terrorist attacks.

Interestingly, three years after imposing general legislative measures against terrorism in Resolution 1373 of 2001, the Security Council appeared to provide a definition of terrorism in 2004 – 'criminal acts, including against civilians, committed with the intent to cause death or serious bodily injury, or taking of hostages, with the purpose to provoke a state of terror in the general public or in a group of persons or particular persons, intimidate a population or compel a government or an international organization to do or abstain from doing any act, which constitute offences within the scope of and as defined in the international conventions and protocols relating to terrorism'.[40] This is quite a narrow approach that combines a generic definition but ties it to the existing treaty crimes. This shows the reality that the generic definition is more of symbolic importance given that terrorist acts are already defined in the suppression conventions. The adoption of a definition by the Security Council is quite important in deflecting the criticism that 'it is precisely the absence of a legal definition of terrorism that makes it possible for the hegemonic power (read "United States") and its followers to determine the international public enemy on a case-by-case basis'.[41]

Most definitions agree that civilians are the main targets, though some would include military targets. Some definitions refer to the political, ideological, religious motives of the terrorists and include reference to the purpose of creating extreme fear in a person, group or population. Most definitions refer to the purpose of intimidating the population or compelling a government to do or abstain from doing something. The political argument to exclude freedom fighters – those fighting for self-determination – is not legally justifiable especially if a definition is confined to attacks on civilians since attacks on civilians can never be justified. In addition, the political argument to include state terrorism within any definition is not legally justified since states come within the rubric of mainstream international law so that international humanitarian law and human rights law in effect prohibit states from committing acts of terrorism. It is regrettable that states cannot be stigmatised as terrorists when they have engaged in such acts against civilians within their jurisdiction or elsewhere (for example by sponsoring insurgents who engage in such acts), but with states still controlling the direction of international law there is little possibility of this happening especially when the move away from the concept of state crimes is borne in mind.

Thus an acceptable definition should cover serious criminal acts (the main examples of which are those found in the existing suppression treaties) against civilians with the purpose of causing extreme fear in the population or part of it, with the aim of intimidating a population or part of it, or compelling a government or organisation from doing or abstaining from some act; irrespective of the political, ideological or religious motive behind it.[42]

Soft law on terrorism

Another way of making progress in producing a more coherent legal framework is through non-binding soft law produced by the General Assembly as opposed to hard, immediately binding law, produced either by a treaty in force or by Security Council resolutions adopted under Chapter VII. There is a great deal of international soft law on terrorism. Important in this regard is the General Assembly Declaration on Measures to Eliminate International Terrorism, adopted by consensus in 1994.[43] The resolution defines terrorism as 'criminal acts intended or calculated to provoke a state of terror in the general public, a group of persons or particular persons for political purposes . . . whatever the considerations of a political, philosophical, ideological, racial, ethnic, religious or any other nature that may be invoked to justify them'. Interestingly there is no exception for national liberation movements even with OIC states included in the consensus – possibly because General Assembly resolutions are not immediately binding, though such resolutions are normative or at least they use normative language.[44] It shows though that there is no principled objection to the definition.

The measures agreed upon by states in the resolution must be adopted in accordance with human rights law and include duties on states to: refrain from organising, encouraging or tolerating terrorist activities and to take appropriate practical measures in their territories against terrorists; ensure the apprehension, prosecution or extradition of perpetrators of terrorist acts, in accordance with their national law; conclude special agreements, bilateral, regional and multilateral and develop model agreements on cooperation; cooperate in exchanging information; implement existing treaties and harmonise national laws in accordance with them; ensure that asylum is not granted to those that have undertaken terrorists acts, and that refugee status is not granted in a manner contrary to these provisions.

Soft law has been developed and could be developed much further to be specific in forms of cooperation: extradition, legal assistance, execution of foreign penal sentences, recognition of foreign penal judgments, transfer of criminal proceedings, freezing and seizing of assets deriving from criminal conduct, intelligence and law enforcement information gathering and sharing; and the creation and recognition of regional/sub-regional judicial spaces.[45] For example if extradition fails and the host state is unwilling to try the terrorist suspects, there should be transfer to a third country. There should be pre-established procedures for this. In addition, states should offer themselves as fair trial venues. A move away from bilateralism (for example in extradition treaties), towards multilateralism, would improve the legal framework for tackling terrorism,[46] as would a general recognition that acts of terrorism cannot be covered by the political offence exception built into some extradition regimes.[47]

Furthermore, there is much greater compatibility between the soft law approach of the Assembly and the hard law approach of the Security Council than is readily conceded. Council Resolution 1373 of 2001 tries to strengthen cooperation; so soft and hard law can work together.[48] The Counter Terrorism Committee (CTC) established by that resolution has produced a directory of recommended best practices, codes and standards in implementing 1373.[49] The Counter Terrorism Committee Executive Directorate (CTED) also serves as an intermediary for contacts between potential donors of technical assistance and recipients, and maintains an online directory of assistance providers. For example in the UK, the Department for International Development (DFID) offers technical assistance on some police and law enforcement matters.

In 2006 the General Assembly adopted by consensus the Global Counter Terrorism Strategy,[50] which develops many of the measures in the 1994 Assembly Declaration but also takes account of Security Council resolutions and mechanisms including the CTC (though it calls on it to work with states at their request), and the 1267 Committee (though it calls on it to ensure fair and transparent procedures). This amounts to a general recognition of the Security Council actions in this area, but also represents an attempt to balance the Council's actions with human rights protection, and by emphasising traditional principles such as state consent. The movement of the membership towards the Security Council antiterrorist regime is made clearer in a later Assembly resolution again adopted by consensus,[51] which reminds states of their obligations under relevant treaties but also under Security Council resolutions including 1373, 'to ensure that perpetrators of terrorist acts are brought to justice'.

In general the Assembly is more concerned with human rights and with a policy of trying to dissuade disaffected individuals from using terrorism by tackling the causes of terrorism.[52] The Assembly also puts more emphasis on states to tackle terrorism, and less on the UN, though the UN will help with capacity building for weaker states to combat terrorism by building indigenous law enforcement, intelligence infrastructure and border patrols to stop terrorist infiltration.[53]

Terrorism and the International Criminal Court

National criminal courts are the normal fora for trying individuals suspected of terrorism, and this remains the case despite the burgeoning international legal framework. Both the suppression conventions and the Security Council's action make this clear; but there is force in the idea that the most heinous terrorist crimes should be tried by an international tribunal. The idea of an international criminal court has for a long time been linked to the issue of terrorism. In the 1930s the League of Nations put forward this link in failed treaties, but it was not until the late 1980s that the idea of having such a court with jurisdiction over terrorist offences was put forward by President Gorbachev of the Soviet Union. However, the treaty produced at the end of the process, the Rome Statute of 1998, did not include terrorist crimes, concentrating instead on the core crimes (genocide, crimes against humanity and war crimes) generally recognised by the international community as giving rise to individual responsibility, in effect creating a new and more universal version of Nuremberg.

Terrorist crimes, though, were included in earlier versions, even the 1998 Draft Rome Statute, which in draft Article 5 covered crimes of terrorism in three distinct offences. First, the general offence of 'undertaking, organizing, sponsoring, ordering, facilitating, financing, encouraging or tolerating acts of violence against another State directed at persons or property and of such a nature as to create terror, fear or insecurity in the minds of public figures, groups of persons, the general public or populations, for whatever considerations and purposes of a political, philosophical, ideological, racial, ethnic, religious or such nature that may be invoked to justify them. . . .' Secondly, it covered any offence in six of the suppression treaties.[54] Thirdly, it prohibited the 'use of firearms, weapons, explosives and dangerous substances when used as a means to perpetrate indiscriminate violence involving death or serious bodily injury to persons or groups of persons or populations or serious damage to property'.

Terrorist crimes were not included in the final treaty for a number of different reasons: there was no agreed definition of terrorism since some Islamic states wanted national liberation violence exempted; there was a fear in some states that it would politicize the Court; others had a feeling that such crimes were more suited to national prosecution and were often not serious enough to be prosecuted internationally.[55]

It was recognised at Rome that serious terrorist crimes may be caught by the definition of crimes against humanity in Article 7 of the Rome Statute, namely 'any of the following acts (murder, torture, imprisonment . . .) when committed as part of a widespread or systematic attack directed against any civilian population, with knowledge of the attack'. 'Attack directed against any civilian population' means a 'course of conduct involving the multiple commission of acts . . . against any civilian population, pursuant to or in furtherance of a State or organizational policy to commit such attack'. This would seem to cover the type of attack mounted by Al-Qaeda against the US, subject of course to the jurisdictional limitations of the Court so that the crime must be committed on the territory of a state party or by a national of a state party, or if the situation is referred to the Court by the Security Council.[56] Furthermore, the Court would come into play only when national courts are unable or unwilling to try suspects,[57] which might serve to strengthen and provide some supervision of the 'extradite or prosecute formula' contained in the suppression conventions.

One of the key features of the Rome Statute is the relationship it establishes between the ICC and the Security Council. The Security Council may refer cases to it, and may also block cases being brought before the Court at least temporarily. While it could use its power to refer terrorist atrocities that amount to crimes against humanity, or indeed war crimes if terrorist acts amounting to breaches of the Geneva Conventions are committed during armed conflict, it cannot refer terrorist crimes per se. Instead, it has shown that it has the competence to establish *ad hoc* tribunals, not only for the core crimes, as with the ICTY and ICTR, but specifically to try terrorist crimes when it established the Special Tribunal for Lebanon in 2007 to try those suspected of being behind the terrorist bombings of 2005 that killed former Lebanese Prime Minister Rafiq Hariri.[58]

The role of the Security Council

Looking in more detail at this pivotal body, in the 1980s the Security Council confined itself to condemning certain terrorist acts.[59] It continued this practice in the post-Cold War period,[60] but it also adopted measures against states – in 1992 against Libya for its support for international terrorism and for its harbouring of the two Lockerbie suspects,[61] measures which ended in 2003; and against Sudan in the period 1996–2001 for Sudanese support for terrorism and for harbouring individuals suspected of the assassination attempt on the President of Egypt.[62]

Towards the end of the late 1990s as the threat of international terrorism emerged the Security Council has developed a targeted sanctions regime involving the freezing of funds, assets and resources of individuals suspected of terrorism or supporting terrorism. Recently such measures have been adopted against those involved in the assassination of Lebanese President Rafiq Hariri in 2005 (followed by the establishment of the above mentioned Special Tribunal),[63] but even before 9/11 such measures were adopted against the Taliban and Al-Qaeda in 1999,[64] following the 1998 African embassy bombings. The 1267 (Taliban and Al-Qaeda) Committee has listed entities and individuals as associated with the Taliban and Al-Qaeda (the current consolidated list has nearly 400 individuals and over 100 entities on it). Under this regime there is an obligation on states to freeze the assets of the individuals and entities listed, and to impose travel and arms embargoes. In 2004 the Security Council set up the 1566 Working Group to recommend practical measures against individuals and groups,[65] though it failed to achieve consensus on extending the listing process beyond the Taliban and Al-Qaeda.[66]

There has been a significant debate on whether Resolution 1267 overrides the human rights obligations of states due to a combination of Articles 25 and 103 of the Charter. In its Declaration on Combating Terrorism (SC Res. 1456 of 20 January 2003) the Security Council, meeting at the level of Foreign Ministers, declared that states 'must ensure that any measure taken to combat terrorism comply with their obligations under international law, and should adopt measures in accordance with international law, in particular human rights, refugee and humanitarian law'. This amounts to institutional *opinio juris* to the effect that mandatory Security Council resolutions demanding that the assets of named individuals be seized do not require or enable states to by-pass their human rights obligations. Those assets must be frozen, and other measures taken against individuals, in accordance with the human rights obligations of member states including those arising under a regional treaty. A member state would be in compliance with 1267 if it froze the assets of a named individual but he was given reasons for the freezing order and had the opportunity to challenge it before a court. The lack of adequate human rights mechanisms at the Security Council level does not mean that they are also rendered inapplicable at the domestic or indeed regional levels by means of a Security Council resolution. This would mean that the European Court of Justice was correct in the *Kadi* case of 2008, in contrast to the House of Lords a year earlier in *Al-Jedda*, though the outcome in both cases was an attempt to balance between the security needs of the state and the human rights of the suspected terrorist.[67]

The Security Council must be content that each state, or indeed regional organisation, will incorporate its decisions while respecting the states' human rights obligations under both treaty and customary law. In its *Kadi* judgment of 2008 the European Court of Justice found that the European Union's incorporation of obligations under the targeted sanctions regime initiated by Security Council Resolution 1267 (1999) violated European fundamental rights of Mr Kadi who had been listed by the Council's 1267 Committee and therefore had his assets frozen without recourse to a remedy, but the Court gave the European bodies the chance to redraft the regulations in a way that was human rights compliant.[68]

Prolonged arbitrary detention of terrorist suspects rather than the seizure of their assets was the issue before the UK House of Lords in the *Al-Jedda* case of 2007,[69] and so the Court had to consider the extent to which the right to liberty and security of person under the European Convention on Human Rights was overridden by Security Council Resolution 1546 of 2004 on Iraq. Mr Al-Jedda had been detained without charge or trial for several years for 'imperative reasons of security' in that he was a suspected terrorist, an undeniable breach of his rights under article 5(1) of the European Convention.[70] The Court felt that the only way of interpreting Resolution 1546 was to permit the UK, for imperative reasons of security, to override Mr Al-Jedda's right to liberty but only to the extent necessary to achieve security.[71] Lord Carswell gave the most far-reaching judgment in this regard when he stated that the power to intern may lawfully be exercised by the UK but only in such a way 'to minimise the infringement of the detainee's rights' under the ECHR.[72] In particular he identified a number of safeguards including 'the regular review of the continuing need to detain each person and a system whereby that need and the underlying evidence can be checked and challenged by representatives on behalf of the detained persons, so far as is practicable and consistent with the needs of national security and the safety of other persons'.[73]

From its sanctions against certain states supporting terrorism in the early 1990s and targeted sanctions against individuals in the late 1990s, the Security Council started after 9/11 to legislate more broadly on terrorism. Resolution 1373 obliges states to criminalise the financing of terrorism; to suppress terrorist groups; deny refugee status to terrorists; prevent the movement of terrorists; bring terrorists to justice; and establish terrorist acts as serious domestic crimes. It did not provide a definition of terrorism (until 2004) which meant that its resolutions were subject to wide interpretation by states in their implementing legislation. Further it has moved away from making individual determinations of threats to the peace in relation to terrorist acts towards determining that all acts of terrorism (whether international or not) are threats to international peace.[74]

The implementation of the measures demanded in Resolution 1373 is monitored by the Counter-Terrorism Committee (CTC) through mandatory state reporting. There appears to be a high degree of compliance.[75] In 2004 the Council created a CTED (Counter-Terrorism Committee Executive Directorate) to provide the CTC with expert advice, to conduct what are called 'expert assessments' of each member state, and to facilitate, but not provide itself, technical assistance to states.[76] In December 2009 the Executive Director of the CTED reported that the 'closer interaction with member states, including through . . . visits, has given CTED new insight into how countries are managing their counter-terrorism strategies and policies, the vulnerabilities they are facing and the technical assistance they may require'. Further, he reported that the CTED Global Implementation Survey 'contains global assessments across the major thematic areas dealt with in the resolution, notably counter-terrorism legislation, border control, law enforcement, countering the financing of terrorism, and international cooperation. It also looks at the field of protecting human rights while countering terrorism'. He concluded by emphasising that 'in our technical assistance facilitation work we are also as a matter of course, encouraging governments to incorporate human rights training in professional training courses related to counter-terrorism, with the aim of ensuring that countries are able to address the challenge of terrorism without compromising fundamental human rights'.[77] The 2009 Global Implementation Survey of the CTED identified a range of problems with a number of states in implementing counter-terrorism strategies pursuant to Resolution 1373, principally the lack of any definition of terrorism (or vague and overbroad definitions) in domestic legislation, the practice of torture and ill-treatment especially at the investigative stage, arbitrary executions, hidden detention, and the practice of returning individuals to states where there is a significant danger of their being tortured in violation of the principle of *non-refoulement.*[78]

Resolution 1373 has been characterised as legislative by some commentators, and therefore questionable when considering the Council as an executive body.[79] Resolution 1373 was legislative in the sense that it required states to adopt provisions derived from the 1999 Terrorist Financing Convention, thereby circumventing the requirement of consent (the treaty at the time was not even in force), but by and large it put the emphasis on states to adopt national legislation which would fulfil the very broad provisions of 1373. It certainly was not meant to be directly effective supranational legislation, and the evidence is that some states have used its broad terms to justify quite wide-ranging internal legislation. Its definition of terrorism in 2004 was too late in some senses to reverse the trend in national legislative provisions and definitions. Between 2001 and 2004 many states put in place new legislation on terrorism based on their own definitions. To 'legislate' against terrorism even indirectly as the Council did in 1373, without a definition, was very suspect in terms of the basic requirement of the rule of law, but states did not object because they could used the mandatory requirements of the Security Council decision as a basis for their own wide-ranging legislation against dissidents as well as terrorists.

The Security Council's response to terrorism has moved from condemnation to the utilisation of its coercive non-forcible powers, first against states and then non-state actors. But it also has the power to authorise military measures.[80] Under the UN Charter there are two exceptions to the prohibition on the use of force – when states exercise their right of self-defence in response to an armed attack and when the Security Council authorises military measures. The responses to acts of terrorism to date have been taken under the right of self-defence not under Security Council authority. So for example in relation to the US response to 9/11 by using force against Afghanistan in 2001; and the Israeli actions of 2006 against Lebanon in response to Hezbollah attacks, and of 2009 against Gaza in response to Hamas rocket attacks, both the US and Israel invoked the right of self-defence.

Of course invoking the right of self-defence is not the same as the legitimate exercise of the right. It is necessary to look for international acceptance that there was a lawful exercise of the right. The Security Council seemed to recognise the right of the United States to use force in self-defence in response to 9/11 in Resolution 1368,[81] although it was not without ambiguity.[82] In relation to Israel, there was no such endorsement though it was not until a number of weeks passed after Israel's ground offensive into Lebanon that the Security Council united to call for a cease-fire.[83] In relation to the three-week Israeli offensive in Gaza in January 2009, the Security Council acted more quickly to call for a cease-fire and a withdrawal of Israeli forces.[84]

The Security Council can authorise military action in response to threats to the peace and arguably its authority should be sought in instances that do not clearly justify the right of self-defence. However, the arguments over the Iraq war in 2003 when an authorising resolution was sought but not adopted shows the difficulties of taking a Security Council route to get approval for military measures, though the invasion of Iraq was not a response to terrorism despite US attempts to link Saddam Hussein to Al-Qaeda. Sometimes the Council's reluctance to authorise military action may be due to self-interested vetoes or the threat of them by the permanent members but on other occasions it might act as a genuine bar to imprudent military action.

The right of self-defence

Under the UN Charter the right of self-defence in Article 51 has traditionally been interpreted to allow for self-defence by one state in response to an armed attack by another, though the text states that the right of self-defence is triggered 'if an armed attack occurs against a member of the United Nations', thus not precluding armed attacks by non-state actors nor defensive action in response to them.[85]

There appears to be wide agreement that the response to the 9/11 attack by Al-Qaeda was the exercise of the right of self-defence in response to an attack by a non-state actor, but there is considerable doubt about how wide that 'precedent' is.[86] At its narrowest it might be confined to its facts: a massive terrorist attack against a state by an organisation with a past history of attacks on US targets, combined with the promise of future, perhaps imminent, attacks.[87] In addition, there was the almost unique strong relationship between the Taliban regime and the terrorists, though neither commanded or controlled the other. There was also a strong moral impetus to the response with many references to the 'evil' of terrorism.[88] Finally, there was a strong condemnation of the attack across international organisations – in the Security Council, the General Assembly, NATO and the EU.

At its widest the precedent could be drawn to concentrate simply on the threat, no matter how imminent, an approach embodied in the National Security Strategy promulgated by President Bush in 2002, which declared that the US would take pre-emptive action in response to a terrorist threat, no matter how remote.[89]

The future development of the right of self-defence in response to terrorist attacks and threats of attack may lie somewhere between the two poles. If there is strong evidence that an armed attack will emanate in the immediate future from a terrorist group found within a state, then it may become established law that the target state can take anticipatory action to strike at the terrorists before they launch their attack. There must be both strong evidence of planned imminent attack (Iraq 2003 shows how hard evidence, as distinct from intelligence, is crucial), best shown by the fact that attacks have already emanated from there, and then the response must be necessary and proportionate. Necessity must be shown by the fact that the host state cannot deal with the terrorists and the only way of neutralising the threat is by military means; and proportionality signifies it must be directed against the terrorists not against the host state unless it comes to the aid of the terrorists.[90] Proportionality was violated in Israel's offensives against Lebanon in 2006 and Gaza in 2009 and arguably in the US-led invasion of Afghanistan in 2001, though the Taliban's close relationship with Al-Qaeda meant that it would have been difficult to target Al-Qaeda alone. However, the fact is that the operation was directed at both from the outset, and has led to the operation having two prongs – a mainly US-led assault against Al-Qaeda still acting under the right of self-defence; and an escalating conflict between a UN authorised NATO force (ISAF – dominated by the US) and the Taliban.[91] An interesting analogy that would justify limited, surgical, extra-territorial operations against terrorist bases has been drawn with the use of force to protect nationals in danger in another state, practice which has been accepted as lawful despite the strict wording of the Charter which suggests any use of force on or against the territory of another state is unlawful.[92]

Though the invasion of Iraq in 2003 was legally justified by the UK and US because of a breach of Security Council resolutions,[93] American rhetoric in the build-up to the war was that this was to remove Saddam as a threat to the US.[94] The general rejection of the legality of the war is largely a rejection of the doctrine of pre-emptive strikes, against either terrorist threats or, as with Iraq, the threat of WMDs. The negative reaction to Iraq also makes it harder to establish that middle ground mentioned, that armed force should be allowed in response to imminent attacks, whether by terrorists or by WMDs. The consensus that was achieved in the international community after 9/11 was lost in March 2003. It will be difficult now to build a true consensus to allow for anticipatory self-defence in response to threats that have not yet materialised, even imminent threats. Those advocating anticipatory action have to rely instead on the silence of the majority of states as a sign of acceptance. Silence undermines the legitimacy needed for the emergence of a new norm.

Conclusion

In the future it might be suggested that states only resort to force in extreme cases where there is strong evidence of an imminent attack being launched from another country. In such cases, bearing in mind the time constraints, the state should first try to seek the authority of the Security Council, then, if not forthcoming, obtain the support of regional bodies such as the EU and NATO. The 'war' paradigm should be used cautiously and sparingly, otherwise the conflict will expand and a continuing and ever-escalating state of hostilities will ensue.

For less pressing threats of terrorist military action then the Security Council should be informed and should be persuaded to authorise military action if the threat becomes imminent. In the meantime the Council and regional bodies could impose measures short of the use of force against individuals and groups on the basis of them being a threat to international peace and security. This would be a welcome return to the situation of the Council dealing with individual instances of serious cases of terrorism, rather than taking a more blanket legislative approach.

In cases falling below this, states should rely on a mixture of cooperation and lawful coercive techniques (which clearly would not include unlawful rendition flights, the torture of suspects, their prolonged arbitrary detention, or acts in violation of the principle of *non refoulement*) to ensure that suspected terrorists are brought to trial, working within existing bilateral, multilateral and regional cooperation regimes. Further, the criminal justice paradigm should be strengthened by consolidating the raft of treaties, agreeing a definition, and by allowing both the International Criminal Court and the Security Council to play a role in the treaty regime. A consolidated treaty should not only define terrorism, it should strengthen the methods of cooperation, especially the 'prosecute or extradite' formula to ensure strong prosecutions or more efficient extradition. Supervision of this obligation should be given to a treaty committee (or the existing CTC). There should be a facility for hyperterrorist incidents to be referred to the International Criminal Court; and there should be a recognition that in cases of international terrorism that constitute threats to international peace, the Security Council has a crucial role to play.

Furthermore, Security Council activities as regards terrorism should not be seen as by-passing or over-riding the criminal justice approach. The 1267 Committee's listing of individuals and entities should be a prelude to their trial for involvement in terrorism. Listing should not be seen as an alternative to trial and criminal punishment, but as an interim step.

The CTC's and CTED's supervision of state obligations as regards terrorism should be seen as improving the existing inefficient treaty regimes, but also checking that states have not violated human rights norms in their implementing legislation. The Security Council could play a crucial role in balancing the security imperative and human rights concerns given that 'many of the world's anti-terrorist laws suffer from the endemic malaise of imprecision. The dangers of bad draftmanship are obvious; one of the potential dangers is the criminalisation of legitimate dissent'.[95] There has to be a balance between security and human rights concerns in the Security Council anti-terrorist regime, something that is being increasingly recognised though more could be done in this regard.[96]

There are constitutional problems as well as legitimacy concerns with the Security Council becoming a general legislator and so its actions should be directed at being compatible/complementary to existing regimes rather than overriding or supplanting them. The Security Council's legitimacy would be improved in this regard if it were part of a consolidated treaty regime to deal with terrorism, just as it has a relationship to the International Criminal Court in the Rome Statute. Though this has been problematic, the Darfur reference in 2005 was something of a breakthrough.[97]

Given that the Security Council has done so much in relation to international terrorism, and done it by virtue of its Chapter VII powers, it might be time to see if the rest of the membership is willing to return to the issue of a comprehensive consolidated treaty, which would recognise the role of the Council but would serve to restrict what seems at the moment to be an ever-expanding Council competence that increasingly impinges on criminal justice concerns. In exchange Islamic states may be willing to lift their objection to a definition that does not exclude national liberation struggles. This should be the case because in 2004 the Council effectively defined terrorism without any reference to self-determination. A return to consensus, but effective, treaty-making is what should be sought. It seems correct to declare that 'due to the impact of mass terrorism, the right to self-determination has been gradually thrust into the background. There is a stronger will today than hitherto to make it clear that terrorist acts are unjustifiable in *any* circumstances . . . .'[98] However, the window of opportunity that opened after 9/11, which might have brought consensus on issues of international law and terrorism, may have been closed by the narrow choices made by major states to pursue the 'war on terror' by military means in preference to developing legitimate and effective mechanisms of national and international criminal justice.

3 Al Qaeda and networked international insurgency

Andrew Mumford*

Al Qaeda represents one of the foremost clear and present dangers to global security in the contemporary world. The group has a presence in over forty countries and is capable of perpetrating acts of catastrophic destruction, as witnessed on 9/11, as well as targeted acts of violence, such as the bombings in Bali, Madrid and London. Much academic ink has been spilt since 11 September 2001 in a parenthetic scramble to understand and explain the origins, evolution and meaning of Al Qaeda's global *jihad*. However, this chapter asserts that there is widespread miscomprehension of the threat posed by Al Qaeda. There has been an overt *tactical* emphasis on the network that has led to the common application of the misnomer 'terrorist group', as a result of a fixation with the events of 9/11 and the failure to appreciate the essentially insurgent nature of Al Qaeda's very creation in Soviet-occupied Afghanistan in the 1980s. The contention here is that analysis needs to shift to the *strategic* level in order to perceive Al Qaeda as an insurgent movement given the network's ubiquitous political endgame primarily via its intention to recast the political *status quo* in 'apostate' Muslim countries, its global presence, and its utilisation of terrorism as one of many tactics applied to fulfil its goals. In order to transfer the analytical scope of Al Qaeda from the tactical to the strategic level, and hence recast our understanding of the group, it is essential to first clarify the tangible differences between terrorism and insurgency. This will then permit a projected historical analysis of Al Qaeda's operations and organisation to be cast in a new analytical light, namely that seemingly disparate Islamist groups, far from being contained local insurgencies, should be viewed holistically as contributing to the grand strategic aims of the wider *jihadi* cause, as Al Qaeda conceives of it. Indeed, much of Al Qaeda's functional abilities, structurally and operationally, are indebted to the group's harnessing of the effects of globalisation, conceptually in terms of its transnational presence as a consequence of porous borders and the erosion of state sovereignty, and technologically in regard to instant global communications, the relative ease of international travel, and swift financial transactions. As a consequence of Al Qaeda's global insurgency there is a need to

* I would like to thank Richard Aldrich, Caroline Kennedy-Pipe, and Kevin Murphy for their helpful comments and critiques during the preparation of this chapter.

reappraise the current plans in place in Western states vulnerable to Al Qaeda attack. Traditional domestic counter-terrorism platforms are simply inadequate to deal with an international *jihad*. Indeed, solutions to the problem cannot be adequately conceived whilst there is a pervasive misconception of the actual threat itself. As the former British Security and Intelligence Co-ordinator, Sir David Omand, observed: 'without a greater degree of convergence of understanding over what and who we are fighting, and what strategy we are actually to fol-low, it is hard to see how the world-wide threat can be contained and eventually eliminated.'[1] Such a hurdle will not be overcome until analysis of Al Qaeda can surmount the tactical obsession with terrorism and become strategically observant of what John Sullivan and Robert Bunker have labelled the '*jihadi* international, with Al Qaeda at the vanguard.'[2]

Terrorism and insurgency

To differentiate between terrorism and insurgency, two terms often misused inter-changeably, is not to merely engage in a facile semantic debate. The variances are on a qualitative, teleological and analytical level. Such discrepancies must be addressed if Al Qaeda is to be adequately conceptualised in its global context. Although definitions of such phenomena are subject to perennial contestation, a broad consensus has emerged. In essence, terrorism is a primarily symbolic tool of political violence applied tactically and often indiscriminately to ensure coercion through fear. An insurgency is a strategic effort to subvert, overthrow and then recast an existing status quo via a combination of political and violent means.[3] Therefore, not only must we distinguish terrorist from insurgent groups by their varying emphasis on tactical targeting, notably the level of discrimination in their attacks (insurgent groups have a far greater propensity for the bombing of specific targets, such as embassies or symbols of 'occupier' power, and for attacking mainly military and political targets as opposed to civilians) but we must also consider the difference of strategic endgames held by terrorist and insurgent groups. Although variations of both groups may hold similar ideological beliefs, the crucial discrepancy is that insurgent groups' overarching aim is to seize con-trol of the state apparatus, as contrasted to purely symbolic terrorist acts that are designed primarily to disrupt or force a change in policy by existing elites. The contrasts between terrorism and insurgency have been muddied in recent years with the rise of the debate surrounding 'new terrorism'. Proponents of the notion of 'new terrorism' pointed to an emergent tendency during the 1990s for terror-ist groups to undertake attacks of catastrophic violence, driven by unshakeable ideological or religious fanaticism to achieve fundamental overhauls in regional or even global governance.[4] Yet arguably such analysis unwittingly describes characteristics of insurgent groups, particularly given the nature of their strategic objectives. Leaving aside the 'new' terrorism debate given the implicit presence of insurgent-related factors in the description of 'new' terrorism,[5] the differentiation between terrorism and insurgency therefore, can be epitomised by the variances in the character, scale and, most importantly, the purpose of the violence used.[6] It is important to bear such distinctions in mind when analysing Al Qaeda, firstly in regard to our interpretation of the threat they pose, and secondly in relation to our conceptualisation of the response to their threat.

Conceiving of Al Qaeda as an insurgent group is only one step to appreciating the fundamentals underlying the 'War on Terror'. Indeed, Western notions of insurgency itself have been moulded by the so-called 'classic' Maoist rural uprisings of the Cold War era whereby insurgents, largely communist, bound themselves within the parameters of a particular state or region. Such outmoded paradigms, however, do not render the classification of insurgency null and void. Al Qaeda and their affiliates share with by-gone insurgents the desire to overthrow an established ruling political and social order, but what transcends previous insurgencies is the sheer scope and span of the Islamist *jihad*. By seeking to depose the 'near enemy' (the perceived 'apostate' Muslim regimes) and strike out at the 'far enemy' (the West), the global *jihad* takes on the hallmarks of an international insurgency. The insurgent in the post-Maoist era of guerrilla warfare is defined by a new set of tactical and operational traits. As Thomas Hammes has noted, such emergent patterns include: the establishment of networked coalitions of insurgents; the escalation of the insurgent cause onto the international stage; the ability to self fund; and the representation of a variety of motivating factors within the movement.[7] Al Qaeda has displayed striking characteristics, particularly since the mid-1990s, which encapsulate the inherent insurgent qualities of the movement, distancing itself from the terrorist misnomer. Terrorist groups do not issue Declarations of War, as Osama bin Laden did on behalf of Al Qaeda in 1998.[8] Neither do terrorist groups carry out atrocities commensurate with acts of war, as Al Qaeda arguably did on 9/11. This insurgent movement is not constrained by concerns harboured by 'traditional' terrorist groups of limiting the number of civilian casualties in their attacks due to concerns over the legitimacy of their cause. In part this is due to the ubiquity of martyrdom in the *jihadi* conception of Islam as well as through the blanket interpretation of all Americans and other Westerners, civilian or military, as being complicit in Western hegemony and the perceived injustices and insults meted out to the Islamic world. Indeed, such is the animosity towards the West, particularly the US, in large parts of the Muslim world that mass casualty attacks perpetrated by Al Qaeda do not necessarily alienate mass popular opinion in such countries, but can indeed mobilise it in support of what is construed as the oppressed rising up against the oppressors. In short, the ends overshadow the means. Furthermore, Al Qaeda's tactic of not claiming the credit for successful attacks against America or 'apostate' regime targets, such as the Khobar Towers military barracks attack in Saudi Arabia that killed nineteen Americans in 1996, runs contrary to conventional terrorist wisdom where there is often a clamour to be associated with events.[9] This can be explained, firstly by Al Qaeda's desire to utilise terrorism as one of many tactical tools to achieve a wider strategic goal. This one tactic alone should not define the group, nor blinker the political and military authorities. Secondly, it demonstrates that the instigation of violence is not their only aim. By delegating credit for attacks it sends a very clear message that that the *jihad* against the West is not limited to a small band of ideologues but is in fact a tangible sentiment that is actionable around the world. Thirdly, such behaviour so 'uncharacteristic' of a terrorist group helps underlie the point that Al Qaeda is not merely a terrorist group with a difference. Its characteristics, strategy, tactics, organisational structure and its international presence indicate that Al Qaeda is indeed a global insurgent movement with a clear political commitment to dismantling the existing world order and rebuilding it in their own image. Terrorism is not the motive or the perpetuating catalyst, but is part of the far wider ideological struggle able to be perpetrated by a global network of myriad affiliates united by a shared strategic vision and a common tactical repertoire.

The global Islamist insurgency

At its inception during the Soviet occupation of Afghanistan, Al Qaeda was engineered to channel funds to the *mujahideen* insurgents who utilised guerrilla tactics to repel the Soviet Army. From its earliest days the group has been linked explicitly with insurgency as a strategy for bringing about political and social change through paramilitary force. The so-called 'Afghan Arabs' dispersed across the globe in the wake of the Soviet withdrawal in 1989 in order to promulgate revolutionary Islamism and helped nurture fledgling insurgencies in the Balkans, Chechnya, Sudan and Somalia, and elsewhere. The Afghan war was the crucible in which Al Qaeda and the current Islamist insurgency was forged, as it ensured, as Marc Sageman has argued, that the disparate *jihadists* 'started to analyse their common problems with a more global perspective, transcending their countries of origin'.[10] If the Soviet invasion of Afghanistan stirred *jihadi* sentiment across the Muslim world and awakened a sense of an Islamist revival, it was the arrival of American troops in Saudi Arabia, the site of the two holiest places in Islam, during the 1990–91 Gulf War that provided the real transformation of Al Qaeda from a defensive, reactionary insurgent group to an offensive, proactive organisation. This shift was formalised with Osama bin Laden's 1996 self-justified *fatwa* against America and the 1998 creation of the World Islamic Front as an umbrella organisation for the *jihadi* movement. However, this change from localism to globalism was by no means assured. Fawaz Gerges has noted that it was not until after the Gulf War that the strategic priority of Islamist groups shifted from the 'near enemy' to the 'far enemy'. In Gerges' view, the transnational nature of *jihadi* training and movement was to facilitate the necessary military skills and knowledge to instigate the overthrow of the authorities in their own countries and not explicitly to generate a global network of strategically cohesive insurgents.[11] Spearheaded by Osama bin Laden's deputy in Al Qaeda, the Egyptian ideologue Ayman al-Zawahiri, the push towards globalism came from a small minority within the Islamist movement and does unveil an internecine division within the wider Islamist movement between what Fawaz Gerges labels the 'religious nationalists' who focus internally on overthrowing regimes in the Muslim world, and the 'religious transnationalists', epitomised by Al Qaeda, whose global belligerence takes the *jihad* to the West.[12] It is this strategic schism, polarised by the differing emphasis on endogenous and exogenous revolution, which we shall see later ensures the need for both domestic counter-terrorism and international counter-insurgency co-operation in order to undermine the holistic threat posed by the Islamist *jihad*.

Structurally, Al Qaeda has been able to foment a global *jihad* by adopting an organisational arrangement that is, in David Kilcullen's words, 'more like a self-synchronising swarm of independent but co-operating cells than like a formal organisation',[13] in contrast to the more hierarchical terrorist groups Western states have been accustomed to countering, such as the IRA and ETA. The former Deputy Supreme Allied Commander of NATO, General Sir Rupert Smith, has helpfully applied botanical phraseology when depicting Islamist insurgent groups, in particular Al Qaeda, as having 'rhizomatic' nervous systems whereby growth derives from the roots even if they become detached from the stem above the ground.[14] Despite the flexible cell-based nature of the wider movement, Al Qaeda retained a core leadership, which was divided into three major committees: military operations, finance, and theological studies. The latter group is responsible for administering the religious justifications for Al Qaeda's perceived *jihad* as well as running a network of religious schools that nurture the next generation of devoted fighter. The finance committee is responsible for channelling funds, from both legitimate and illegal ventures, to enable the other branches to function. The military branch is the most obvious public embodiment of Al Qaeda's international presence, disseminating military training at specialist camps as well as planning and executing terrorist and paramilitary operations. The retention of a potent core leadership was severely tested after the US-led invasion of Afghanistan in October 2001, disrupting the Taliban-guaranteed safe-haven Al Qaeda enjoyed. The efficacy of post-9/11 centralised control over the *jihad* is subject to fierce academic contestation, as the 2008 exchange between Bruce Hoffman and Marc Sageman in *Foreign Affairs* demonstrated. This debate pitted Sageman's 'leaderless jihad' theory that Al Qaeda is now disparate and maintained by informal grassroots radicalisation against Hoffman's view that, in his words, 'bin Laden still matters' as Al Qaeda's core leadership is reconstituting in Pakistan and reasserting control over the wider *jihad*.[15] Despite salient points made by both authors, we should be wary of overtly dichotomising the state of Al Qaeda's leadership. A central core has always had to rely on a self-perpetuating grassroots movement to contribute to a cohesive, if not entirely co-ordinated whole. This is in large part due to the emergence of three major regional hubs of Al Qaeda cells, in the Arab region, North Africa and South East Asia, which has allowed the organisation to 'shift control over operations from the vertical to the horizontal as necessity dictates'.[16] Demonstrative of such capabilities was the 1998 bombings of the US embassies in Tanzania and Kenya, which marked a watershed in Al Qaeda's operational abilities. Firstly, it attested that the group could and would strike outside their traditional sphere of operations in order to undermine the 'far enemy'. Secondly, it was to prove the point at which Al Qaeda would have to decentralise the planning and execution of future attacks if the *jihad* was to be globally effective and the network remain operationally functional.[17] After 1998 the involvement and responsibilities of the core leadership of Al Qaeda were limited to financing and training. The potency of the regional theatres of operation for Al Qaeda is attested by the fact that in line with the core leadership they 'share a common tactical style and operational lexicon . . . (and) follow general ideological or strategic approaches aligned with Al Qaeda pronouncements . . .'[18] The core and the dispersed hubs are further connected by personal links between insurgents who have shared combat experiences, for the older generation repelling the Soviets from Afghanistan in the 1980s, whilst the latest wave of recruits will undoubtedly be tied by the common denominator of attendance at a training camp in Afghanistan or Pakistan. These are the ties that bind a seemingly disparate global movement by granting it an invigorated sense of purpose and mutual justifications for combat. David Kilcullen also points out that there are additional social and economic binds that partially homogenise the movement, notably an 'intricate network of private patronage, financial obligation and mutual commitment'.[19] Given such a degree of interconnectivity between hubs and cells of Al Qaeda it would be short-sighted to perceive the regional affiliates as essentially localised insurgencies with unique causal factors and domestic political goals (present though they are). Instead analysis should lean towards interpreting seemingly localised Islamist insurgencies as constituting the sum parts of the whole. Groups across the *jihadi* spectrum offer logistic, financial and political support for each other's campaigns and contribute to a shared pool of anti-Western, pro-*jihad* propaganda.[20] Such trends lend themselves to a picture of not only a state-free actor capable of transcending national boundaries but of also being, in Brian Reed's term, a 'sovereignty-free actor . . . not bound by the traditional concerns of states, yet they still have sufficient resources to initiate global action on their own authority and influence the course of world affairs'.[21] Therefore, the inter-connectivity of Al Qaeda's affiliate groupings combined with their immunity from accountability makes for a potent international insurgency capable of promulgating and executing operations with the aim of achieving a shared strategic goal. This has been able to occur in large part due to the harnessing of some of the side-effects of globalisation, notably the increasing porosity of state borders and instant global communications.

Transcending and undermining the state in a globalised world

In the era of globalisation, politics is increasingly conducted transnationally and this shift has therefore increased the scope for discontent and violent reaction by non-state actors on the global level concomitantly.[22] Yet despite the fact that the perpetrators of the global *jihad* are essentially 'stateless' this should not prohibit the conceptualisation of Al Qaeda's strategic mission as an insurgency. Analysis needs to overcome state-based definitions of insurgency that emanate from the 'classic' counter-insurgency era of the mid-twentieth century when mainly rural, Maoist-inspired guerrillas operated within the boundaries of a particular state (i.e. Malaya or Vietnam) for the express control of that state. The gradual erosion of the hegemony of the state in the era of globalisation should therefore encourage a reappraisal of not only the geographical criteria of an insurgency but also force us to re-evaluate the global horizons of the strategic missions of both insurgent and counter-insurgent in the so-called War on Terror. Contemporary *jihadis* are not constrained by Westphalian notions of secular sovereignty and statehood and are indeed willing to 'use the technology of globalisation in their quest to go beyond the nation-state in the pursuit of their vision of transforming regions, and indeed the world, to meet ideals fuelled by their interpretation of religion'.[23]

The disintegration of state authority, epitomised by the proliferation of 'failed states' in the post-Cold War era, has had a direct impact upon the ability and likelihood of non-state actors instigating an insurgency to fulfil their political goals as ungoverned, or even ungovernable, spaces became contested. Given the overt politicisation of insurgencies and the pervasive challenge to state authority which is an inevitable consequence of a non-state violent uprising, we must, therefore, understand the changes to the international system of statehood in order to fully understand the nature of the global insurgency that poses a threat to it. Some analysts have gone too far by suggesting that Al Qaeda's strategy is a 'global insurgency fought against the Westphalian system of states'.[24] The relationship between Al Qaeda and the state is more complex than that. The state system itself is not the *casus belli* for Islamists. The grand strategic imperative of establishing the supra-national theocracy of the Caliphate would of course demolish the Westphalian system, but in terms of realistic and communicable strategic aims held by *jihadi* groups the expulsion of occupying foreign armies and the imposition of *sharia* law in Muslim countries are the most prominent. Indeed, the *jihadist* movement is itself characteristic of what John Sullivan and Robert Bunker have labelled a 'virtual state' whereby they 'possess standing armies, treasury and revenue sources (even if it derives from criminal enterprises), a bureaucracy or "civil" service, intelligence collection and analysis organs, welfare systems, and the ability to make alliances (with state and non-state entities)'.[25] This encapsulates the paradoxical relationship Al Qaeda has with the state. Organisationally it has taken on certain common structures and processes (indeed, through its symbiosis with the Taliban regime in Afghanistan between 1996 and 2001 it could be said to have taken control of a state in its own right), yet it is ideologically and militarily geared towards the fundamental dismantling of Western and 'apostate' state power in favour of a pan-continental Caliphate.

As the consequences of globalisation have affected the conduct of world politics on an international and national level, the sub-national effects are particularly resonant especially in terms of how it has shaped the operational conduct of insurgent groups such as Al Qaeda. Michael Fowler has pointed to three factors that have conditioned the proclivity towards analysis of insurgency on a global scale: 'the openness of the world political and economic system after the fall of communism, availability of technology, and the free flow of ideas across borders around the world'.[26] However, it is this second of Fowler's factors, the availability of technology, which has catalysed the Islamist insurgency onto the global level above other causes. Information age technology has become so widely available that it has provoked a profound change in the way in which insurgent groups can communicate, operate and function. The dawn of the internet has, above other technological innovations, created multiple avenues for the distribution and exchange of both Islamist propaganda and training material. In short, the technological prowess of the West is being skilfully manipulated by its enemies to undermine its very existence. Robert Cassidy has miscast the nature of Al Qaeda's operational outlook when he depicts the group as 'twenty-first century Luddites since they reject technological change and globalisation . . .'[27] Even a cursory analysis of Al Qaeda's propaganda distribution, recruitment techniques and operational reach in fact demonstrates that the group has actually embraced technological change and aspects of globalisation, such as email, internet video postings, instant wired money transfers, and mobile phone communication. Al Qaeda has harnessed global technology for its own purposes in order to manipulate aspects of its asymmetric advantages over the Western nation state. In short, it is not the material by-products of globalisation that Al Qaeda rejects, but the underlying cultural and political value system that underpins it. The internet has become the 'medium of choice' for *jihadi* groups, as demonstrated by the exponential rise in fundamentalist websites, from just 14 in the year 2000 to over 4,000 by 2005.[28] The internet serves as a news portal for Islamists where developments in conflicts and politics can be disseminated free from Western perspectives. Furthermore, the internet provides for the open dissemination of propaganda, including videos of hostage executions and improvised explosive device (IED) detonations, as well as acting as a training platform where tactical manuals can be downloaded and militaristic lessons learned. It can also offer an outlet for expression in a non-violent way where the dissent, anger and activism of Islamists is channelled through the conduit of the worldwide web.[29] The widespread access to commercial technology created by the West's information-based economy allows contemporary insurgents to exploit the relative anonymity of cyberspace given the trillions of electronic transactions and interactions taking place every day. The proliferation of mobile telephones and laptop computers for use by Al Qaeda operatives (for example, the Madrid train bombs were detonated by mobile phones) is reflective of the parallel decrease in cost and increase in the availability of such communication equipment. This harnessing of the technology that has sustained the process of globalisation has aided the efficiency and effectiveness of Al Qaeda's global insurgency to the extent that 'anyone with a computer, a modem and a credit card is limited only by his imagination and intelligence in developing information from the political level to the tactical'.[30] Indeed, such technological innovations have allowed individuals to feel part of a wider virtual Islamist community that stretches around the world. Globalised technology has permitted Islamist diasporas to be informed and involved in the insurgency, including its current form in Afghanistan, from a distance by arranging logistical and financial assistance at the click of a button. Yet it is not just the technology of Western states that is being used against it. One other major consequence of globalisation that Al Qaeda operatives are astute to exploit is the increasing simplicity and decreased cost of international travel and the subsequent porosity of state borders. This has eased the movement of insurgents for training and fighting purposes, as the growth of Western-based Islamists visiting Pakistani camps or indeed entering Afghanistan to conduct insurgency operations has demonstrated. Porous borders, firstly in the context of Western integration and secondly in terms of ungoverned or contested spaces in conflict areas, has conditioned the global Islamist struggle to become an insurgency by osmosis. As Roger Scruton has argued, Al Qaeda's global *jihad* 'is an implacable summons to war, issued by globe-trotting Muslims, many of them extremely wealthy, and most of them sufficiently well versed in Western civilisation to be able to exploit the modern world to the full . . . With Al Qaeda, therefore, we encounter the real impact of globalisation on the Islamic revival'.[31] Such a threat, so global in its scope yet localised in its actions, poses a unique problem for the Western liberal state to address. Global warfare marred the twentieth century, but the totalising nature of conventional conflict is ill-suited for the nuances of asymmetric insurgency. What is clear is that Al Qaeda's conflation of terrorism as a tactic and insurgency as a strategy necessitates a hybrid response.

The liberal state and counter-insurgency solutions

By differentiating between insurgency and terrorism, thus altering how we *perceive* the threat from Al Qaeda, the fundamental nature of the *response* is therefore transformed. Insurgencies are, in essence, a 'whole-of-government issue' whereas terrorism remains a mainly law enforcement problem.[32] The entrenched political and social motivations of an insurgency can lead to an assumption that the insurgents are extreme representatives of what can essentially be a quasi-legitimate grievance at the heart of a certain society or political system. Terrorists are, conversely, popularly held to be criminals pursuing misguided and illegitimate goals. Consequently, the Western liberal state has held that the latter can be suppressed by legalistic measures, yet the former requires a fundamental reappraisal of the political system and measures sought to keep the population of the affected country or region 'on side' in recognition of the social appeal of the insurgent's message. The 'War on Terror' is therefore a misnomer, applied solely for political reasons. The conflict is about more than securing the American homeland and it requires more than domestic legal restrictions, financial monitoring and intelligence gathering.

Before 9/11 Western liberal democratic states largely conceived of and implemented counter-terrorist responses on the nation-state level. The endogenous threat perception negated the need to formulate a global strategy.[33] What 9/11 did was to shake the West out of its state-centric mentality and brutally awaken it to the potent threat posed by non-state networked actors. This requires, as John Mackinlay has quite rightly pointed out, a change in direction from the 'crudely kinetic procedures of counter-terrorism to a genuine, politically-led counter-insurgency campaign'.[34] What has become clear since 9/11, and the subsequent invasions of Afghanistan and Iraq, is that existing national and international security structures, including domestic police and intelligence services in Western states, have found it immensely challenging to adapt to the new operational environment that has superseded the traditional state-on-state or internal threat situation. The transcendence of state boundaries in the international *jihadi* insurgency, both operationally and ideationally, has meant that the national security of states, and broader global peace and security, now has to be interpreted interdependently. This can be achieved in part by the creation of closer co-operational relationships between the elements constitutive of state security (diplomatic, intelligence and military provisions) and those organs of both sub-state security (the police) and international security (such as Interpol and NATO) in order to foster an exogenous and endogenous prevention and response capability. However, the insurgent nature of the *jihadi* threat should not lead to assumptions that the only way to counter the movement is through military means alone. This was never the case even in the so-called 'classic' era of counter-insurgency in response to Maoist guerrillas in the 1950s and 1960s.[35] Law enforcement and criminal justice mechanisms should be granted priority status to maintain standards of civil liberties, human rights and transparent jurisprudence in bringing suspected insurgents to justice. The military does nevertheless have a crucial role to play, yet one that differs from previous counter-insurgency experience. What must be remembered about the current insurgent battlegrounds of the War on Terror is that it has actually been the invading Western coalition that has instigated the conflict and has forced the *jihadi* fighters to become reactive to the Bush Doctrine. Thus we have an inversion of the traditional formulation of the insurgents attempting to permanently change the status quo, and instead have witnessed the Western 'coalition of the willing' acquiesce to a strategy of pre-emption, overlooking certain crucial law enforcement aspects of a hybrid counter-insurgency campaign (most notably the lack of impetus in tracking down and bringing to justice key figures in the *jihadi* insurgency, such as Osama bin Laden and Ayman al-Zawahiri). In short, there needs to emerge a concerted effort that focuses on political, legal, intelligence, military and crucially cultural issues pertaining to countering the *jihadi* insurgency, built on a local, national and international level, cutting across and between the multi-variate levels of global security. However, the attainment of such a strategic balance has been lacking. Paul Wilkinson has accused the West of suffering from 'a failure of leadership and a failure to mobilise global support for a genuine multi-national, multi-religious and multi-pronged strategy to unravel the Al Qaeda network and to win the crucial battle of ideas'.[36] It is this battle for ideas within the wider Muslim world that is as important as the military battle against insurgents, and is one that is suffering from neglect in the grand strategy of the War on Terror. The utilisation of 'soft power' in conjunction with 'hard' military power is central to any counter-insurgency campaign, and it will help ameliorate the distrust and hatred of the West in parts of the Muslim world as a precursor to not necessarily 'winning' the 'hearts and minds' of those in Islamic countries, but at least placating them. This can be achieved by firstly erecting ideational barriers between Al Qaeda's fundamentalist message and the thoughts and actions of vulnerable communities, and secondly by appreciating that the battle for 'hearts and minds' lies as much in good governance in insurgent areas as it does in protecting the liberal values at home that the West purports to stand for. This in part helps foster local and regional solutions to a global problem.

We therefore can see that in order for the Al Qaeda threat to be adequately suppressed there is an obvious need for domestic counter-terrorism to be conjoined with a wider, transnational politico-military counter-insurgency strategy.

Western counter-terrorism strategy is commonly premised on 'the 4Ps': prevention, pursuit, protection and preparation.[37] Such criterion is readily transferable to the counter-insurgency paradigm, and holds some valuable strategic pointers. Given the internationalisation of the Islamist *jihad* it is necessary to evaluate any attempt at the prevention of Al Qaeda attacks at the global level, and particularly in the context of their insurgent strategy. Prevention must include the close monitoring of international border crossings, especially into countries where known Al Qaeda camps are functioning. This will therefore reduce the pool of would-be insurgents armed with the knowledge and inspiration to initiate attacks in their home countries. Tighter restrictions on the flow of money between *jihadi* groups has been implemented by close international financial co-operation since 9/11, and this must continue if Al Qaeda is to be prevented from operating effectively. There is a clear need for the prevention plank of any strategy to acknowledge both domestic and international concerns. Western liberal states must prevent the radicalisation of the young generation of Muslims by concomitantly engaging with and listening to their concerns whilst marginalising fundamentalism through concerted police action upon active instigators of violence. Internationally, prevention can be achieved through co-operation and assistance with governments most susceptible to Al Qaeda attacks in an attempt to help allies build more effective, and more discriminate, counter-terrorist capabilities. The need to pursue known Al Qaeda operatives is perhaps the one strand of any effective strategy that transcends into the realm of international counter-insurgency most obviously. Again, given the global networked nature of Al Qaeda, the pursuit of the fighters and sponsors of the insurgency necessitates not only a truly international effort, but also inevitably requires the utilisation of military force – a facet not associated with counter-terrorism *per se*. Indeed it was the ultimate failure of coalition forces to pursue and apprehend any of the major Al Qaeda or Taliban figures after the invasion of Afghanistan in October 2001 that has arguably led to an increased inability to prevent further attacks due to the mere potency of their myth, propagated by regular video and audio messages. However, the outcome of the pursuit of Al Qaeda operatives will not only be predicated on an effective and realistic intelligence assessment process, but must be conducted in accordance to due legal procedure that reflects the very premise of the Western liberal state. Quite simply, prevention cannot be reconciled with contradictory double standards. The notion of protection in a counter-insurgency strategy must be extended not only to citizens threatened by acts of domestic terrorism, but also to the citizens on the frontline of the War on Terror in Afghanistan and Iraq. The security of the civilian population in an insurgency scenario has been a central tenet of counter-insurgency thinking since its modern inception in the mid-twentieth century. Connected to the notion of winning 'hearts and minds', the protection of civilians does more than just encourage support for the counter-insurgency mission but also aids the prevention of future attacks by instilling confidence in the military effort amongst the indigenous population and retarding any nascent resentment or radicalisation as a result of the military presence. Finally, the conception of anti-terrorist preparation is equally applicable when dealing with an international insurgency, given the need to construct a coherent, achievable and well-resourced counter-insurgency campaign. Strategic planning is a vital element in any conflict, and the War on Terror is no exception. Indeed, the lack of post-war planning in the run-up to the Iraq invasion arguably contributed to the proliferation of Islamist violence in the aftermath of Saddam Hussein's toppling.[38] Holistically, the central '4Ps' of a domestic counter-terrorism strategy, designed to curtail the internal Al Qaeda threat in Western liberal states, are well suited to be elevated and applied to an international counter-insurgency level. This, in part, has been appreciated by President Barack Obama, whose 2009 review of the campaign in Afghanistan acknowledged that the fight against Al Qaeda abroad has consequences at home, therefore justifying an operational synergy between foreign counter-insurgency and domestic counter-terrorism measures: 'Our overarching goal remains the same: to disrupt, dismantle, and defeat al Qaeda in Afghanistan and Pakistan, and to prevent its capacity to threaten America and our allies in the future'.[39] The strategic nuances of the Al Qaeda threat are evidently applicable to an insurgency scenario and therefore, if the security and resilience of the Western state is to be secured during this tumultuous period, then a reappraisal of such a threat, as well as the required response, is vitally necessary.

Conclusion

The direction of the American-led 'War on Terror' since the invasion of Iraq in 2003 has led to a tangible increase in the threat posed by transnational networked Islamist insurgents. Despite suffering the loss of its Afghan haven, the scattering of its hierarchy, and the failure to make inroads into overthrowing 'apostate' regimes, Al Qaeda has been re-energised by the American foray into Iraq. A new wave of recruits flocked to its ranks, as training and operational franchises functioned in areas on the Afghan-Pakistani border, not to mention the crucible of Sunni belligerence in western Iraq. This region came to be dominated by the affiliate group 'Al Qaeda in Iraq', a branch founded by the notorious Islamist guerrilla Abu Musab al-Zarqawi (killed in a US air raid in June 2006) who merged his Al Tawhid wa Al Jihad group with Al Qaeda in October 2004. Similar to the effect of the Afghan war on emerging *jihadi* sentiment in the 1980s, the war in Iraq turned into an ersatz laboratory for guerrilla warfare where radicalised insurgents engaged the 'occupying forces' in urban conflict on a daily basis, sapping coalition morale and resources. These insurgents operated against a backdrop of vitriolic anti-Western, mainly anti-American, opinion throughout the Islamic world. In many ways, Al Qaeda is more dangerous now than it was in the immediate aftermath of 9/11.[40]

The evolution of the threat posed by Al Qaeda, from a disparate band of poorly-armed guerrillas to a global network of technologically adept insurgents, has presented the Western liberal state system, in terms of both its continued security and its continued relevance as an actor in international affairs in the era of globalisation, with a virulent and violent obstacle. Indeed, the ascendancy of asymmetric warfare in the post-Cold War, and now especially post-9/11 world, has come to represent, in Rupert Smith's assertion, the 'near completion of a circle' in conflict terms, whereby the inter-state total warfare of the last century subordinated the sub-state actor to the nation-state for the purpose of victory, swinging round to the new paradigm where the sub-state actor has come to turn on the state through the use of 'terrorist attacks or the use of force outside the framework of the state'.[41] The threat to states is, as has been maintained throughout this chapter, both endogenous and exogenous: endogenous in terms of *jihadi* sleeper-cells, training camps or operational bases that are known to have a presence in over forty countries worldwide, and exogenous in terms of the networked nature of these cells that encourages international co-operation, aided by the causes and consequences of globalisation, that can wreak damage upon individual states and the system of statehood as a whole as Al Qaeda aims to accomplish the reinstatement of the theocratic Caliphate and topple 'apostate' Muslim states. As a consequence of this multi-pronged threat, a multi-pronged response must be formulated. Notions of Al Qaeda as a terrorist group do not do justice to the grand strategy of their *jihad*. Neither too have they adequately encapsulated the paramilitary nature of Al Qaeda's tactical arsenal. A counter-insurgency strategy comprised of the most rudimentary yet elementary facets of minimum force and cultural sensitivity must be enacted in the frontline of the War on Terror. This must be utilised alongside a political counter-insurgency platform, which actively discourages support for the *jihad* via a prudent and measured foreign policy in the Muslim world (arguably a hard task given the international fall-out from the invasion of Iraq), and a legal counter-insurgency platform that utilises a honed intelligence network to pinpoint the prime leaders and backers of the insurgency, and ensure a police-led 'decapitation' policy that culminates in criminal proceedings and not indiscriminate bloodshed. The West must do its own bit to stop fanning the flames of an already powerful fire. Therefore, by assessing the threat holistically, strategically and tactically, the state response can be equally holistic, ensuring the safety of the Western liberal state, its citizens and its values, during a most turbulent period in its evolutionary history.

4 Ethical and legal reasoning about war in a time of terror

James Connelly and Don Carrick

In this chapter we argue that reliance on the law in and of itself is insufficient to address the complex issues at play in war in a time of terror. However, this does not mean that the solution lies in a substitution of a legalistic conception of ethics for a reliance on legalism per se. Addressing the moral dimension requires addressing it with the use of appropriate forms of moral reasoning and these forms of moral reasoning cannot be reduced to a sort of ghostly ethical double of a legal code. On the contrary, it is a substantive requirement for forms of moral reasoning adequate to the complexities and nuances of modern warfare. Accordingly, we seek to show that moral reasoning is inescapable; that it cannot be reduced to rules, tick boxes or codes; that there are no algorithms which can be relied on to provide answers in the absence of moral reasoning; and also to give a sense of how moral reasoning in this territory proceeds.

The focus here is on moral reasoning, not moral theories. A moral theory is an attempt to encapsulate and determine moral reasoning by constraining it within the framework of a certain principle or constellation of principles. Thus, for example, utilitarianism focuses on consequences of actions, not the independent moral quality of actions, and, in particular, asserts that we judge consequences by aggregating the balance of loss over gain and comparing the net sum of different actions or proposed courses of action. Classically this was framed as aiming for the greatest happiness of the greatest number; in modern utilitarianism it tends to be framed as the maximising of people's preferences, whatever those preferences are. A utilitarian approach therefore is reductive in the sense that it seeks to ground all moral reasoning in a single principle or constellation of closely related principles. However, irrespective of whether this claim can in the end be justified or not, irrespective of whether morality can be reduced to calculation of net aggregate consequences, it is palpably the case that actual moral reasoning always combines concern for consequences with concern for the rightness or wrongness of certain actions as such. To assert that certain actions are right or wrong in themselves is a feature of what is referred to as the deontological approach to moral theory. In this approach, the right is not regarded as simply that which maximises the good, where the good is specifiable independently of the right. (For example, in utilitarianism the greatest happiness is the good and the right action is that which maximises it.) In a deontological approach, on the contrary, the right and the good are specified independently, from which it follows that there might be constraints on the pursuit of the good; an action might be 'the right thing to do' even if it doesn't maximise overall welfare, and the 'wrong thing to do', even if it does. In real moral reasoning, both features – the right and the good – are always present and in real moral reasoning there are constraints on the reduction of the goodness or badness of actions to consideration of their consequences alone. What has become known as Just War Theory comprises both deontological and consequentialist elements. This shows that the dichotomy between these forms of moral reasoning is a false one in practical moral reasoning. They are often presented as alternatives, sometimes even as alternatives that can be chosen at will or whim to fit the circumstances. This is not so. Real moral reasoning is a complex affair which necessarily comprises both.

Over the past forty years, after the Vietnam War, just war theorising, which had been largely ignored in mainstream reasoning about war and international relations under the hegemony of 'realism', began to reassert itself. Traditionally it was the province of theologically based reasoning deriving ultimately from authors such as Aquinas. However, in its modern incarnation (in which the lead was taken by Michael Walzer in his influential *Just and Unjust Wars*, originally published in 1977), it was recast as a secular theory, one not unrelated to its origins in the Catholic church, but conceptually independent of it and essentially the distillation of many centuries of reasoning on the justice and conduct of war. But we are wary of continuing to refer to it as 'a theory'. A better way to characterise it is as a *tradition* of moral reasoning. It is not a theory in the way that utilitarianism is a theory, both because it includes elements of both deontological and consequentialist reasoning and also because it does not seek to reduce all reasoning on war to a single explanatory principle. As George Lucas suggests, it is a 'mode of normative discourse, a philosophical tradition of reflection on the moral constraints of both prudential reasoning and political practice'.[1] Just war theory or tradition (henceforth JWT) should therefore be thought of both as an *approach* to moral reasoning about war (drawing on the accumulated wisdom of practical reasoning about war) and as a *resource* comprising the most salient conceptual and moral distinctions distilled over centuries of reasoning. It should not be thought of as an answer-generating machine operated by turning fact and value inputs into neatly minced outputs at the single turn of a handle. It is a way of reasoning, not a substitute for it. We return to these themes later. For the moment we will inspect some features of the history of JWT.

In ancient Rome the fetials (*fetiales*) were a college of priests who had special responsibility for maintaining peaceful relations among the Latins. They would oversee the making of treaties, declarations of war, and other such functions . . . If it was decided that a grave breach of the peace had in fact occurred, such that a just war would be warranted, the fetials would first approach the guilty city to demand redress. If, after a certain length of time, no satisfaction was given, war could begin.[2]

Two millennia later, a remarkably similar ritual was followed in the long run-up to the March 2003 invasion of Iraq by the US-led coalition, albeit with UN weapons inspectors taking the place of the fetials. So when it was judged that Saddam Hussein was indeed 'threatening a grave breach of the peace', and when he failed to 'satisfy the demand for redress', then war could begin, and it did. But that is not what would have happened in ancient Rome. The procedure then for legitimating going to war was a two-stage process. After the fetials had made their report to the Emperor that the war in question was legally permissible, the members of the Senate (that is, the representatives of the Roman people) still had to decide whether it was just to do so. In other words, advice had been given that Rome *could* go to war (a matter of legal authority, within the realm of law); the question remained as to whether Rome *should* go to war (a matter of ethical permissibility, within the realm of morality). This procedure constituted the required 'public declaration' in two senses; firstly, by way of making an open offer to the enemy or opponent to take every opportunity of redress short of war, and secondly by way of inviting all parties involved in the domestic decision-making process to deliberate on the morality of the intended decision. In our modern example, therefore, the Bush and Blair governments possibly satisfied the first dimension by giving Saddam every opportunity to 'come clean' about the WMD, but ignored the second, by failing to refer the matter to the appropriate 'legitimate sovereign' – the UN Security Council – to debate the ensuing morality of the case.

The outcome was that the USA, Britain and their allies went to war on the flimsiest of pretexts – many still argue that there was, in fact, *no* legal justification for the invasion – and without any morally convincing support for the venture. The fact that the Bush administration had deemed the invasion to be a necessary response to the events initiating the so-called War on Terror was assumed to be sufficient explanation. By implication, therefore, compliance with the traditional fetial preconditions was deemed unnecessary: a hindrance rather than a help to the self-styled crusade against the 'forces of evil'. In this chapter, we shall argue that such a view is both misleading and dangerous, and the Iraq venture has proved to be nothing more than an exercise in what philosopher George Lucas has aptly dubbed 'vigilante justice'.[3] The old rules can, and should, continue to be applied for so long as the War on Terror continues; the rule of law and the demands and constraints of morality must be restored to their rightful place in the scheme of things. We begin with a brief analysis of the reasons why there was no clear investigation into the ethical aspects of the Iraq invasion.

One major cause of this omission was an undue reliance on an unquestioned equivocation between law and morality: an unspoken assumption that if something is legally required, permitted or forbidden, then it is also, automatically, morally required, permitted or forbidden. But this assumption is deeply flawed. Uncritical reliance on it has been a major contributory factor in the development of a way of thinking about war that relies far too much on this narrow view. In fact, the true history of the relationship between law and morality is one of tensions and conflict rather than harmonious coexistence.

Such tension and conflict are reflected in the ongoing dialogue between the adherents of the two major schools of thought in the world of jurisprudence concerning the nature of law, namely the 'natural law' school and the 'legal postivist' school. The central point of difference between the schools lies in their diametrically opposed view of the conceptual connection between law and morality, with naturalists maintaining that there is a *necessary* connection between them and positivists maintaining that there is not, that, at best, the connection is only contingent. Travelling down these different paths has in turn led those concerned with thinking about war to favour one or other of two paradigmatic modes of discourse, the first being JWT (which can be termed the ethical paradigm), the second being International Humanitarian Law (IHL) (which can be termed the legalist paradigm).[4] The function of each is to critically interrogate the justness of going to war (*jus ad bellum*) and the justice of actions in war (*jus in bello*).[5] Now, it is reasonable to say that in modern times, and especially since the coming into being of the United Nations Charter in 1945, the legalist version has been favoured over the ethical but, as we shall see, the ethical version has never really gone away and has recently resurfaced. However, in order to better appreciate the complex interaction between the two, it is also necessary to know something of the history of our ways of thinking about justice in war. We begin with an exposition of the development of such modes of thought, during which we will pick out the various justifications offered for going to war in at particular times in history. We then conduct a critical examination of the strengths and weaknesses of the respective paradigms as exemplified in their application to the wars of the late twentieth and early twenty-first centuries, and we plot the limits of their usefulness.

Historically, ethics came first, as it were, in the form of the application of what became known as 'natural law' theory to interrogate the justice of war. In the West, this natural law based approach dominated reasoning on the topic from about the fifth century BC (which saw the appearance the first written record of a debate about such matters in the form of the 'Melian Dialogue' in Thucydides' *Peloponnesian Wars*[6]) until the seventeenth century AD. During the intervening two millennia, a variety of theologians, philosophers, lawyers and statesmen developed and refined JWT into a recognisably modern form: it is in the fifth century BC that the term 'just war' makes its first appearances in the learned writings of the time (it may well have been coined by Aristotle). Importantly, JWT was treated at that time (that is, before the accretion of theological undertones) as an essentially *secular* doctrine based on pragmatic considerations about when it was justifiable to go to war even though notions of religious or holy war still underlay the reasoning.[7] It is for this reason that the notion of self-defence, which would later come to be regarded as central to the justification of *any* war, was regarded by the ancients as meaning 'a war in defence of one's religion', even if this meant going on the offensive in order to do so.[8] So, for the people of the ancient world in the fifth century, the just war was primarily an *aggressive, offensive* war; a war of conquest (in pursuit of honour, glory and power) and, sometimes, a war of *punishment*.

However, the ethical paradigm did not last long before the legalist paradigm came to take centre stage. In the first century BC, Roman lawyers such as Cicero further refined the tradition into a legal model, exemplified by the procedure of the fetials. At this point in the unfolding of the relationship between law and morality, the distinction between them was more of a procedural than a substantive nature. The law emphasised compliance with an established procedure, scrupulous adherence to which rendered the war in question legal and thus, as Cicero expressed it, avoided invoking the anger of the gods. Further, the procedure embodied one, and perhaps two, moral considerations which we would now characterise as 'last resort' and 'legitimate authority'. Even so, this implicit concession to morality did not protect the Roman system from subsequent abuse by an over-reliance on the letter, rather than the spirit, of the law. The visits of the fetials to, for example, the Gauls, involved little more than the making of an offer that could not be refused; 'either surrender and become slaves and vassals of Rome, or else suffer the consequences'. The Romans had unapologetically reverted to the Greek model.

But following the collapse of the Roman Empire in the West, the Catholic Church became the principal global power, and development of JWT reverted to the theologians. An unhappy period in history then followed, during which the idea of holy war resurfaced in the form of the Crusades and *jus ad bellum* 'became polluted with some dark religious dimensions like self-righteousness, inflexibility, demonization of others and fanaticism'.[9] St Augustine, writing in the fourth and fifth centuries, effectively (although not entirely successfully) reconciled the aggressiveness of the Old Testament warmongers with the near-pacifist approach of the Christians. Nevertheless, he was still somewhat equivocal as far as the legitimacy or otherwise of holy wars was concerned and, building upon a distinction between 'the innocent' and 'the guilty', regarded even defensive wars as involving an element of punishment of the guilty aggressor. Then, in the twelfth century, St Thomas Aquinas produced a codified version of JWT, somewhat simplified, but nevertheless in a form that was recognisably modern, and which became the foundation upon which the present forms of JWT were built. After implicitly suggesting, *contra* Augustine, that holy wars could never be justified under any circumstances, Aquinas argued that three basic stipulations – what we would now call necessary and sufficient criteria – had to be satisfied before going to war. It must be declared by a *legitimate authority* (in this, Aquinas anticipated the idea of a head of state), it must be fought for a *just cause*, and those undertaking the war must have *right* (that is, morally worthy) *intentions*. Later commentators added a total of four more criteria namely, and very briefly, *last resort, reasonable hope of success, proportionality* and *just means*.

The sixteenth century saw a further strengthening of the requirement that the only just cause for war was self-defence, with the Spanish commentator Francisco de Vitoria completing the secularisation process by making it clear that *all* communities, religious or not, had a right not to be attacked and a right to defend themselves if they were. He was, however, very much opposed to the idea of the pre-emptive strike, remarking that 'It is quite unacceptable that a person should be killed for a sin he has yet to commit'.[10] He also added a salutary warning that any decision to go to war should only be made after careful consideration and after seeking the opinions of the wise (that was, of course, also the point of the second stage of the fetial procedure).

It can reasonably be said that at that point in history, the ethical paradigm of JWT had reached its zenith. From then on, over the subsequent five hundred years or so, we find the legalist paradigm gradually returning to prominence until, in the seventeenth century, Hugo Grotius produced his monumental *On the Laws of War and Peace*. This extremely influential work was, in spirit (if not in form), the direct ancestor of all the codes, conventions and laws that followed. It was written at the height of the worst excesses of the wars of religious Reformation and Counter-reformation, and at the dawn of the most destructive of these, the Thirty Years War. Grotius was determined to construct a framework within which a proper decision procedure could be followed, with the intention that the moral underpinnings of JWT could find expression in law.

The same century also saw the signature, in 1648, of the Treaty of Westphalia which effectively created the modern nation-state system. These two events marked the start of a another process of refinement and codification that would eventually lead to the emergence of what we now call IHL or the Law of Armed Combat (LOAC) and the adoption into nation-state legal systems of the various Conventions, Treaties and Protocols, so as to control relations between states and to ensure that war was indeed a last resort when negotiations to avoid it had completely broken down. War would then become, in Carl von Clausewitz's famous characterisation, 'the continuation of political intercourse with the admixing of other means'.

The period from the seventeenth century to the end of the nineteenth did not see any major developments in JWT as such, at least as far as *jus ad bellum*[11] was concerned: the tradition was found to be more or less adequate for dealing with large-scale inter-state wars, greatly assisted by the exponential increase, from the mid-nineteenth century onwards, in international recognition of the aforementioned Conventions, Treaties and Protocols which, broadly speaking, had turned the moral rules, principles and guidelines of JWT into concrete law.

But there is another crucially important piece that has to be fitted into our JWT jigsaw before it is complete, namely the notion of *human rights*. The key players here were John Locke and Immanuel Kant (both of whom actually perceived themselves as working *outside* the Just War Tradition). They were living at a time not only of religious wars, or wars of conquest, but of *civil* wars, and they were witness to the gross infringement of the rights of hundreds of thousands of individuals of their own countrymen, not just those of – to paraphrase the notorious words of Neville Chamberlain in a more recent era – the citizens of a far-off country of which they knew nothing. This was war on one's own doorstep. Locke therefore insisted that, henceforth, governments had to respect the basic rights of each individual citizen if they were to be perceived as legitimate and thus deserving of the respect of those citizens. Kant, in turn, took this theme to an international, cosmopolitan level and also considered in great detail what ought happen after a war was over: he was the first major figure to seriously address the problems of *jus post bellum* and the idea of the just peace. In time, and following upon the lessons learned from the First and Second World Wars (particularly the latter, involving as it did the horrors of the Holocaust and the morally disturbing cases of the firebombing of German cities and the use of the atomic bomb on Hiroshima and Nagasaki), the work of Locke, Kant and their successors would lead to the landmark 1948 Declaration of Human Rights, which enshrined human rights protection and established its connection with the legitimacy of the state, once and for all. Add to that the creation of the United Nations Charter in 1945, and it would appear that the legalistic paradigm has triumphed. All nations signing up to these codes bound themselves, for all time, *to follow the rules* as to when they could go to war and as to what they could (and could not) do once they were actually at war.

But there is another strand to the thread of the development of human rights legislation that we must examine before we can consider ourselves fully theoretically equipped to interrogate the reality of New Wars. The path taken towards full recognition of human rights was not a smooth one. During the late eighteenth and early nineteenth centuries, UK politics and political decision-making was in thrall to the utilitarian theories of Jeremy Bentham and John Stuart Mill, to which we alluded at the beginning of this chapter, which maintained that the right action to take on any occasion was that which promoted the greatest happiness of the greatest number. The rights of the individual – the natural rights, at least – were a secondary consideration in the calculus, to the point at which Bentham was notoriously able to declare that talk of (natural) human rights was 'nonsense upon stilts'. Added to this was the related fact that the legal positivists were dominant in the field of jurisprudence. This had a vital consequence for the understanding of the relation between law and morality. Legal positivists such as John Austin maintained that the law is the command of the sovereign backed by the threat of sanctions. On this view it followed that the law should be obeyed simply because it was there, regardless of whether it had a *moral* grounding: the fact that it has been imposed by the relevant legitimate authority is in itself sufficient to demand compliance.[12]

The UN Charter (UNC) of 1945 finally confirmed the dominance of the legalist paradigm, providing an internationally recognised legal framework within which JWT could operate and by which UN member states could agree to be legally bound. This was a voluntary contractual relationship, rather than an imposition by a higher authority of laws which had to be obeyed. To this day, some commentators are confident that '[l]aw now offers an institutional and doctrinal space for transforming the boundaries of war into strategic assets as well as a vernacular for legitimating and denouncing what happens in war'.[13] So, for a brief period after 1945, it looked as though the Charter would work as planned: at last the lawyers had an apparently clear set of legal positivist 'black letter' or 'bright line' rules, regulations and procedures to be followed without the requirement for recourse to any underlying ethical principles.

However, this ideal did not survive the trauma of the Vietnam War. By the end of that unhappy conflict in the early 1970s, the voices of the lawyers had ceased to be of any relevance and the voices of protest were essentially speaking the language of JWT.

Where does this leave the debate? Between the end of the second world war and the end of the 1960s, as we remarked earlier, the JWT was largely dormant: on the one hand its rationale was assumed to be subsumed under the UNC and it was largely understood in legalistic terms; on the other hand, forms of ethical protest against war tended to derive from pacifist positions, positions of opposition to all war. The JWT does not prescribe pacifism – on the contrary it maintains that some wars are just and some unjust, some ought to be fought and some ought not to be fought. However, following Vietnam, the distinction between justified and unjustified wars came to the fore, together with a recognition that the serious question of whether a particular war was justified or not could not be reduced to its mere abstract legality. Were legality and morality always hand in glove, then to answer the question of legality would *ipso facto* be to answer the other and *vice versa*. But this is not so. To assert that the 2003 Iraq war was illegal, according to international laws and protocols, is not in itself to say anything definitive about its morality. A course of action might be legally permitted but morally or pragmatically or prudentially wrong. For many reasons, one does not do everything that one might be legally permitted to do; conversely, there are cases where a course of action might be technically illegal and yet, because the moral imperative is so clear, the law has to be over-ridden or changed. Again, the law may grant permissions or 'rights' to certain actions, to which there might nonetheless be moral duties to abstain in the exercise of the legal right. For example, a bank might have a legal right to foreclose on a home loan on which a borrower has defaulted, but a moral duty to abstain out of mercy if the borrower has attempted in good faith to meet the obligation, and genuinely intends to do so.

In general, the UNC has typically been the starting point for all *jus ad bellum* considerations: those wishing to find just grounds/legal authority for going to war in the late twentieth/early twenty-first centuries for any reasons other than self-defence have looked to the UNC to provide them. However, there is a vital point that can be, and often is, easily obscured: judgement. Following laws or rules requires judgement – legal judgements by definition require judgement – even though the tenor of black letter law and of legalistic interpretations of legal codifications of JWT tends to overlook or obscure this point. No matter how 'black letter' a piece of law is; no matter how 'bright line' it might be, the need to exercise judgement can never be eliminated. This is both a logical and a practical point.

Even in a case where it is clear to all that a particular rule or principle applies in a clear cut way, there is still the need to exercise what Kant called 'determinant' judgement, which is to recognise both the rule and the particular case and to see that one should be subsumed to the other. In other cases this might, however, become progressively more difficult: it simply might not be obvious whether a particular case is an instance to which the rule applies. As we move to this end of the spectrum of judgement we move to what Kant termed 'reflective' judgement in which the moral judge has to decide not whether a rule governs a particular case, but somehow to work out what rule there might be that could possibly govern this case, in the absence of any rule that obviously already does so. This requires acute and concentrated moral reasoning in which all the powers of moral judgement and reasoning are brought to bear.

Consider how this applies to the JWT. There is a danger that JWT itself is open to treatment as a sort of moral algorithm, as a set of tick boxes in which a sufficient number of ticks yields the result 'this war is just'. This might be glossed by talking of necessary and sufficient conditions: but this begs the question, as it supposes either that there is a clear lexical ordering between the principles of JWT such that A is more important than B which is more important than C and so on, so that we can decide, by progressing through the more important to the less important, whether a war is just or not. Or, again, if all of the principles are taken to be equally important, does that mean that *all* of them have to be satisfied before a war can be declared just? But, as Lucas points out, this is hardly satisfactory either. Some principles (such as legitimate authority) had much greater importance and sali-ence at a time when such authorities were few and far between and the definition of what counted as such unsettled: but following the Treaty of Westphalia in 1648 it is far less of an issue. If that is the case, is satisfying that criterion to be held as significant and important as satisfying (for example) the criterion of proportion-ality? That would be absurd: but what follows is not that there is a defect in the JWT, but rather that there is a defect in the way that it is sometimes treated as a moral algorithm. As we have seen, there is another compelling reason for refusing this conclusion, which is that JWT as a whole is made up of several interlocking elements, each related but also requiring separate treatment. The answer to the question of proportionality or right intention is not satisfied by an answer to the question of just cause or reasonable prospect of success. Each of these elements requires concentrated independent moral judgement or, in its legal variant, legal judgement. Thus an interim conclusion is that the legal understanding of JWT can-not be sustained, if it suggests (together with other ways of understanding JWT) that it consists of a check list which can be completed in the absence of fully devel-oped moral reasoning. Again, even where it is recognised that judgement (whether it be legal and moral) is required, it cannot be reduced to a matter of satisfying necessary and sufficient conditions as though it were a unified theory in which once all the buttons are pressed, all systems are go. If it is ever treated that way, it is wrong to treat it that way.

Another way of making this point is to observe, with Lucas, that some approaches to reasoning about just war are compliance-based; that is, they:

> resolve disputes by appealing to compliance, either with established interna-tional laws and customs, or (in the case of philosophy) with lists of necessary conditions arising from a longstanding and authoritative tradition of schol-arly discourse over many centuries. By contrast, Walzer, and other propo-nents of applied ethics, invite readers instead to engage directly in a kind of moral casuistry by citing, describing, and analyzing specific historic cases or hypothetical examples, and then testing what might be termed their 'pre-theoretic moral intuitions' on the historical cases or hypothetical examples cited. From this procedure, they then elicit more general, action-guiding

reasons or governing normative principles that resolve or explain the cases, or lead . . . to challenging or revising conventional wisdom about the meaning or application of such principles, such as the 'principle of double effect'.[14]

Let us amplify this point. JWT is a guide to action, or to be more precise, a guide to thinking about action; it cannot be (and ought not pretend to be) fully comprehensive and complete – any more than any other moral theory can be. Here the same issue arises for JWT viewed as a non-codified moral theory as arises for any other moral theory: no moral theory, whether utilitarian, virtue ethics or deontology, can be regarded as a means to generating simple conclusions, still less as something to be used to justify conclusions already reached on other grounds. Each can help moral reasoning but moral reasoning cannot be reduced to any of them.

Practically speaking, of course, ethics and law have been intertwined in a complex relation over many centuries. At certain times this relationship seems to have achieved a sort of equilibrium: it seemed for a while that the UNC had effected a seamless merger of JWT and law and to have settled on one clear justification (self-defence) for engaging in warfare. However, the remaining catch-all provisions in the UNC have proved to be singularly inadequate for providing clear legal/ethical justifications for any state engaging in anything other than wars of self-defence. For example, certain wars of humanitarian intervention, such as Kosovo in 1999, were clearly illegal and started without UN sanction: but it might be argued that they were morally justifiable. Other wars, such as that in Iraq in 1991, were both legal and morally acceptable (from the point of view of *jus ad bellum*, although not necessarily from the point of view of *jus in bello*). Michael Walzer notes that:

> I don't believe that the bombing of Iraq in 1991 met just war standards; shielding civilians would certainly have excluded the destruction of electricity networks and water purification plants. Urban infrastructure, even if it is necessary to modern war making, is also necessary to civilian existence in a modern city, and it is morally defined by this second feature.[15]

All of these cases test both the legal justifications for war and also the application of JWT to modern wars. The difficulty in some of these cases – perhaps especially in these cases of humanitarian intervention and pre-emption – is that once they have happened there is a tendency to revert to a consequential utilitarian mode of reasoning in which the justification of the war is held to reside in its consequences. But how long does one wait for the consequences? And, assuming that ultimately the wished-for consequences finally ensue, how far can they be laid at the door or to the credit of the original intervention? In other words (even if one accepts the utilitarian premise of the argument) how is it possible to prove the counterfactual, that is, to know what would have happened in the absence of the intervention and to reliably claim that the good consequences were the *results* of the intervention.

The Iraq war of 2003 (definitely illegal and morally dubious) and Afghanistan (arguably both legal and moral as constituting self-defence proper) also bring in the growing importance of *jus post bellum* considerations (as in Brian Orend's work) as a consideration of increasing relevance and importance at strategic level.

Michael Walzer makes a point of saying that JWT, 'from the beginning . . . had a critical edge' and that 'it is, in fact, doubly critical – of war's occasions and its conduct'.[16] Hence we cannot ignore the issue of *jus in bello*; we must consider both the justifiability or otherwise of both the occasions of war (*jus ad bellum*) and also its conduct. In addition we should direct our attention towards the post-war settlement and consider how the use of various means in the conduct of war might be right or wrong per se and also valuable or a hindrance to the post-war settlement. The vital point to remember is that means are not neutral in relation to ends: they carry over into their ends and their effects live long after their initial employment. Indeed, one of the most important criticisms of any theory which sharply distinguishes means and ends is to note the fact that ends and means necessarily intertwine, with no clear beginning or end to either, and means in turn becoming ends and ends in turn means.

So what are the limits on what is permitted in the conduct of warfare in the twenty-first century? In a post-9/11 War on Terror, is anything permissible and anything justifiable? Is the War on Terror a genuine war in the first place? What counts as self-defence in a War on Terror? Do the traditional distinctions such as that between combatants and non-combatants still have any value? In short, can we still apply JWT to the War on Terror and to fighting terrorism, or do we now have no choice but to become hard-line realists and begin to think the unthinkable about, for example, condoning the use of torture to elicit information?

We do not propose to try to answer all these questions. Let us consider one by way of illustration. In recent discourse the notion of self-defence has been extended beyond its previous bounds, and the interpretation of self-defence now includes not only pre-emptive strikes, but preventive strikes – strikes not against an enemy's actions, but against its anticipated possible actions in the future. However, the enemy itself is typically not easy to identify or target and may be embedded in a civilian world (sometimes in the midst of another sovereign state with which the proponent of self-defence is not at war) where it is hard to locate and strike it without enormous collateral damage. These considerations raise vital questions concerning sovereignty and the justification of collateral damage. The justifications are typically utilitarian – it is frequently the case that innocent civilians are the victims in attempts to target a particular person or people, where the attack is not directly on the state itself but on a group harboured by or residing within the state. These facts, at the least, modify the application of standard responses in the targeting of innocents in war in which no one is seen as innocent and hence it also alters the applicability or justifiability of the doctrine of double effect.

Let us further illustrate this through consideration not only of the decision to go to war but also the conduct of the war itself. In the past it has often been argued that these decisions and the associated forms of moral reasoning are matters primarily for civilians (in the case of *jus ad bellum*) and high ranking officers (in the case of *jus in bello*). But this is not any longer the case, as the very notion of the 'Strategic Corporal' indicates.[17] The point is that the actions of those at the bottom of the command chain can have consequences at operational level that go up through tactical to strategic and political levels. This is of particular relevance in 'wars amongst the people' where it is strategically and tactically necessary to win as many hearts and minds as possible, and where a single mistake can set back the whole campaign. There are moral and prudential reasons for 'Strategic Corporals' to be aware of and familiar with the rudiments of moral reasoning about the conduct of war. Further, this is made more pressing by the simple fact that war in the present world is media war in which instant worldwide publicity given to any illegal or unethical actions (as always, it is the bad actions which stand out and attract attention). This suggests that it is necessary to maintain the moral high ground at all times; there are many who would argue that the Bush administration forfeited it through the method and manner of detainment at Guantanamo and the use of interrogation methods including torture. It might indeed be argued that the distinction between *jus in bello* and *jus ad bellum* is no longer as distinct as it was previously thought to be. War is made and re-made on the ground and the justifiability of war can be directly affected by the actions of those on the ground – the Strategic Corporal – who are responsible for its conduct.

However, we have to be careful in asserting that, simply because war is being fought in a 'time of terror', therefore there needs to be any sort of profound change to the rules or criteria of *jus in bello*. What has changed, it seems reasonable to assert, is that the focus now lies mainly on the two key areas of discrimination and proportionality. And this brings us to another example, that of the 'doctrine of double effect'. The doctrine distinguishes the intended results of an action from its unintended (but foreseeable) results and maintains that there are circumstances (on the assumption of proportionality) in which because it is impossible to achieve an intended result without causing harm to non-combatants, as an unintended side effect. But this does not, of course, sanction just any action of which it might be said 'I intended to kill those persons and not those, therefore my action is justified.' The doctrine requires that there is no alternative, that the target is of sufficient importance, that every effort is made to minimise harm to non-combatants, and so on. And this is, again, a matter of moral judgement and not one to be answered automatically either by saying it is forbidden (on the ground that some non-combatants might be harmed) or that it is always permitted (on the grounds that overall the consequences are beneficial). Elizabeth Anscombe expressed the point succinctly:

> There is a great distinction between attacking a group of persons directly, and killing them accidentally in the course of attack on others. But yet another distinction must be made. It is a different thing, while making one group of persons a target, to kill others by accident, and to make a group of persons a target, in order – by attacking them all – to attack some members of the group who are persons who may legitimately be attacked. The first case involves no sin; the second involves murder and is not an example of double effect. It has been claimed as such by some who, defending blockade, allow that civilians are not a proper military target, but who argue that attack may be made on a

whole group of persons which includes both civilians and combatants. This claim cannot be allowed.[18]

The underlying difficulty here is, as Walzer argues, that JWT is not a pacifist doctrine: it is used to justify war and it is heavily weighted towards realistic estimation of the consequences of actions. It does not lead to the view that non-combatants will never be injured or killed. If the principle of non-combatant immunity is strengthened so that it becomes an absolute rule on the killing of all non-combatants then the theory would converge on pacifism. In his view the ethic of the JWT is an ethic of responsibility:

> which requires critics to attend closely to what soldiers try to do and what they try not to do. The refusal to make distinctions of this kind, to pay attention to strategic and tactical choices, suggests a doctrine of radical suspicion. This is the radicalism of people who do not expect to exercise power or use force, ever, and who are not prepared to make the judgments that this exercise and use require. By contrast, just war theory, even when it demands a strong critique of particular acts of war, is the doctrine of people who do expect to exercise power and use force. We might think of it as a doctrine of radical responsibility, because it holds political and military leaders responsible, first of all, for the well-being of their own people, but also for the well-being of innocent men and women on the other side.[19]

With this in mind, Walzer seeks to modify the doctrine of double effect, both to make its application more stringent and also to show where it is clearly justifiable to engage in actions which result in death or injury to non-combatants.[20] Others wish to deny the validity of the doctrine itself, in any of its forms. T.M. Scanlon, for example, argues that although the doctrine 'correctly identifies certain actions as impermissible, it provides the wrong explanation of why they are impermissible'.[21] Why does he argue this? Principally it is because, in his view, intention is not necessarily relevant to the permissibility (or otherwise) of an action. What matters is what effects the action will bring about. Consideration of intention might help us understand what someone was trying to do in performing a certain action; it might help us judge the moral character of the agent; but what it will not do is provide us with a tie-breaker whereby we can judge, of two actions with the same or similar consequences, that one is permissible and the other not permissible. Scanlon notes that 'what is of fundamental relevance in these cases is the effects of an agent's action on the world around her (or what it is reasonable to expect those effects to be). Her intention is relevant . . . only because it tells us something about these effects'.[22]

Christopher Waters argues that 'when the rule of law in international relationships fails, the results can be deadly. However, the core rules themselves are generally clear – both with respect to the (il)legality of a conflict and the conduct of hostilities – and breaches of the rules are actually much rarer than commonly perceived'.[23] He adds to this the observation that international law seeks to minimise the use of force and that if it fails to do so, it aims at providing tools which 'can be used to protect the victims of that armed conflict'. We agree with Waters that not only is there 'a significant overlap between legal and strategic concerns' and that 'in many areas, a purely legal calculus does not and cannot displace the necessity of an ethical one as well'.[24]

Throughout this chapter our concern has been to explain the role of ethical reasoning and moral discourse in relation to war, its occasions and conduct. This is clearly not to deny the vital role of law but rather to insist that reliance on law and its forms of reasoning narrowly conceived can never be sufficient. This is both because it in itself requires acts of judgement which necessarily move it away from simplistic reliance on the supposed clarity of black letter or bright light legal propositions. It is also because where the law runs out, moral reasoning and judgement have to take over: after that there is nothing else.

Part II

International law and security

5   Law and war in the global war on terror

James Gow and Rachel Kerr

The post-Cold War period has seen substantial evolution in the relationship between law and war.[1] It has seen considerable development in the field of the Laws of Armed Conflict as well as considerable change in the character, if not the nature, of contemporary warfare and marked developments in the international political arena, most notably regarding action in response to threats to international peace and security.[2] Although the full impact of these changes has yet to be realised, the relationship between war, crime and legitimacy has been brought sharply into focus with regard to a number of recent events that have given rise to heated debate.[3] From decisions about whether and when to use force, to dilemmas over how force should be deployed, issues of legality and legitimacy have featured prominently. The changing character of warfare, leaving behind more conventional forms, has stretched and tested a body of law designed, in the main, for conventional armed conflicts, requiring reflection, adaptation, interpretation and, in some cases, possibly requiring new legal instruments. This chapter considers four areas, in this context, that have given rise to heated debate in the context of the 'war on terror': extended discussion of self-defence to the notion of 'targeted killings'; the issue of detaining quasi-Prisoners of War in the context of a form of transnational conflict that, as a non-international, is not covered by the Geneva Convention on Prisoners of War; irrespective of their formal status, the abusive treatment of individuals detained by US and coalition forces in camps based at Guantanamo Bay and elsewhere, including the difficult topics of rendition, torture and abuse that came to mark the US mission; extension of the latter, the juridification of armed conflict – with the UK example to the fore.

Targeted killing and 'active' self-defence

The United States appeared to push the envelope of law and practice concerning 'targeted killings' and the use of Unmanned Aerial Vehicles (UAVs), often called 'assassination' attempts, against leaders and prominent members of Al Qaeda.[4] *De facto*, this practice arguably had precedents, albeit ones covered otherwise by a self-defence, or enforcement action, where the 'targeted killing' was formally not the mission, even if this was the genuine purpose of an action, for example, against a 'command and control' position officially. Examples of this included the attack on Momir Qaddaffi's home in Tripoli, in 1986, an attempt to kill Saddam Hussein on the last night of operations in 1991 and an attack on Slobodan Milosevic's residence in 1999. The same approach could be said to have covered the 1998 US cruise missile attack on targets in Afghanistan, understood to have missed Osama bin Laden by a matter of minutes – yet that attack was certainly an attempt to get bin Laden himself and was the start of operations to target Al Qaeda cadres. In early 2006, an attack was launched against a target in the Pakistani border region close to Afghanistan, where bin Laden's deputy Ayman al Zawahiri and other Al Qaeda leaders were thought to have been – but once again, the prime targets escaped shortly before the strike hit. On other occasions, for example in Yemen, in 2002, US forces used UAVs with televisual capabilities to locate and destroy members of Al Qaeda. However, America's critics have questioned both the legality of such actions and their practical benefit.

There are two key aspects to the discussion of the lawfulness of targeted killing under international law, one based on the limitations imposed by existing law and the other about the difficulty of moving to a radical new approach. Under the sovereignty doctrine and traditional interpretation of the right to self-defence, the targeting of an opponent's leaders is not allowed, given that the fundamental premise is mutual recognition. That would be significantly compromised if those exercising sovereign rights were to be targets in war. However, actions such as these are legally questionable, whether carried out as an act of extended self-defence – a US doctrine developed, *inter alia*, in the context of action against Libya in 1986 – or as part of an international peace mission. Israel was the only country explicitly to have invoked a policy of targeted killings, which it based on a notion of 'active self-defence'.[5] The UK and the US had consistently condemned Israel's action as illegal and unlawful. Yet, the US appeared, in practice, to have begun a similar policy as part of the War on Terror, and consulted Israeli government lawyers on their legal interpretations and preparations to resist legal challenges to the policy in the US and elsewhere.

Anne-Marie Slaughter posited an alternative, radical approach: to have the UN Security Council declare individuals such as Saddam or Milosevic to be 'threats' and to authorise the use of 'all necessary means' as an enforcement mechanism under Chapter VII of the UN Charter to remove them – implying, if necessary, to kill them.[6] Aside from the reluctance of states to move in this direction and the practical difficulties of both agreeing and implementing such a resolution, there was a sound logic to the proposal. Rather than making whole populations under such authoritarian and dangerous rulers suffer with sanctions, or bombing, superficially it made great sense to decide to target the leader, or leaders – something already developed regarding 'smart sanctions', where economic, political and cultural measures were applied against individuals. However, the realities of diplomacy and the reluctance of ordinary political leaders to sanction a principle that might mean their becoming an immediate target, as well as the moral ambiguity surrounding this notion, left the proposal as a discussion point.

There were also uncertainties regarding the effectiveness of targeted killing; however, the record here was more clear-cut, with clear benefits possible in the short-medium term, although the longer-term political effect might lead to a legitimacy deficit. Israel has been the most prominent and successful exponent of targeted killing and, although brutal, the policy has been effective. Use of this approach to remove leaders of groups using violence against the state was highly effective in disrupting the command and control structure of organisations. The calculation is that once a level of 25 per cent of the command cadre has been killed, the remaining cadre cannot function properly any more, as the rate of loss is such that it cannot be made up by new recruits who require training, reducing efficiency and at the same time encouraging enemies to hide for their own security rather than expose themselves by preparing and initiating attacks. The net effect, in the Israeli case, was to generate a salient drop in the number of attacks in Israel. In a crude statistic, Israeli Defence Minister General Yaakov Amidror, speaking in 2005, reported a fall from 140 deaths a month to 50 a year since the policy began in response to the al-Asqa 'Intifada' in 2000.[7] This apparent effectiveness made it popular among Israelis, in general. However, a study by the Bank of Israel that connected share activity to the occurrence of targeted killings revealed that killing military targets boosted confidence, while targeting political figures drained it.[8] This indicated perhaps that worries emerge if the action is not clearly perceived as war-like.

It was possible, then, to point to success in deterring and disrupting attacks by employment of targeted killing against terrorist or insurgent enemies. But, there was a strong and conventional case that placed emphasis on hearts and minds in combating irregular forces operating among the people. In this context, the use of targeted killings could be seen as counter-productive in the longer-term, as it generated widespread hostility, fuelling extremist approaches and probably reducing the chances of deeper and lasting security. However, these effects were significantly reduced, as the Israelis discovered, if so-called 'collateral damage' could be minimised or avoided. If only 'military' personnel were struck, the legitimacy deficit could be mitigated. However, the US record on limiting 'collateral damage' was not strong, as numerous civilian deaths and the subsequent outrage confirmed in the failed attempt to kill Zawahiri. America's apparent adoption of a terrorist assassination, or targeted killing policy, was a radical step, questionable in legal terms. Yet, generally, it was effective. Although it caused opposition and accusations of inhumane and careless 'collateral damage', the hard evidence in US intelligence analysis indicated a stronger record than critics allowed. For example, claims of ten innocents killed in one case in Pakistan reported by the BBC were wrong, with only half that number killed, and those five included Abdullah Hamas al-Filistini, a senior Al Qaeda figure.[9] There were other less immediately obvious aspects to the use of UAVs for targeted killing operations, however. The record of regular military operatives was significantly better than that of either CIA or private military security operatives in conducting these actions, with most 'collateral' killing the result of action involving the latter two.[10] There was, therefore, a case for mounting attacks of this kind in the context of the 'new' form of warfare – even if, as noted above, some prominent figures called for a total ban on their use. The US was likely to increase its use of these operations, therefore, despite longer-term legitimacy considerations. The latter were offset by the likely benefits of destruction, disruption and deterrence effectuated by targeted killings.

Prisoners of non-war, or quasi-prisoners of war: the Guantanamo conundrum

The US detention facilities at Guantanamo Bay, Cuba, were marked by criticism. Guantanamo was controversial as soon as the initial Camp X-Ray became public at the end of 2001. That temporary facility was replaced early in 2002 by Camp Delta, with proper, purpose-built accommodation. The legal basis for detention was a particularly acute matter of US domestic and international controversy, calling into question the legitimacy of the US position. This led, at times, to an apparent US softening of its approach in response to the pressure, but not, given Washington's perceptions of necessity, to its overall policy. Even when the newly elected President Barack Obama made an immediate commitment to closing the Guantanamo facility within a year, he was unable to keep to it. The imperative to do something with those held there prevailed over the new Administration's desire to abolish the camp. Commonly discussed as 'Guantanamo justice', that label was a misnomer, given that for all but a few, justice was not the reason for their incarceration. The main issue was what to do with those captured in action against the US and its allies, or in other ways but part of hostile activity (notwithstanding the possibility of mistaken identity). They were not detained as suspected criminals, in the context of what the US regarded as the Global War on Terror, but as enemies who were not to be returned to the battle space. This was a parallel to the practice in conventional wars, where prisoners of war are captured and held so that they cannot return to the fight. This aspect of the issue was little recognised or understood – and was damaged by association with questions of abuse of detainees there and, more pertinently, elsewhere. Guantanamo continued to be damaging in terms of support both domestically and internationally for the Bush Administration's 'War on Terror', however, as it was perceived as undermining the values it was intended to protect.

Camp Delta and its predecessor, Camp X-Ray, were contentious and wrapped in legal controversy and challenge. While the intricacies of US constitutional and human rights law, as well as the internal politics of the Bush Administration, cannot be fully considered here, it is clear that the US position on Camp Delta had some foundation in a novel circumstance – how to handle 'non-prisoners of war'. US lawyers had worked out a scheme that sought to meet the new situation, which involved a legal grey area.[11] Hundreds of Taliban, Al Qaeda or other 'personnel' had been captured in Afghanistan, initially, while others were detained, over time, elsewhere. As non-state actors and, also, arguably, as members of a clandestine organisation, albeit quasi-military, they were deemed not to be covered by the Fourth Geneva Convention on Prisoners of War. That covered only regular military personnel. At the same time, most of these individuals were not detained as criminal suspects. A major fallacy in much of the criticism of the Guantanamo arrangements involved assertions that these individuals had been detained without charge, when, in fact, there was no question of criminality, for the most part, only of detaining individuals as a security provision.[12]

If these detainees were not technically prisoners of war, then they were civilians. Detaining civilians who are none the less engaged in hostile action means that, in effect, a new category is required. Discussion of the Geneva Convention categorises such individuals 'unprivileged belligerents', at times. This term was eventually adopted by the US under the Obama Administration, but for several years under the Bush Administration, the US named this not-genuinely civilian category as 'unlawful combatants'. It should be noted, of course, that neither of these terms actually appears in the Conventions themselves. The detention of civilians as a security measure in the context of armed conflict, aliens on territory under control and occupation of territory is allowed, as a security provision under the Fourth Geneva Convention (Arts. 41, 42, 43, 68, 78 and Section IV), even though the terms on which that was drafted did not foresee the circumstances of transnational and international insurgency in which the US found itself. Thus, technically, those detained were not Prisoners of War under the conventions, although the US conceded, in time, that, while seeking to work in the spirit of the Geneva Conventions, as far as possible, it had to extend limited protection in accordance with Geneva III to former members of the Taliban in Afghanistan.[13] However, in the US perspective of a Global War on Terror, which was a war in terrain beyond existing legal provision, these were the equivalent of Prisoners of War, but could not be so by name, in terms of the Convention. Therefore, the 'unlawful' did not denote criminality, but rather reflected the fact they were not belligerents in the sense of Convention III, and their detention was more, though never explicitly, linked with the provisions available in wartime for detention of those deemed to be enemy combatants.

In addition, having secured Congressional approval for a global 'war', Presidential Authority under the relevant act of Congress gave the President apparent *carte blanche* and was also used as part of the legal underpinning for the Guantanamo Regime. Beyond this, it is fair to presume, the naval facility there was selected because it was ostensibly outside US sovereignty and Federal jurisdiction,[14] in principle. This, it was believed, placed it outside the reach of US civil liberties provisions (something that had emerged, retrospectively, regarding the detention of ethnic Japanese Americans and Japanese aliens as a provisional security measure in America during the Second World War). While the US military controlled the Guantanamo facility, it was subject to Cuban sovereignty. Realistically, that sovereignty was unlikely to be invoked. Thus, if not watertight, the Administration lawyers had come up with an arrangement that implicitly and explicitly drew on existing instruments of law, in some instances, and approaches, none of which wholly or formally applied, in order to create a detention arrangement that nestled in a legal space between US domestic law and instruments of international humanitarian law. This was an effort to mix pragmatics with potential legal justification in highly unusual conditions.

However, over the years, there were legal challenges to these arrangements in US courts, as well as increasing international socio-political and strategic pressure.

Camp Delta became a lightning rod and focal point for criticism of, and opposition to, Washington and its policies. Some chinks in the Administration's legal armour emerged. The detentions were challenged in the US courts, with some success in a case regarding a US citizen detained on US soil, who it was deemed could not be held on the same terms as those detained elsewhere in the world. The US Supreme Court considered whether the US Constitution allowed the president to order indefinite detentions, although there was a differentiated approach here to US citizens and non-nationals,[15] as well as recognition of the need for military and security precautions.

The overwhelming majority of the detainees were deemed to be 'unlawful enemy combatants', as noted above. This meant that they were not protected persons as Prisoners of War, under Geneva III, as noted already. Formally, therefore, the Convention did not apply – although some international lawyers questioned the manner of this determination.[16] This left the detainees in a legal black hole, which permitted the US military to detain them indefinitely as a security measure. At the same time, the decision to hold them at Guantanamo meant that they were outside US sovereign territory and therefore not necessarily subject to the jurisdiction of US courts and human rights legislation. None the less, the US Supreme Court ruled that there was effective US authority at Guantanamo, given that it was a military facility exclusively under US authority, which meant that US law could apply. Thus, the only jurisdiction applicable, in practice, was that of the US military and the US Constitution (although theoretically there might be challenge under Cuban sovereignty, in reality there was no scope for this). Following the ruling, the US military and the CIA were obliged to begin a programme of periodic individual reviews – a process that would be consistent with requirements regarding protected persons detained under the Geneva Conventions.

As a result, the Administration found itself in what no longer appeared to be such a watertight legal position. It was still, though, an arrangement that had ensured the Administration the benefit of a great deal of time. Because they were detained as combatants and as a security measure, issues raised by Human Rights Watch (HRW), such as their having been detained for two years without charge, had limited relevance.[17] The HRW report condemned the US authorities for detaining individuals at Camp Delta without charge and without rights of access to counsel. In particular, the HRW report called on the US Supreme Court to rule that detentions at Camp Delta were illegal and contravened the US Constitution. The report built on strong criticism in the US and around the world for provisions to try some of the detainees using Special Military Commissions. The arrangements for those trials created concerns with even America's closest allies, Australia and the UK, expressing clear concerns about some aspects of the proposed framework and engaging in considerable quiet diplomacy seeking to ensure that certain standards were maintained. However, it was always unlikely that either the HRW report challenge, or international concerns, would bring significant change in the US approach.

After initial difficulties and some mistakes at the original temporary detention facility at Camp X-ray, it seemed that the detainees had relatively good, though basic, conditions – not that this was the widely shared perception of the Camp, which continued to be both a source of, and focus for, complaint. The International Committee of the Red Cross/Red Crescent (ICRC) had been permitted access to ensure good conditions. While the ICRC did not refer to the conditions, quite unusually, it publicly raised grave concerns about the detention of three children under the age of 15 and an undisclosed number aged 15–17. The Human Rights Watch challenge, while a sign of significant concern in the US about Camp Delta, could not provoke a change in policy, either directly or through the courts, even if there were some changes of approach.

All of those detained at Camp Delta were detained there as a security measure. However, a small number of them faced possible trial before US Special Military Commissions – so in early 2006, nine cases had been identified (although others earlier slated for possible trial, including two Britons, had been returned to their home countries). Even before the final arrangements for these trials were in place, however, several aspects of them caused concern in the US and elsewhere. Washington's closest allies, Australia and the UK, despite their allegiance, engaged in significant quiet diplomacy with regard to the arrangements for their own nationals listed to be tried. This resulted in the return of those persons, in the end, when the US did not agree to essential provisions. In the UK, the two citizens who had been listed for possible prosecution were released after returning to the UK.

Among the concerns addressed was the death penalty. There was agreement between London and Washington, in line with longstanding practice on extradition cases from the UK to the US, that the death penalty would not be applied, although it was otherwise part of the penal arsenal at these commissions. London and Sydney supported the Guantanamo arrangements, although with reservations, and would certainly have preferred the US to be responsible for holding these individuals and, if relevant, trying them. This was the case with the two British citizens deemed to be 'high risk', who, none the less, were transferred to the UK, in the end.

Among the major concerns expressed by some countries were the rights to defence and to appeal. Under the military justice terms of the Commissions, only Department of Defense appointed lawyers were permitted – initially and for some time – to act as defence counsel. However, as time progressed, Australia secured agreement that its nationals would have access to lawyers of their own choice, while a military lawyer would formally lead the defence. Similar terms emerged regarding nationals of other countries, such as the UK. However, such developments would be limited, as the scope for manoeuvre was relatively limited. A key area of difficulty was lawyer–client confidentiality, which was not available, as such restricted contact as was possible, in a few cases, was subject to the provisions for military monitoring of conversations. The right to appeal was also a difficult – and breaking – point in negotiations with the closest allies. They would not countenance proceedings with no right to appeal and would not accept a right to petition the US President as anything like an acceptable substitute.

The right to appeal is a basic principle of the US and other Western liberal legal codes, and although not a right, appeals have generally come to be admitted under the US military code. However, the Special Military Commissions would involve no right to appeal. Those convicted would have the right to petition the President, but this was not regarded as satisfactory either by international lawyers and human rights commentators, or by governments friendly to Washington. Even if, at best, the right to petition the President had been reconfigured as a right to appeal, perhaps with the President's deferring to some form of judicial panel appointed for that purpose by the President, the proceedings would still have been open to major criticism. The scope for changing the structure and procedures was so small as to rule out notable changes, aside from downsizing and restructuring, which is what occurred, even after President Obama had initially suspended the Commissions, had them reviewed and sought new arrangements. However, the latter were different in nuance only. Their essence remained the same, leaving Obama perhaps to rue his stark condemnation of the commissions as a 'dangerously flawed legal approach'.[18]

Obama's travails reflect those encountered by the previous Administration, which had sought to lessen the impact of Guantanamo as both a lightning rod for political opposition and terrorist recruitment. In August 2005, the US Administration announced that it would soon be prepared to release seven of nine British citizens detained among the almost 660 individuals held by the US at Camp Delta. These were not the first detainees to leave Guantanamo – already 84 individuals who had been detained had been released as posing no threat, while four medium threat cases had been transferred to Saudi Arabia for indefinite detention. The transfer to British custody actually took some months. It only occurred when terms had been agreed under which the British authorities could guarantee that these individuals, classified as 'medium' threats, would face prosecution, be detained or prevented by some other action, such as tagging, from participating in terrorist activities. However, the prior announcement and the fact that they were British citizens meant that they were likely to gain greater public attention than previous releases. This was probably the intention of the Administration as the US prepared to release some of those it believed no longer needed to be detained, either for purposes of gathering information, or as a protective security measure to ensure that those individuals did not engage in hostile action against the US. Individuals from other countries were to follow the same trajectory at a later stage.

The responsibility for dealing with these individuals fell on the home country in each case, in particular, for ensuring that they would not be able to engage, once more, as combatants against the US and its allies and partners (although, according to US Secretary of Defence Donald Rumsfeld, some of those released had returned to the field). This was likely to be an unwelcome responsibility in some countries, which had quite probably been content not to have to deal with the problem of those individuals, whom it would be hard to hold in the same kind of detention, in most cases, in other Western countries. The same would be true on US sovereign territory itself – a problem raised in the US judicial system and by critics around the world.

The Guantanamo detentions and possible trial arrangements continued to generate enormous criticism, both in the US and internationally, calling into question their legitimacy. This was significantly damaging in the conduct of the Global War on Terror and badly undermined the need to win hearts and minds in the struggle to separate potential supporters of those violently opposing the US by promoting liberty and justice as US and Western values. Instead, it added to anti-US sentiment, bolstered by the concerns of Washington's closest allies. However, given the security imperative as judged by the US defence and intelligence agencies, and the seeming strength of the Administration's cleverly crafted legal position, technically – which, at a minimum, would take a very long time to unpick – the US approach could not change in any significant way, as Obama found. Indeed, only a Supreme Court broadside ruling really managed to change anything throughout this period. Therefore, any apparent softening of the position under Obama was no more than that – apparent, but not substantial. Experience showed that whilst each concession for the nationals of some countries might alleviate some of the challenges to Guantanamo justice, they almost inevitably added another. At the same time, those from countries that showed little interest were ignored, and perceptions of inequity were likely to grow. This sense was amplified by the international furore concerning other US practices that flouted, or played with, legal boundaries, and which some sought to justify in the context of the new circumstances of war.

Rendition, torture and abuse

The American Civil Liberties Union (ACLU) brought a legal case against the US Administration, in December 2005, alleging that the CIA's programme of 'extraordinary rendition' – where it effectively kidnapped terrorist suspects around the world and kept them in a secret network of detention facilities outside the US – was against both US and international humanitarian law. The ACLU legal action fuelled already intense debates concerning US treatment of detainees in the Global War on Terror, which also included accusations of torture and disputes with the US Senate over this issue – all of which played into the hands of both domestic and, crucially, international opponents and critics of the US.

The Bush Administration consistently found itself on the wrong side of criticism regarding its policy of detaining terrorist suspects. The issue had previously been focused on the detention facilities at Guantanamo Bay, Cuba, which provoked negative discussion around the world, as well as in the US itself, as seen in the previous section, and which remained the subject of legal challenge. It was also negatively affected by the striking images of prisoner abuse at the Abu Ghraib prison in Baghdad.[19] Although these images and the actions they depicted were not part of any formal policy and completely separate from other issues of detention,[20] they merged into one in the international public discourse and were seen as examples of an overall coherent policy – which they were not necessarily. Despite the prosecution and very public sentencing of those involved in the Abu Ghraib incidents, as well as other less publicised cases (the total number of those court-martialled exceeded thirty, while more than another fifty were reprimanded).

In November 2005, the *Washington Post* reported that the CIA ran a network of secret detention facilities around the world that involved at least eight countries, including at least two in Eastern Europe, and that people disappeared into these so-called 'black sites', about which only a very small number of people in either the US or those countries had any knowledge, and even fewer knew the locations.[21] Alternatively, candidates were transferred to the custody of third states for detention and interrogation. The report also suggested that torture and abuse might take place at those sites. In addition, ABC's television news investigative team revealed that the CIA had been authorised to use six 'enhanced interrogation' techniques, some of which, at least, raised concerns about possible torture.[22]

Finally, and perhaps most damagingly, the Republican Senator for Arizona, John McCain, proposed an amendment to the $440 billion defence authorisation bill that made clear that torture and other cruel and inhuman acts (the language of the Torture Convention, ratified by the US in 1984) were banned. McCain, a Vietnam veteran famous for having being cruelly tortured while a Prisoner of War, had clear authority on the issue, which was supported by 90 of the Senate's 100 members (raising the curious prospect that in the country that for over 60 years, including the Cold War, had promoted itself as the beacon of liberal democracy and human rights, there were 10 members of the senior legislative body who appeared to support torture, although this was indeed more apparent than substantive, as there were different reservations on the law itself). However, the Administration caused a stir, further fuelling the composite view among critics and opponents that it supported torture, when Vice President Dick Cheney requested that the CIA should be excluded from the amendment. Responding to the criticism that followed this statement, President Bush explicitly declared that the US did not engage in torture, without qualification. And in response to ABC's report on 'enhanced techniques', CIA Director Porter Goss denied that the CIA engaged in torture in an interview with ABC's Charles Gibson, placing particular emphasis on the conclusion that torture does not work as a chief reason.[23] But that denial and the information that provoked it left little doubt that Agency engaged in practices that were questionable in many eyes and might be criminal in the US, but, unlike the activities regarded as torture, might be useful in the Global War on Terror.

The first of America's contentious approaches involved 'extraordinary rendition'. Rendition effectively constitutes a form of kidnapping, albeit for a legal purpose. It is against the law in most liberal democracies (although France, for example, as well as the US has used this approach), in line with provisions on human and individual rights, and is a breach of the basic doctrine of international law, the right to non-interference in internal affairs, if carried out on the territory of another state. The US, perhaps reflecting its frontier traditions, including those of the posse and bounty hunters, familiar from Hollywood Westerns, allows more scope than others for this activity. However it reflects this cultural heritage, it is the case that the US legal system has allowed for rendition and related activities, such as bounty-hunting, and continues to do so, in more restrictive ways. The process previously allowed those wanted to be apprehended and 'rendered' to the appropriate authority, often involving an indictment in one jurisdiction in another jurisdiction and transfer to the jurisdiction of indictment. This is no longer formally authorised in the US for inter-state activity,[24] though in practice, where there is bail money at stake, for example, it still occurs (with bail bondsmen employing bounty hunters to track down those who have broken bail), even though, technically, having identified the location of the wanted person, they should inform the relevant authorities, and often, bounty hunters only have authority in one state, as different rules apply in different states (including the prohibition of rendition in Kentucky). However, while rendition is an accepted, but problematic, practice in the US historically and, in more limited forms, presently, it poses international problems. Already, this issue provoked differences concerning war crimes suspect detentions in the former Yugoslav lands, where some NATO countries would not sanction operations to detain suspects in Serbia, for example, despite the legal authority of the International Criminal Tribunal for the former Yugoslavia (ICTY)'s statute as a binding instrument under Chapter VII of the UN Charter, overriding other parts of international law because such action would have been illegal under their own country's laws, leaving personnel involved open to possible prosecution (in contrast, the formal UN missions in Bosnia and Kosovo meant that NATO forces had legal status there, giving them authority to carry out detention operations in those places). Over one hundred suspected terrorists were apprehended in this way during the 'War on Terror', raising serious concerns and prompting parliamentary inquiries in countries such as Canada, Italy, France, Sweden and the Netherlands, all friendly countries and most of them formal allies. The CIA had been responsible for kidnapping citizens or residents of those countries, simply picking them up from the street, or their homes, bundling them to an airport somewhere and onto a CIA flight to an unknown location. The CIA and the Administration clearly believed that this direct action, avoiding the need for lengthy legal processes with the countries involved, which would alert suspects to the CIA's knowledge, in any case, were practical. However, in causing significant friction with friendly, very closely allied countries and their security and intelligence services, the activity had a significant downside, which was amplified in the international struggle to win hearts and minds. This practice reinforced the sense in many quarters that the US was a law unto itself, not respecting either the sovereign or individual rights of others, and operating double standards as it criticised other countries each year for torture and other human rights abuses – including some of the countries to which it sent those rendered by the CIA, where, the ACLU and other critics suspected, torture and abuse might occur.

The second contentious element in America's approach concerned what were labelled 'enhanced interrogation' techniques. Some caution needs to be exercised over use of the term 'torture' regarding US activity. The denials of torture by the President and the CIA Director reflect their understanding (and that of their legal advisors) concerning torture, which, in the narrowest legal and technical terms, involves the infliction of physical or mental pain.[25] This may be distinct from other categories of activity, which some practitioners would label 'stress' techniques, and which, under a Presidential Finding of 7 February 2002, were specifically authorised as 'enhanced interrogation' methods, albeit that each of the six methods identified by ABC required specific approval at high level before use. But there was a sharp problem over this in the US: certain stress techniques might be regarded as borderline, or even wholly unacceptable.

There were inter-agency differences about the use of these techniques, even within the US, adding to their contentious character. The CIA's 'enhanced methods' went far beyond anything that the FBI was allowed to do. The Bureau had the most conservative approach, believing that even to suggest that the death penalty might be applied would be a breach of the Torture Convention, based on the legal theory that an implicit threat might cross the mental pain threshold. The US military had generally taken a conservative approach, but had a set of enhanced methods involving some stress techniques, such as sleep deprivation, authorised early in the War on Terror. But, after the Abu Ghraib incident became public, these were stopped. However, some methods that continued to be used by the CIA were not used by the military because, *inter alia*, they would contravene military law, if carried out by someone on the Pentagon payroll. Thus, the CIA's position, while argued not to be torture, exceeded that of other principal security agencies in the US. The FBI and some more senior CIA officers (who had refused to take training in, or use, the enhanced methods) believed that the stress techniques would breach the 5th, 8th and 14th amendments of the US Constitution if applied on US soil. The White House, the Justice Department and the CIA lawyers all believed that because the methods were used against non-nationals outside US soil, they did not breach the law. However, non-government lawyers rejected this interpretation,[26] as well as that offered by Senator McCain and his backers in the Senate, whose amendment made sure that any technical loophole was closed, when the Bush Administration finally dropped its opposition.

While there were differences over the use of 'enhanced interrogation', all branches of the US Administration agreed that torture was unacceptable. There were two reasons for this – legality and pragmatics. In terms of the law, there was little doubt that torture was against both US and international law. Having ratified the Torture Convention in 1984, the US adopted its provisions as US Law. However, even had it not done so, the crimes applicable under the Convention were classified as 'international crimes', meaning that they fell into a category so serious that, in theory, they could be prosecuted in any country, no matter where the offences were committed, or the nationality of the accused. Reinforced by the elements of the US Constitution mentioned above, this meant that torture was wholly unacceptable, morally and legally.

The second reason torture was rejected – and a significant factor in US ratification of the Convention – was the consensus among practitioners that it was not useful. Professional interrogators concur that, as a means of gaining information, it is highly unreliable, at best. In most cases, it is believed, those under interrogation will say what they believe the interrogators want to hear, in order to end the torture. However, what they say is very often wrong, as it has been invented only to gain relief. While there might be situations in which torture would produce useful information, there is no way of knowing if this is the case, while, it is believed, 95 per cent of information can be gained by other psychological means when deployed by professional interrogators. The only clear case of success using torture came in the Battle for Algiers – and that, ironically, involved French military interrogators' discovering from an Algerian captive that their own French government was engaged in secret negotiations that would essentially betray them, the military.[27] Otherwise, torture is seen either as a measure of the interrogators' lack of skill, or as a purely sadistic activity meant to intimidate not only the victim, but also others in society. In this sense, those with experience of interrogations tend to agree that torture is counterproductive in terms of its impact on 'hearts and minds', both those of opponents, and one's own side.

'Enhanced methods' lay at the heart of the debate. In the understanding of some practitioners, action that some observers might believe to be 'torture' might be 'stress' techniques, in that they are argued not to cause physical or mental pain. This blurs the 'cruel and inhuman' treatment aspect of the Torture Convention – although the McCain amendment left little room for discussion. While torture was agreed not to work, opinion was divided within the CIA regarding the 'enhanced methods' approved for use. These resulted in at least three deaths, while practised by inexperienced officers, but also proved successful in gaining valuable information – most notably in the case of Sheikh Khalid Mohammed, the architect of the September 11 attacks on America.[28] Particular concern surrounded 'waterboarding', a practice where the detainee was made to believe that they were drowning. This measure was especially controversial, as it contravened US military law. US military personnel in Vietnam and, even a century ago, in the Philippines were given criminal convictions for using this practice. Something like 'waterboarding' clearly caused distress, as, by the CIA's admission, its own officers lasted an average of 14 seconds in exercises.[29] Unlike clear acts of torture, these techniques were believed to offer benefits. However, even if such actions are not deemed to be torture, they were probably still 'cruel' or 'inhuman'.

Accusations of torture and admissions of practices deemed by the US to be legitimate provoked major concern in the US about conduct of the War on Terror and the legitimacy of so-called 'enhanced' methods of interrogation. While some of the measures adopted, such as rendition and enhanced interrogation, might have had some practical benefits, and were argued to be necessary at times, they were quite probably counterproductive. They raised problems in terms of both US law and the activities of other branches of the US government, as well as prompting criticism and challenge from civil liberties activists. Those domestic problems and challenges, along with the accusations and admissions – even if the US did not technically use torture – significantly undermined Washington's attempt to win hearts and minds in its international struggle with Islamist terrorists. At the same time, the focus on lawfulness and normative standards confirmed the centrality, however, of these elements in setting the boundaries of war and its alternatives.

Law enforcement

The US was not alone in the shadow cast by issues of abuse. While the US struggled to invent ways in which to handle issues, the UK struggled to handle them within existing legal frameworks. But the attempt to enforce the relevant law proved difficult and reinforced the sense in which legal and ethical issues play a major role in the scope of contemporary warfare. The 'judicialisation of armed conflict',[30] or 'juridification of war',[31] has meant that Western governments and armed forces have come under ever-increasing scrutiny. The media play a powerful role in this, framing discourse about the just character and rightfulness of both cause and conduct of whatever action is taken'.[32] In this context, allegations of wrong-doing present serious challenges to acquiring and maintaining public support for any use of force in the short, medium and long term. This dilemma is particularly acute with respect to the use of force in pursuit of stated humanitarian objectives, as in Kosovo, and in operations where the competition for 'hearts and minds' is crucial, as in Iraq and Afghanistan.[33]

The UK Government and military leaders faced a series of allegations of war crimes by British forces operating in Iraq in 2003–4. The cases, and the way in which they were dealt with, highlight a serious set of dilemmas for the military and their civilian leaders and for civil–military relations, as well as presenting operational challenges for the use of force in the modern world. These cases were also especially challenging because of the political context surrounding them, so that the ramifications of dealing with allegations of abuse reached far beyond the immediate victim and perpetrator and their families. Allegations of war crimes fed vigorous debate around key issues of responsibility for the war, support for British forces involved and the impact on the civilian population of Iraq.

A number of allegations were made against British forces, some of which resulted in judicial proceedings. In the *Trooper Williams* case, which was referred by the Army Prosecuting Authority to the Crown Prosecution Service and the Metropolitan Police, Williams was charged with murder in September 2004 and the case was committed to trial at the Old Bailey – a rare example of a member of the British Armed forces being charged with murder whilst on active duty[34] – where it eventually collapsed.[35] In 2004, relatives of six Iraqis killed by British forces brought a claim under the seeking judicial review of the Secretary of State's alleged failure and/or refusal to conduct independent inquires into their deaths, to accept liability for those deaths and to pay just satisfaction. Five of the six cases involved shooting incidents in which Iraqi civilians were killed or fatally injured and died later.[36] The last case, concerning Baha Mousa, was the most controversial and was very different in nature. Whilst the first five involved soldiers' opening fire in combat situations, the Mousa case concerned the alleged abuse of Iraqi civilians in British custody. The treatment of Baha Mousa and others at the hands of British soldiers was seen by many as situated in the wider pattern of abuses already identified above. For some, however, the case was no more than an exercise in scapegoating, and certain sectors of the right-wing press were vociferous in their indignation at the fate of the Commanding Officer, Colonel Jorge Mendonca[37] – even though it began to seem possible, following a public inquiry, that Mendonca might eventually have a case to answer.

Mousa, 28, died in Basra on 15 September 2003 after being subjected to numerous assaults over 36 hours when he was in the custody of British soldiers from

1 Queen's Lancashire Regiment (1 QLR).[38] Mousa, together with six others, was arrested on the morning of Sunday 14 September following a raid on the Haitham Hotel in Basra where he worked as a receptionist (Operation Salerno). Found inside the hotel were rifles, AK47s, ammunition, grenades, a sniper scope, timings believed to be indicative of bomb making devices, forged identity documents and a large quantity of Iraqi money, all of which appeared to confirm intelligence that the hotel, together with others in the city, was being used as a base for insurgents and extremists.[39] Accordingly, employees at the hotel were taken to a Temporary Detention Facility (TDF) at the 1 QLR Battle Group Main Headquarters whilst it was determined whether or not they should be interned on the basis that they posed a threat to coalition forces.

It was alleged that they were subjected to ill-treatment at the hotel, prior to being arrested and taken to the TDF,[40] but the majority of the beatings took place at the TDF. It was alleged that much of the abuse was to keep the detainees in the stress position as part of the conditioning procedure set out in 1 QLR's procedure for detainees/internees. The detainees were made to stand with their backs against the wall, their knees bent so that their thighs were parallel to the ground and their arms outstretched in front of them, again parallel to the ground.[41] The precise cause of Mousa's death was unknown, but pathologists agreed that it was either postural asphyxia or the net result of his multiple injuries.[42] At the post mortem, it was reported that his body had 93 visible external injuries, strangulation marks, broken ribs, and a broken nose.[43] Another of the Iraqi civilians had such serious injuries to his kidneys that he suffered renal failure, and others had identifiable injuries consistent with being assaulted, being punched or being kicked.[44]

The court martial opened on 7 September 2006 at Bulford Military Court Centre and lasted just over six months. The Crown presented evidence of systematic abuse, including making prisoners stand in stress positions, subjecting them to verbal and physical abuse and inhuman and degrading treatment, including being kept in the toilet area for three hours and being made to drink a soldier's urine.[45] In particular, the Crown made reference to 'the choir', which consisted of Corporal Payne striking one detainee after the other so that they called out in pain.[46] The situation was described as 'an apparent free-for-all with solders acting in the belief of total impunity'.[47] In support of the negligence charges, the prosecution alleged that the noise coming from the detention facility was such that it must have been heard by soldiers nearby: 'We are not dealing in this case with an isolated incident of ill-treatment carried out behind closed doors. We are dealing, are we not, with the systematic ill-treatment if not inhuman treatment over a period of at least 36 hours done quite openly, coupled with shouting and bawling and the banging of a metal pole for a great deal of that time.'[48]

Corporal Payne pleaded guilty to one count of inhuman treatment, and became the first British soldier convicted of a war crime under the International Criminal Court Act.[49] He was jailed for one year and dismissed from the army. The second and third charges, of manslaughter and perverting the course of justice, were dropped on the basis of the Judge Advocate, Mr Justice McKinnon's determination that there was no case to answer. With regard to the former, he said that the case against Payne collapsed because Crown could not show that he was responsible for all, or even a substantial part, of the multiple injuries sustained by Mousa, there having been 'numerous assaults over the 36 hours by other unidentified persons or intruders not under Corporal Payne's control'.[50]

Justice McKinnon also determined that there was no case to answer with respect to Lance Corporal Crowcroft, Kingsman Fallon, Sergeant Stacey and Colonel Mendonca. This owed to a wall of silence – or collective amnesia among all of those involved, with versions of 'I don't remember' being used over 600 times.[51] The remaining two defendants, Warrant Officer Davies and Major Peebles, were acquitted a month later. With respect to Crowcroft and Fallon, the Crown had been unable to pinpoint a victim or an injury as attributable to either of the accused. Indeed, the majority of the injuries appeared to have been sustained in the 26 hours following the end of Crowcroft and Fallon's guard duty, during which time, 'the beatings and ill-treatment of the detainees continued and intensified'.[52] Moreover, as was the case with the charges against Sergeant Stacey, Private Lee, on whose evidence most of the Crown's case was built was, 'in all respects, a hopeless witness'.[53] So, they were in the same situation as 'all those soldiers whom I shall not name, [who] frustrating though it may be, the Crown has acknowledged by its failure to charge any of them that there is, as is the fact, no evidence against them'.[54]

The rationale for finding no case to answer in respect of Colonel Mendonca was somewhat more convoluted and substantially more controversial. Mendonca was one of the most highly decorated Colonels in the British Army and had enjoyed a distinguished career, with rapid advancement through the ranks to full Colonel. He was awarded an MBE and the Distinguished Service Order medal for service in Iraq. It was Colonel Mendonca himself who initiated the formal inquiry that resulted in charges being brought.

As already stated, Mendonca was charged with negligently performing a duty by failing to take such steps as were reasonable in all the circumstances to ensure that Iraqi civilians being held at the temporary holding centre under his command were not ill-treated.[55] It was not suggested that he condoned the abuse, but that, as a Commanding Officer, he 'either failed to impose a sufficiently robust culture of intolerance towards such abuses or failed to have a sufficiently firm grip on his soldiers'.[56] The Judge Advocate found that since the charges against Mendonca dealt purely with events after 13 September 2003, and not with either the delegation of responsibility for the processing and treatment of detainees to the Battle Group Internment Review Officers (BGIROs, Major Royce and Major Peebles) or the procedure and operation of the processing of detainees adopted by 1 QLR on the basis of FRAGO 29, issued by the Brigade Headquarters, Mendonca could not be held criminally responsible: 'no witness has given any evidence to the effect that Colonel Mendonca did anything he should not have done or that Colonel Mendonca failed to do something he should have done in relation to the charge against him. [. . .] The ill-treatment on 14 and 15 September 2003 was a "one-off" occurrence which Colonel Mendonca had no reason to believe was taking place until he was informed of the death of Mr Baha Mousa'.[57] However, following the Baha Mousa public inquiry, Mendonca's position became more questionable, as it emerged that he had not even visited the TDF following the death, telling the inquiry only that he visited once at the end of their first day of detention and that they were not hooded and quiet at that point. Some interested observers find this either barely credible or negligent, and that it is 'entirely foreseeable that the Commanding Officer, Mendonca, is likely to face criminal charges'.[58]

This case more than any other brought to the fore a series of issues around the legitimacy of the war in Iraq, the conduct of the British Army in Iraq and the wider stresses and strains of operating in such challenging and difficult circumstances. The controversy highlighted a deeper sense of malaise among the military about the Iraq war relating to fears that they are bearing the burden of illegitimacy.[59] In some quarters, it was seen as a politically motivated witch-hunt. The case also raised doubts about the capacity of the military justice system to deal with such cases: 'Despite an interim payment of compensation by the MoD to the receptionist's family, a three-year investigation and a six-month court martial of seven soldiers, costing £20m, nobody has ever been found responsible for Mousa's death.'[60] Although it was acknowledged by the Judge Advocate that Mousa's injuries were the result of numerous assaults over 36 hours, his conclusion is damning: 'And yet none of those soldiers have been charged with any offence simply because there is no evidence against them as a result of a more or less obvious closing of ranks.'[61] Even more damaging was the perception that this was merely the 'tip of the iceberg'.[62] The public inquiry into Baha Mousa's death certainly confirmed the doubts about the military justice system, as admissions of having lied to the investigation and the court martial were made.[63]

Conclusion

Each of the areas considered above highlights a different set of dilemmas inherent in the changing relationship between law and war. They demonstrate the difficulties of operating in situations such as that encountered in Iraq where lines between war fighting and policing and between combatant and non-combatant are increasingly blurred. Application of the law is never straightforward, and is further complicated by the changing character of warfare, and what constitutes an armed conflict, as well as by blurred distinctions between war, peace and occupation, and difficulty in drawing distinctions between combatants and civilians, and, regarding all and each of these, which legal regime pertains to a given situation at a given moment. As one senior military officer commented, 'What's faced the British Army in Iraq has been more acute than anything for generations'.[64] It has been lamented elsewhere that 'one of the many darker ironies of twentieth century history [is] that, just as codification of laws respecting non-combatants achieved further refinements, a whole surge of revolutionary struggles, civil wars and insurgencies have made discriminate warfare more difficult than ever to implement'.[65] Add this to increased scrutiny and raised expectations of clinical strikes and low-casualty warfare and the problem is compounded.

The Laws of Armed Conflict and International Humanitarian Law may be in need of change in some respects, but they are only part – and quite likely an early part – of a phase of change regarding issues pertaining to the laws and war and the relationship between them. War is changing and will continue that change for decades ahead. As it changes, the law, which has already begun to change, will continue to evolve in relation to changes in armed conflict and the political environment. The foregoing chapter has reviewed a number of legal-conceptual-practical areas that reflect change and that have raised sharp problems and generated heated debate. The practice of targeted killings, especially using UAVs, brings a new dimension to armed conflict and the basis on which it is done is open to question, especially where those practising this phenomenon are not uniformed military personnel. The question of what to do with prisoners when the 'war' is not the kind of war for which the law was drafted goes to the fine boundary issues of defining 'war' and 'non-war' and therefore the status of those involved and who is protected by the law, at which point, in which cases. The false blurring of this issue in principle with those of *habeas corpus* and criminality in the discussion around Guantanamo is, clearly, a fallacy, if the issues are closely and genuinely considered. Yet, there is discomfort surrounding this position, and even more, the blurring is understandable when it overlaps with questions of a far darker nature, as was the case with Guantanamo. The record of abuse of detainees in US custody at Guantanamo and, even more, elsewhere in the world, and their effective kidnapping and transfer to third countries, in some cases easily obscured other matters requiring fine tuned attention. However, such abuse and the torture to which it is symbolically linked, while never condonable, are also products of the new era of warfare. In particular, they are manifestations of the way in which the focus at the core of warfare has shifted from physical destruction and winning a trial of combat and strength, to one of winning a struggle of wills, in which values and ethics – including adherence to legal standards and the avoidance of damaging images of wrongdoing – are central. As shown in the final section, in particular, while the legalisation of war is more advanced than ever before, this is creating pressures on armed forces as they attempt to keep their house in order while doing what they have to do – and recognising that what they have to do has altered with the changing character of warfare. Recognising the centrality of these legal issues is essential, given that such issues of definition affect judgements on conduct, and, so, ultimately, on legitimacy.

The growing pains of change are marked by challenges regarding the law. Understandable, though not always justified, criticism focused on legal issues has been at the heart of a process of re-conceptualisation and re-definition. In the context of change, the legal-political issues marked the boundary of 'war' and 'non-war'. It also marked the core of growing pressures on those engaged in the conduct of warfare, with allegations of unlawfulness made as armed forces were deployed in novel circumstances that some deemed illegitimate, as well as charges of criminality over how those forces acted in those situations.

6 Security, discretion and international law

Aidan Hehir

The idea that the end of the Cold War would herald 'the age of enforcement' in terms of international human rights law assumed that the enforcement mechanisms within the architecture of international law were dormant – i.e. that they existed but weren't being used. In fact the application of Chapter VII in 1990s, for example, demonstrated the extent to which the legal architecture was a conscious product of political expediency which left the Permanent Five members of the Security Council (P5) with considerable discretion. The legal mechanisms for addressing intra-state crises in the UN Charter were not designed to eliminate political judgement. The limited innovations which have occurred in the contemporary era have preserved the Security Council's power of discretion.

This chapter argues that responses to intra-state crises will always be inconsistent so long as the body empowered with the sole authority to legitimise the use of force – namely the P5 – is mandated only to *choose* when to act, rather than compelled to do so. Those seeking consistency in responses to intra-state crises thus must target the discretion inherent in international law regarding the use of force rather than lobbying individual states to 'do the right thing'. Hence the logical end point of the argument in favour of consistency has to be the creation of an independent body with the authority to pass judgement on a particular situation and if necessary to deploy military force when a situation reaches a pre-defined nadir. Such a reform – though highly ambitious – would obviously have implications for humanitarian intervention, but, this chapter argues, also improve the regulation of the use of force more generally and in particular address some of the issues raised by the highly contentious use of force characteristic of the US-led 'war on terror'.

'Something must be done'

The debates on humanitarian intervention in the 1990s, perhaps uniquely, involved a discussion about both law and politics which generated considerable inter-disciplinary debate. The specific catalysts for this debate were two-fold; the question of the internal responsibilities of states, and the corollary regarding the international community's right to intervene (not only in the military sense) in the domestic affairs of states. The refrain 'something must be done' periodically rang out in

the face of humanitarian crises and the Rwandan genocide precipitated an out-
raged chorus of 'never again!'. Yet, precisely *who* should do 'something' quickly
emerged as a contested issue.

The end of the Cold War led many to assume that cooperation at the UN would
be more achievable and precipitate the development of a culture of timely and
effective responses to humanitarian crises. The UN-sanctioned imposition of
no-fly zones in Iraq certainly fed this optimism and for a period a sense of 'eupho-
ria' overcame the UN.[1] In the landmark Resolution 688 in 1991 the Security Council declared, '[The Security Council] Condemns the repression of the Iraqi civilian
population in many parts of Iraq, including most recently in Kurdish populated
areas, the consequences of which threaten international peace and security in the
region'. This signalled a new willingness on the part of the Security Council to
broaden its interpretation of its Chapter VII powers to include intra-state humanitarian crises. The provisions of Chapter VII outline the circumstance under which
the Security Council may sanction the use of force. Under Article 39 the Security
Council can determine 'the existence of any threat to the peace, breach of the
peace, or act of aggression' and decide what measures need to be taken. If peaceful measures fail then the Security Council, acting under Article 42, can sanction
more robust measures '. . . as may be necessary to maintain or restore international
peace and security'. Stretching this provision of the Charter to include humanitarian crises provoked some controversy; indicatively, the Independent International
Commission on Kosovo (IICK) noted, 'At present the Charter does not explicitly give the Security Council the power to take measures in cases of violations
of human rights'.[2] Whether the application of Chapter VII powers to intra-state
humanitarian crises is consistent with the Charter was, therefore, of some doubt.[3]
Nonetheless, in the context of the inertia that characterised the UN's response to
crises during the Cold War this concern with legal procedure was seen as somewhat academic.

Simon Chesterman, however, notes that Security Council action under Chapter
VII during the 1990s was haphazard, leading to 'ambiguous resolutions and con-
flicting interpretations [of Chapter VII]'.[4] The sanctioning of action, according
to Chesterman, 'depended more upon a coincidence of national interest than on
procedural legality'.[5] In addition, when the Security Council used Chapter VII
during the 1990s the supporting resolution invariably deemed the action to be
exceptional. Indicatively, the sanctioning of action in Somalia in 1992 was premised on it being 'an exceptional response'; the deployment of troops in Rwanda
in 1994, through Resolution 929, was described as 'a unique case'; Resolution
940 sanctioning action in Haiti recognised 'the unique character' of the situation and stated that Haiti's 'extraordinary nature . . . [required] an exceptional
response'. Additionally there were a number of instances when the spectre of
inertia returned, most notably in Bosnia and during the Rwandan genocide. This
inconsistent use of Chapter VII angered many who accused the Security Council of
hypocrisy.[6] Interventions sanctioned under Chapter VII thus clearly become more
commonplace but the selective application of this provision has been a cause for
concern. The idea, therefore, that the removal of the Soviet veto and the end of

bi-polarity, coupled with the rise in prominence of global civil society agitating for more focus on human rights, would precipitate the initiation of effective remedial action by the Security Council was demonstrably disproved. The P5, regardless of any ideological or political rivalry, continued to treat situations on a case-by-case basis determining action on the basis of their respective national interest rather than either humanitarian need or procedural legality.

The inconsistent response to crises in the 1990s, therefore, highlighted the extent to which the international legal architecture's enforcement mechanisms were ultimately predicated on the disposition of the Security Council and the P5 in particular. There was certainly no shortage of human rights legislation; since 1945 there have been a number of international treaties proscribing certain violations of human rights. Todd Landman's statistical analysis of human rights law in the post-Charter era concluded that there has been 'an expansion in both the breadth and depth' of the international human rights legal regime and that 'an increasingly larger set of human rights has found positive legal expression, while on the other hand a larger number of states have ratified these main instruments'.[7] It is clear, therefore, that states, at least since 1945, have been willing and able to agree on certain universal human rights laws.

Compliance with these laws, treaties and commitments has been manifestly erratic, however; over the course of the 20th century, far more people were killed by their own governments than were killed by all wars put together. This has much to do with the fact that human rights law constitutes a different sub-set of international law from the laws governing inter-state relations. As Malgozia Fitzmaurice states, 'Human rights treaties are not contractual in nature and do not create rights and obligations between States on the traditional basis of reciprocity; they establish relationships between States and individuals'.[8] States, therefore, may well agree amongst themselves on standards they *should* uphold domestically but ultimately, under the current system, the self-regulation of compliance with these agreements limits the effect in the inter-state context the original treaty can have. Non-compliance with human rights treaties results in negative consequences only for the domestic citizenry and not other signatories to the treaty. In this respects, as Louis Henkin notes, 'compliance with human rights law ... is wholly internal'.[9] The only exception is the possibility that the Security Council will determine that a situation warrants a Chapter VII intervention, yet as noted the invocation of this provision is discretionary and historically has been a function of a coincidence of interests among the P5.

'A realist core'

The contemporary tenets of international law derive from the process of law formation orientated towards defining the rights afforded to states, and the remit of the international institutions established to regulate them. The emergence of the sovereign state in the 17th century led to the gradual development of rules governing relations between these political entities. While international law expanded in the 18th and 19th centuries the legal system at this time was undermined and abused by the more powerful states and lacked a constitutional base. In the pre-World War I era:

> the dominant powers determined the criteria by which non-European politi-
> cal communities could be admitted to membership of international society,
> including the degree to which the laws of armed conflict were to apply to the
> non-European world.[10]

States essentially acted without restraint apart from that derived from domestic considerations and the policies of their rivals and allies.[11] Legal codes certainly existed and states often committed themselves to behave in certain ways but the malleability of these codes was routinely exploited. For example, it was agreed that self-defence was a permissible basis for the use of force, hence effectively all acts of aggression during this period, including even Germany's invasion of Belgium in 1914, were legitimised as such.

The establishment of the League of Nations in 1919 was championed by its proponents as a means by which the international system could be better regulated and the use of force curtailed by law. While the aspirations of the League manifestly failed, significant developments in international law with long-term implications *did* occur during the League's existence. The Permanent Court of International Justice was established in 1922, later becoming the International Court of Justice (ICJ) in 1946. The Kellogg-Briand Pact in 1928 constituted a significant renunciation of war as an instrument of foreign policy and the pact's key provisions were incorporated into the UN Charter. The normative remit of international law thus expanded to constrain not just the conduct of war but the grounds on which it could be legitimately waged.

World War II catalysed a shift from idealism to realism in International Relations theory which largely mirrored international politics during the Cold War. In terms of international law, however, World War II accelerated the process of law formation regarding the use of force. The UN Charter constituted an ambitious attempt to constrain the recourse to force and for the first time codified sovereign equality as the basis of the international legal system. The new legal regime attempted to restrict the use of force through the creation of inviolable states of equal legal status thereby preventing, at least in legal terms, the overt use of power in international politics. Andrew Hurrell argues that the evolutionary trajectory of international law in the latter half of the 20th century has been orientated:

> towards a system in which norm creation becomes an increasingly complex
> and pluralist process, in which ideas of equality become more powerful and
> pervasive, and in which specific rules come to be understood and interpreted
> in the light of general legal principles and shared foundational values and as
> part of an increasingly integrated normative order.[12]

The normative goal of pluralist law creation and peaceful inter-state relations could only be realised if the legal subjects of this new regime were afforded equal rights and, crucially, empowered with the right to determine their own fate, hence the need for sovereign equality and inviolability.

The establishment of the UN and the legal rights granted to states should not be seen, however, as a bottom-up process whereby major powers bowed to pressure exercised by smaller states demanding equality and the establishment of an egalitarian regime. Gerry Simpson cites the special powers reserved for the P5 as evidence of what he terms 'legalised hegemony', namely:

> the existence within an international society of a powerful elite of states whose superior status is recognised by minor powers as a political fact giving rise to the existence of certain constitutional privileges, rights and duties and whose relations with each other are defined by adherence to a rough principle of sovereign equality.[13]

Indeed, Hedley Bull cautioned that legal systems always reflect existing power asymmetries; 'any historical system of rules will be found to serve the interests of the ruling or dominant elements of the society more adequately than it serves the interests of the others'.[14] The UN framework was of course designed by the victorious Allies who reserved significant competencies for themselves, most notably the veto powers of the P5. Nigel White describes the veto as 'a realist core in an institutionalist framework – a political core in a legal regime'.[15]

The creation of the Security Council was a conscious acknowledgement that power was a factor in international relations and one which had to be formally recognised in the new international legal system. As Herbert Briggs noted the framers of the Charter sought to ensure that the new organisation would 'work with, rather than in opposition to, the realities of power'.[16] Likewise Dimitris Bourantonis notes that the permanent members of the Security Council were delegated a 'privileged position' and a 'superior status' on the basis that this was necessary to ensure these states would 'offer their political, military, technological and financial support'.[17] The power of the Security Council at the zenith of the new system and the constitutional competencies at their disposal meant that 'the Security Council was left free to *interpret* what it meant to promote international peace and security'.[18] The veto thus served as a means by which the P5 acquired 'the legal and constitutional weapon with which they could defend their interests and position'.[19]

The Security Council is formally constrained by the Charter and exercises its power within the framework stipulated therein. The Council's powers, therefore, 'cannot be unlimited'.[20] In 1948 the ICJ acknowledged the formal constraints upon the Security Council; '[the] political character of an organ cannot release it from the observance of the treaty provisions established by the Charter when they constitute limitations on its powers or criteria for its judgments'.[21] More recently in the 1995 Tadic case the Appeals Chamber of the ICTY declared that the Council must only take action 'within the limits of the Purposes and Principles of the Charter'.[22] Nonetheless, despite these legal constraints, in reality the Council has acted as the principal interpreter of the Charter's rules and hence its own powers. During the course of the negotiations at San Francisco in 1945 Greece proposed that the ICJ be designated as the sole interpreter of the Charter but this was rejected. This has meant that in practice, 'the Charter is what the principal organs do'.[23]

The centrality of discretion

The vast corpus of human rights law lack independent enforcement mechanisms and are reliant on the Charter's provisions. These provisions, covered under Chapter VII, are essentially ill-suited to being applied to intra-state crises. Even if one maintains that Chapter VII, imperfect as it is, *can* be applied to intra-state crises there remains a key barrier to enforcement, namely the interests of the P5. Unless the P5 agree, no enforcement action can be ordered. An example is provided by the provisions of the 1948 Genocide Convention. Article 8 of the Convention states:

> Any Contracting Party may call upon the competent organs of the United Nations to take such action under the Charter of the United Nations as they consider appropriate for the prevention and suppression of acts of genocide or any of the other acts enumerated in article III.

In practice the 'competent organ' of the UN is the Security Council. Thus, if states believe that genocide is occurring and wish to stop it, the matter is referred to the Security Council which then decides what action, if indeed any, to take. By virtue of their veto power the P5 have the discretion to take action; there is no compulsion on the P5 to act when a situation is deemed to constitute a threat to international peace and security and therefore the Security Council's official response to a situation is the product of political calculations thereby necessarily predicating the international legal system's effectiveness on political expediency. For example, the crisis in Darfur has been described as genocide by many NGOs, states (including the US) and UN missions to the region. The matter was referred to the Security Council and while it determined that the situation constituted a threat to international peace and stability, and certain members agreed that the Sudanese government was orchestrating the genocide, no effective action was mandated. Indeed, in 2004 in his testimony before the United States Senate Foreign Relations Committee Secretary of State Colin Powell stated, 'genocide has been committed in Darfur and . . . the Government of Sudan and the Jingaweit [sic] bear responsibility'. Yet he subsequently added,

> no new action is dictated by this determination. We have been doing everything we can to get the Sudanese Government to act responsibly. So let us not be too preoccupied with this designation.[24]

From a strict legal perspective, Powell was correct; his assertion that genocide was occurring only compelled the US to refer the matter to the Security Council – which they did – rather than to take further action. As Yoram Dinstein notes, 'no state acting alone (or even jointly with like-minded allies) has a legal option of resorting to force against another State, with a view to averting genocide or bringing it to an end'.[25] Thus, the US's justification for only referring the matter to the Security Council rather than acting to halt the 'genocide' was arguably legally sound given that the dominant legal view is that a state's acknowledgement of the occurrence of genocide does not require it to take military action.[26] The Security Council is not bound by the Charter to take any action and thus the response to Darfur was the function of political calculations.

The centrality of discretion, therefore, militates against consistency. The obvious solution to this is to reform the decision-making process to limit discretion and introduce measures which would insure an automatic response. Reforming the Security Council – both in terms of its composition and powers – however has proved notoriously difficult not least because of the P5's implacable opposition. Indeed, Bourantonis notes that in the post-Cold War era as the clamour for reform of the Security Council grew the P5 'reached a tacit agreement and adopted a common stance on the reform issue: to resist claims for reform and to do their utmost to prevent discussion on the subject in the UN'.[27] The evolution of the idea 'The Responsibility to Protect' (R2P) illustrates the extent to which the P5 have consistently distanced themselves from any compulsion to take action in favour of the maintenance of discretion.

The Responsibility to Protect

In 2001 the International Commission on Intervention and State Sovereignty (ICISS) published their seminal report *The Responsibility to Protect*. The Report was an attempt to clarify the responsibilities of both states and the international community with respects to preventing and halting egregious intra-state crises. The ICISS privileged the UN as the entity with the legitimacy to order an intervention; all those seeking to launch an intervention, the ICISS advised, must seek the Security Council's approval. The ICISS warned that acting without explicit UN approval ran the risk of undermining the UN and international law more generally. Membership of the UN, the ICISS claimed, carries an obligation not to unilaterally use force but also an obligation to use force on behalf of the UN if so sanctioned.[28] While the ICISS was clear as to the importance of the Security Council it additionally criticised the unrepresentative nature of the P5 and its lack of accountability to the General Assembly. In terms of addressing the biggest issue regarding the Security Council's record on humanitarian intervention – the veto power of the P5 – the ICISS suggested the P5 commit to a voluntary 'code of conduct' whereby,

> a permanent member, in matters where its vital national interests were not claimed to be involved, would not use its veto to obstruct the passage of what would otherwise be a majority resolution.[29]

The 'code of conduct' was a highly idealistic 'solution'. A non-binding agreement in itself is a problematic legal mechanism, while the very idea that the P5 would collectively have no interests in the outcome of a particular intra-state conflict was arguably naive.

In May 2002 the Security Council discussed the ICISS's report; the US 'was noticeably unenthusiastic about the debate' while additionally 'there was widespread opinion in the meeting that if new situations emerged . . . the five permanent members and broader Council would lack the political will to deliver troops and would limit themselves to condemnatory resolution'.[30] The US rejected the idea of being bound to commit troops should the ICISS's thresholds be breached, while China and Russia opposed any diminution of the Council's monopoly on the authorisation of the use of force. At the 2005 UN World Summit the idea of the P5 agreeing not to use their veto powers – the 'code of conduct' – was jettisoned early in the negotiations.[31] The US in particular distanced itself from any initiatives that would have imposed a legal duty to intervene and its support for the final wording was explicitly conditional on the maintenance of discretion. In a letter to the President of the General Assembly prior to the Summit, John Bolton, then US Ambassador to the UN, suggested amending the section in the draft document regarding R2P, arguing, 'the Charter has never been interpreted as creating a legal obligation for Security Council members to support enforcement action'. The draft *Outcome Document* originally read 'The international community, through the United Nations, also has the *obligation* to use diplomatic, humanitarian and other peaceful means, including under Chapter VI and VIII of the Charter to help protect populations from genocide, war crimes, ethnic cleansing and crimes against humanity'. Bolton requested that this be changed to read, 'The international community, through the United Nations, also has *moral responsibility* to use appropriate diplomatic, economic, humanitarian and other peaceful means, including under Chapter VI and VIII of the Charter to help protect populations from such atrocities'.[32] 'Moral responsibility' and 'obligation' are clearly two very different duties.

The 2009 General Assembly debate on R2P did nothing to amend the legal mechanisms or enhance the likelihood of consistency. During the debate the P5 distanced themselves from any automaticity; the UK ambassador cautioned against thresholds or 'checklists' for action, warning, 'Every situation is different'[33] and hence a political decision has to be agreed, while the Chinese ambassador stated,

> the Security Council has a role to play but it must make judgments and decisions tailored to specific circumstances and must act prudently. Here it must be pointed out that the responsibility entrusted to the Council by the Charter is the maintenance of international peace and security.[34]

This reference to maintaining 'international peace and security' is an obvious, and indeed legally accurate, reference to the limits of the Council's raison d'être; while increased pressure has been put on the P5 to 'do something' in response to a number of intra-state crises since the end of the Cold War, humanitarian action was not, and is not, an explicit part of its mandate. There has been no development, therefore, which can be cited as enabling a consistent, impartial response in future;

decisions will continue to be made in an ad hoc fashion dependent on political whims and exigencies.

The deleterious effect of discretion

The previous sections have noted that discretion was consciously built into the Charter, that the remit of the Security Council was shaped by an explicit acknowl-edgement that political calculations would guide the P5 who were mandated to 'interpret' threats to international peace and stability, and that nothing has changed. Why, then, is this problematic and in what sense does this relate to the 'war on terror'?

One of the most controversial aspects of the war on terror was the extent to which the US determined to take unilateral action to defend itself. This was most obviously manifest in the bellicose commitments in the 2002 National Security Strategy and the invasion of Iraq. The 2003 invasion, widely denounced as illegal due to the lack of Security Council authorisation, led to a plethora of books and articles predicting the demise of the international legal system and the reversion to a system based on unilateralism and subjective determinations as to threats, rights and responsibilities. This fear generated by the war on terror, however, owes its origins to a much less controversial intervention which itself is attributable to the discretionary powers of the P5, namely NATO's 1999 intervention in Kosovo.

NATO's intervention dramatically highlighted the contestation surrounding unilateral humanitarian intervention. Conscious of the willingness of Russia and China to veto any proposal sanctioning action against Milosevic's Yugoslavia, NATO circumvented the Security Council. While some legal justification was indeed formally offered, the lack of Security Council authorisation was primarily justified on the grounds that to have done nothing was unconscionable. In terms of objective assessment, the dominant (though by no means unanimous) legal view was that NATO acted unlawfully. The UK House of Commons Foreign Affairs Select Committee concluded that NATO's intervention was 'of dubious legality in the current state of international law'.[35] The finding of the IICK that the NATO intervention was 'illegal but legitimate' has become an oft-quoted and widely accepted appraisal of the intervention.[36]

International law's dependency on the Security Council – itself considered a body of low moral standing – led to the conviction that, as Robertson argued, 'humanitarian intervention cannot be the prerogative of the UN'.[37] This, therefore, catalysed the emergence of the conviction that as the very basis of international law was predicted on the assent of the P5 who were guided at all times by political rather than legal or moral concerns, international law itself was of dubious utility. Given that the P5 included Russia and China, many argued it did not make sense to predicate the legality of humanitarian action on whether or not these notorious human rights violators supported morally legitimate action. As Bellamy argued, 'Why . . . should undemocratic states with poor human rights records prevent a group of democratic states from protecting people in foreign countries?'[38] It was claimed that as both Russia and China so obviously remained wedded to narrow geopolitical worldviews and retained a stranglehold over international law the utility of law was diminished. International law was therefore deemed by some as outdated and certain ostensibly more ethically advanced states should not be bound by provisions.[39]

The widespread disaffection with international law in the area of human rights protection and the general sense that the Charter regime was anachronistic necessarily lent succour to those seeking greater flexibility in their international conduct. It is not difficult to discern, therefore, that the exposé of international law's failings in one area – namely humanitarian intervention – permeated into other areas. The denigration of international law in 1999 logically did not remain localised around the issue of human rights protection. The fact that the US felt compelled to 'go it alone' in the war on terror was routinely justified in a markedly similar manner to the justifications proffered in 1999. The Security Council was denounced as a talking shop hamstrung by the nefarious agendas of the P5 with China and Russia in particular singled out as recalcitrant purveyors of *Realpolitik*. Frustrated with the often glacial pace of reform many argued that the necessary changes to the rules and norms governing the use of force cannot be achieved through consensus. The willingness of China and Russia to veto any substantial reform came to be portrayed as self-interested spoiling by illiberal governments who reflect neither the wishes of their own citizens or world opinion.[40] It was argued, therefore, that change must be forced through by those 'enlightened states' that embody progressive moral rectitude.[41]

The rhetoric of the Bush administration during the war on terror reflected this attitude of disdain towards international law. Former US President George W. Bush outlined his views on the UN's authority by declaring, 'We don't really need the United Nation's approval to act . . . When it comes to our security, we don't need anyone's permission'.[42] Similarly, when planning US military strategy following the September 11th attacks Bush declared, 'I don't care what the international lawyers say; we are going to kick some ass'.[43] The United States 2002 National Security Strategy constituted, according to Jean-Marc Coicaud, 'a significant depreciation of international rules, treaties and security partnerships as they had previously been conceived'.[44] Prior to the invasion of Iraq, President Bush asked, 'Will the United Nations serve the purpose of its founding, or will it be irrelevant?'[45] Failure on the part of the Security Council to support the US was therefore portrayed, somewhat ironically, as a dereliction of duty and a blow to the UN-centred system of international law.

The invasion of Iraq polarized the international community on a number of issues not least its legality. Many argued that the intervening coalition had not only broken international law, they had in fact conducted 'a multiple assault on the foundations and rules of the existing UN-centred world order'.[46] It must be noted, however, that this wiliness to act unilaterally, though often the primary weapon used against the Bush administration, predates the war on terror. Indicatively, William Cohen, US Secretary of Defense from 1997 to 2001, described Security Council authorisation as 'desirable, not imperative'.[47] Indeed, at its Fiftieth Anniversary in 1999 NATO states announced that they would 'prefer' to act with Security Council backing but 'must not limit themselves to acting only when such a mandate can be agreed'.[48] Operation Iraqi Freedom was seen by some as a part of a broader post-Cold War trend in Western policy towards international law. According to Nigel White,

> In many ways the Iraq crisis of 2003 was the culmination of a decade of pressure by the US and UK directed at changing the legal framework governing the use of force contained in the UN Charter, in a concerted effort to widen both exceptions to the ban on the threat or use of force.[49]

The intervention in Kosovo, however, was cited by certain supporters of the invasion of Iraq who pointed out that the Operation Allied Force had also been technically illegal but ultimately legitimate and hence a legitimate template for circumventing the Security Council for the greater good already existed. Anne-Marie Slaughter made the comparison, noting, 'the Bush administration has started on a course that could be called "illegal but legitimate" a course that could end up, paradoxically, winning United Nations approval for a military campaign in Iraq'.[50] Clearly, it would be an exaggeration to claim that Operation Iraqi Freedom was a consequence of Operation Allied Force though the continuities between the two interventions are strong not least in terms of their respective impact on international law.

While the 'coalition of the willing' did proffer a robust legal justification in 2003 this was rejected by the majority of observers. In tandem with the legal rationale many of those supportive of the invasion expressed a desire to change the rules governing the use of force, thereby suggesting in effect that while the invasion may not have been strictly legal international law, the UN system itself had to change to meet the demands of the modern era. Indeed, Tony Blair stated,

> It may well be that under international law as presently constituted, a regime can systematically brutalise and oppress its people and there is nothing anyone can do, when dialogue, diplomacy and even sanctions fail, unless it comes within the definition of a humanitarian catastrophe (though the 300,000 remains in mass graves already found in Iraq might be thought by some to be something of a catastrophe). This may be the law, but should it be?[51]

Yet, the claims made regarding international law's redundancy are compromised by the fact that the very states who have routinely argued that unilateral action was necessary because of the legal shortcomings have themselves resisted changing the basic structure of the system. As Caplan states, 'there is little evidence that the British government or any other major power, is contemplating fundamental UN reform in response to the need to strengthen the organisation's capacity to cope more effectively with humanitarian catastrophes'.[52] This is evident with respect to the evolution of R2P and the lack of any reform with respects to the veto. The rejection of international law, therefore, is arguably born less from conviction and more from expediency. Thus the veto powers of the other P5 states can be seen as beneficial beyond the obvious capacity to block unpalatable proposals. States acting unilaterally can lament the fact that they were forced to do so by the 'Chinese/Russian veto', additionally, when moral pressure builds, states may refer the matter to the Security Council knowing little will occur, and later decry this obfuscation, pointing the finger at other P5 members.

There can be no doubt but that the increase in incidents of, and support for, action without Security Council approval since the initiation of the war on terror constitutes a fundamental threat to the international legal system. According to the United Nations High Level Panel on Threats, Challenges and Changes, diminishing the UN's monopoly on the use of force would fundamentally undermine the authority of the UN and cause a chain reaction of unilateral aggression.[53] Richard Falk claimed after the invasion of Iraq that the UN had been relegated to the role of 'a debating society',[54] while David Malone similarly lamented, 'Above all, the UN was the loser, not in terms of compromise to its principles, but in perceptions of its effectiveness and centrality'.[55] As Kofi Annan warned, 'unless the Security Council is restored to its preeminent position as the sole source of legitimacy on the use of force we are on a dangerous path to anarchy'.[56]

Beyond discretion?

The Charter empowers the Security Council to take action at the discretion of the P5. In the contemporary era the politicised nature of the P5 decision-making process has led to increased rhetorical support for unilateral action often from the very states that seek to maintain the P5's veto power as evidenced by the American invasion of Iraq and Russia's intervention in Georgia. While the present system may well serve the interests of the P5, it constitutes an open wound which left untreated will surely be fatal for international law. For those concerned that the death of the international legal system would plunge us back to the more violent days of the 18th and 19th centuries when malleable norms constituted international 'law', this corruption at the heart of the system has to be addressed. Allowing states to independently determine when force should be used for humanitarian reasons or when they deem a regime to constitute a grave threat to either national or international security is certainly inherently problematic.

Nigel Rodley and Basak Cali note that following NATO's intervention in Kosovo in 1999 three perspectives on the legality of NATO's actions emerged; first the minority view that Operation Allied Force was legal, second the majority view that it was illegal and a third view which held that it was 'a potential harbinger of future legality'.[57] Therefore, while the dominant view was that NATO acted contrary to international law, many who acknowledged this illegality argued, and indeed hoped, that as Operation Allied Force had so emphatically illustrated the deficiencies with the existing legal regime legal reform would subsequently follow. The need for fundamental legal reform was stressed by certain observers conscious of the politicised nature of P5 decision-making and uncomfortable with the permissibility of 'illegal but legitimate' action.[58] Many preferred to find some means to reconcile the two; indicatively Michael Burton asked 'Why saddle legitimate intervention with the stigma of illegality?'[59] Additionally, others feared that without clearer guidelines unilateral intervention would become a more common practice and one which would destabilise the international system;[60] a fear which according to some manifested in 2003 with the US invasion of Iraq.[61] The ICISS, a self-described response to the legal deficiencies exposed by NATO's intervention, noted, 'the issue of international intervention for human protection is a clear and compelling example of concerted action urgently being needed to bring international norms and institutions in line with international needs and expectations'.[62] Additionally while the IICK's conclusion that Operation Allied Force was 'illegal but legitimate' has become an oft-quoted appraisal of NATO's intervention, one aspect of the report which received less publicity was the corollary: 'Allowing this gap between legality and legitimacy to persist is not healthy'.[63]

The problems posed by humanitarian intervention and the nature of the use of force employed during the war on terror share a common genesis; the powers vested in the Security Council. Any legal regime which lacks an independent police force and army and is ultimately predicated on the whims of powerful elites to dispense 'justice' and legitimise the use of force will surely qualify as a 'failed state'. In the absence of clear constitutional guidelines on the use of force, an independent judiciary and a coercive body capable of enforcing the law effectively and consistently, all domestic legal regimes are doomed. It is not surprising, therefore, that the international legal system which displays these characteristics has suffered this fate. What is surprising, however, is the paucity of proposals articulated to address this major failing. While there have been a number of proposals for increasing the membership of the Security Council and changing the voting rights of its permanent members, surprising little has been advanced that would constitute the large-scale reform required. Put bluntly, without an independent international military force and an independent mechanism empowered to determine when this force can be deployed, the debates of the 1990s and the 2000s will continue *ad nauseum* while the perceived legitimacy of international law will steadily erode.

It is surely time, therefore, to focus on curtailing the power of the P5 and establish a means by which the use of force is regulated by an independent entity with the power, should it need it, to deploy military force. Sir Arthur Watts frames the issue in stark terms:

> There is a choice: the international community must either establish an international force to maintain order, or let states perform that function themselves. The framers of the UN Charter attempted the former, but their good intentions have never really been carried through . . . one is left in practice with self-appointed guardians of the peace. However, that cannot be a satisfactory basis on which to organize a legal order.[64]

Meaningful reform would require the establishment of two new entities; an international body – perhaps elected by the General Assembly – to represent the UN and not individual states, charged with determining the legitimacy of a proposed use of force and an international army capable of being mobilised to either lead or support a sanctioned military intervention. This would ensure that determinations that a situation was a humanitarian crisis which demanded external intervention, or that a particular situation/regime was a threat to international peace and security requiring the use of force, would be objectively made and ultimately consistent. Additionally, it would ensure that these determinations would not be mere condemnatory utterances but decrees capable of being enforced by an international force should states decline to volunteer their own troops. These mechanisms could be reserved for those situations where the Security Council fails to respond to a situation which manifestly demands external intervention or when the Council accepts the gravity of the situation but fails to take subsequent action. In this respect the new bodies would not be in competition with the Council but rather substitutes in cases of inertia. Reforming the system so that the authorisation of the use of force was not the sole preserve of the P5 with the discretion to act would mean that unilateral action could no longer be justified on the basis that it was a tragic necessity caused by the unreasonable use (or threatened use) of the veto. Failure to secure the P5's assent could be mitigated by lobbying the alternative non-state body and hence winning objective legitimacy for one's proposed actions.

To state the obvious, such a reform is no easy task; logistically and politically this would require a truly gargantuan change more extensive than any previous legal or political reform. Additionally, any attempt to reform the UN, including the powers of the Security Council, would confront the obstacle posed by the Security Council's veto power; Article 108 of the Charter stipulates that amendments to the Charter must be approved by the P5. In this context 'turkeys voting for Christmas' springs to mind with respects to the likelihood of such reform.

Nonetheless, there are reasons to be somewhat optimistic that such a proposal is not utterly fantastical. The catalysts for the establishment of the International Criminal Court did not stem from the P5 and the fact that three of the P5 have yet to ratify the Rome Statute (Russia, the US and China which has not signed it) has not prevented its operation. There are obvious limits to the International Criminal Court's (ICC) powers, however, and it would be certainly wrong to claim that the court is beyond the interference, both formal and informal, of the P5. Organisations which delegate competencies to non-state-based institutions, such as many EU institutions, clearly constitute examples of international organisations which do operate, at least constitutionally, without the interference or influence of state interest. Individual members of the EU no longer have exclusive power over many competencies traditionally the sole preserve of sovereign states. States will join, or remain members of, organisations which exercise control over aspects of their domestic system if they are convinced that the benefits outweigh the sacrifices and the higher authority is truly impartial.

Ultimately, while the current international legal system constitutes a major advance compared with a hundred years ago, we have manifestly reached the limits of this system's applicability unless we are content to replay the debates of the last twenty years – regarding both humanitarian intervention and the use of force more generally – for another twenty years and beyond. International law will continue to be derided as impotent and hopelessly corrupt unless both the 'who decides?' and 'who acts?' questions are answered in a way which ensures consistency and impartiality. So long as the failings exposed by the debate on humanitarian intervention continue unchecked, they will poison the entire legal system and slowly corrode its legitimacy and efficacy. If I feel that the government, the police and the judiciary are hopelessly corrupt, driven by narrow self-interest and ultimately unwilling to protect me from criminals and external threats generally, then I will literally take the law into my own hands and buy a gun. If my elderly neighbour is burgled I will confront the intruder rather than ring the police as I am uncertain they will react. While this may constitute justice of a kind it is obviously a slippery slope; imbued with self-righteousness and convinced that I alone can mete out justice I may well use my gun for less moral ends, particularly if I am convinced that the police are less powerful than me. In this respect the erosion of law's efficacy in one area can be seen to percolate throughout the entire legal system and it is not surprising, therefore, that intervention in Kosovo and the invasion of Iraq have so many parallels. When law lacks objectivity, consistency and efficacy a vacuum exists which must necessarily imperil stability and peace.

Conclusion

According to Antonio Cassese, 'the system envisaged in the UN Charter for the maintenance of international peace and security . . . has substantially failed'.[65] On the day of the US invasion of Iraq UN Secretary General Kofi Annan stated, 'we must all feel that this is a sad day for the UN and the international community'.[66] International law and the primary body established to regulate it are, therefore, quite obviously in crisis. While it would be an exaggeration to suggest that the various crises currently hampering the efficacy of the UN and international law more generally all stem from the powers of the P5, there can be little doubt but that the P5's position at the zenith of the international legal architecture exercises a corrosive effect on the efficacy of international law and the UN and perceptions as to the legitimacy of both.

States, according to John Mueller, will intervene 'only when their interests seem importantly engaged or where they manage to become self-entrapped'.[67] While this is not an especially controversial or profound statement it does have enormous implications for the current system of international law; so long as the regulation and enforcement of international law is primarily the concern of self-interested states each armed with the power of veto, it is likely that challenges to international law witnessed in the past twenty years will continue. The veto was the cause of the inconsistent response to intra-state humanitarian crises in the 1990s and the 'illegal but legitimate' argument advanced by NATO states in 1999 unsurprisingly expanded beyond the issue of humanitarian intervention as evidenced by the Bush doctrine. The P5 veto facilitates the argument that the unilateral use of force was an unfortunate but necessary option, and this cannot but degrade international law.

'The challenge facing the international community', as Michael Byers notes, 'is to maintain rules on military action that are reasonable, effective and widely accepted'.[68] At present this is manifestly not the case and so long as the regulation of the use of force is a function of the discretionary powers of the P5 this will continue. In reference to the crisis facing international law Franck Berman argues that the solution 'must lie in collective international authority, and more particularly in building up its regularity, predictability modes of operation, and most of all its accountability'.[69] The reforms proposed above, though obviously ambitious and in need of further refinement and detail, are based on principles of objectivity, consistency and effectiveness which, I suggest, must guide the transformation of international law that is so obviously necessary.

7 The human security agenda after 9/11

From humanitarian intervention to peacebuilding

Natasha Kuhrt

This chapter will engage with the widespread assertion that 9/11 and the 2003 intervention in Iraq have 'cast a shadow over the progression of the human security agenda'.[1] Human security has increasingly been posited as an alternative narrative to state security, in part due to its focus on a more normative discourse, and is now at the heart of the United Nations agenda. However, there is a disjuncture between the United Nations' Security Council's (UNSC) responsibility for international peace and security on the one hand, and the assertion of human security on the other. Nowhere is the difficulty more apparent than in the 'Responsibility to Protect' document published three months after 9/11. It will be argued that the human security agenda can be salvaged to some extent by investing in the third 'pillar' of the concept, the 'responsibility to rebuild'. Here, the interconnected nature of threats can more effectively be addressed. If state failure and state weakness represent some of the causes of terrorism, then it seems logical to concentrate efforts on such endeavours, although such projects have their own dilemmas. Unfortunately peacebuilding has become tainted by its association with unilateral efforts in Iraq and its association with the War on Terror in Afghanistan. As Roland Paris suggests, the partial similarities between these two operations and UN operations elsewhere have led to 'equating the Iraq war and international peacebuilding missions as part of an abhorrent phenomenon of "democratic imperialism" or "imperial nation-building"'.[2] Some have even depicted the US efforts at democracy promotion in Iraq and the Middle East as the logical conclusion of pre-9/11 peacebuilding operations. Before turning to an examination of statebuilding after conflict, the issue of humanitarian intervention and UN interventions in general since the Cold War will be addressed.

Since the end of the Cold War and the end of bipolar confrontation a new international power structure has emerged, leaving just one military superpower, and a smattering of 'great powers', including one 'rising' power. The 1991 Gulf War on the one hand appeared to demonstrate a new international consensus on intervention, but on the other was a display of US military power. Alongside this, the apparent growth in the influence of the human rights agenda, in particular the influence of human rights law on the UN agenda, seemed to herald a 'post-Westphalian order, where international law, with its enlarging normative scope, extending writ and growing institutionalisation, exemplifies the phenomenon of globalization'.[3] Moreover, politics and law appeared to be converging, as the UN Charter, a legal-political instrument, was given new life. It seemed as if the purposes and principles of the UN Charter were now in greater harmony: thus international peace and security could now be maintained simultaneously with a respect of 'equal rights and self-determination of peoples' and 'respect for human rights' in Article 1.[4] The prohibition on intervention in violation of a state's territorial integrity in Article 2 remained as an integral component of state sovereignty. However, several developments appeared to be challenging conceptions of sovereignty. The increasing emphasis on human rights, it was clear, could come into conflict with the principle of sovereignty and prohibition on intervention. Whether one sees the human rights component of the Charter as central, in a 'broad construction of positive peace', or whether one sees non-intervention as central, is revealing. Nevertheless, it seemed that the internal matters of states were fast becoming internationalised, in particular as intra-state rather than inter-state conflict was on the rise. In addition, in some of these crises, porous borders meant a spilling over of conflicts and their concomitant problems into a wider region. Indeed, several UNSC Chapter VII resolutions in the 1990s referred to the impact on surrounding regions.

Humanitarian interventions

In the UN Charter itself the relationship between the human rights discourse and those *jus cogens* norms such as territorial integrity and non-intervention is not clear. The lack of clarity as to which should prevail allows states to interpret the Charter as they see fit. Some would suggest that the intervention in Kosovo facilitated this. If it could be argued that there was law 'outside the Charter' that allowed intervention to take place (Just War Tradition) or simply that one inter-pretation of the Charter was that human rights could not be 'trumped' by territorial integrity.

There have been few interventions since the end of the Cold War that can be unreservedly classed as 'pure' humanitarian interventions in terms of motives, and certainly none before that. It has become almost a cliché to suggest that the concept is 'contested'. There has never been consensus on humanitarian intervention and probably never will be (two of the P5 states strongly dispute the existence of such a norm). This is related to concerns regarding state sovereignty which assumes a prohibition on intervention in a state's internal affairs, if not complete authority in a state's own territory. National interests have always been the sticking point. It is useful here to recall that after the disastrous US adventure in Somalia, the US State Department issued PDD-25 which suggested that the US should in future refrain from intervening in situations where the US had no 'clear' national interest. The actual UN resolution was formulated in terms of the need to allow the safe pas-sage of humanitarian assistance; as Nicolas Wheeler says, it was important for the UNSC to 'find a threat to International Peace and Security (IPS) as it would have exceeded its legal competence if it had tried to justify enforcement action on the basis that Somalia had ceased to exist'.[5]

While the intervention in Somalia was critiqued as having failed precisely because there was no national interest, others appeared to be criticised for having 'too much' national interest. Haiti is a case in point (although not technically a case of humanitarian intervention, humanitarian justifications were advanced). Many UN member states, especially those on the UNSC, recognised that this was America's sphere of influence and that other factors related to concerns about refugee flows came into play. If it had not been for this implicit knowledge that US intervention was related to these other factors, the Haiti resolution would likely not have passed. Moreover, as Neil MacFarlane reminds us, Russia was looking for tacit US approval of its operation in Georgia at the time.[6] However, despite the fact that the Haiti intervention was most emphatically not described as a precedent (the UNSC described the unique nature of the situation as demanding an 'exceptional response'[7]), Thomas Franck nevertheless was moved to hail the Haiti intervention as evidence of an 'emerging right to democratic governance'.[8] In fact the relevant UNSC resolution, while seeking to 'restore the rightfully elected government', was widely criticised not only for the fact that the UNSC appeared to be licensing US action in its own 'backyard' (this was particularly abhorrent to certain Latin American states given previous US policies there) but also because scant attention was paid to restoring the rule of law and justice in the mandate of the peacekeeping force.[9] The priority appeared to be to stem the flow of refugees heading for US shores, rather than to bring justice to Haitian society. Therefore we should treat with caution Alex Bellamy's assertion that the 'Somalia and Haiti cases were particularly important because in both cases the Security Council identified human suffering and governance issues as threats to international peace and security, and therefore legitimate objects of intervention'.[10] The same year as the Haiti intervention, the genocide in Rwanda shamefully failed to mobilise the international community.

In stark contrast, Kosovo appeared to be an unprecedented example of multilateral intervention in the name of 'values'. While Kosovo was ostensibly an intervention to put an end to severe and wide-scale human rights abuses, there was also an implication that the type of regime was a factor, so that 'free nations tend to be stable and solid partners in the advance of humankind. The best defence of our security lies in the spread of our values'.[11] While not supported by Russia and China, two of the P5, the intervention was endorsed by a range of developing countries and the intervention was undertaken by NATO (not a regional organisation according to Chapter VIII, but still its multilateral character lent a certain legitimacy). Therefore, the action against Serbia was deemed to be 'illegal yet legitimate' (the verdict of the Kosovo Commission). Herein lies the dilemma: for those inclined to take a restrictionist view of the Charter this was clearly illegal on a strict interpretation of the Charter, and therefore it was impossible to state that this action was clear evidence of an emerging norm of humanitarian intervention; as Ian Brownlie points out for example, the UK envoy to the UN Jeremy Greenstock, while asserting that NATO action in Serbia was legal, made no reference to the UN Charter nor did he invoke any sources of international law.[12] For some, it demonstrated that the Charter needed amendment: thus Michael

Glennon suggested that it was impossible for the UN Charter to 'reflect satisfactorily the realities of the international political system. A correspondence of legal expectations with geopolitical, at least with respect to nerve-centre security issues such as intervention, is essential if the legalist model is to be anything more than window-dressing'.[13]

However, there were also clear strategic interests on the part of the NATO alliance, and in effect the international community had issued Milosevic with an ultimatum based on political demands. For this reason, therefore, the legitimacy of the intervention in Kosovo was called into question by some parties, notably China and Russia, both P5 members. Taking a legal positivist view, however, they argued that it was the erosion of the sovereignty norm with which they were principally concerned: if NATO could intervene in Kosovo today, without UN authorisation, then the next stop might logically be Chechnya or Tibet. In Russia's view the parallels between Kosovo and Chechnya were clear: in both cases Muslim 'terrorists' sought to achieve independence via the use of force.

Russia and China were not the only opponents; for example, as Brownlie notes at a meeting of Foreign Ministers of the Group of 77 held several months after the NATO intervention, ministers 'stressed the need to maintain clear distinctions between humanitarian assistance and other activities of the United Nations. They rejected the so-called right of humanitarian intervention, which has no basis in the UN Charter or international law'.[14] Some of their reservations were probably less to do with the 'humanitarian' aspect of the intervention but to do with the perpetual association of humanitarian intervention and secessionist movements. On a strict reading of norms of self-determination, this should not be achieved externally outside the decolonisation context.

This highlighted the fact that while the Cold War was over, and the West had 'won', among the P5, the upholders of international peace and security, there remained very different interpretations of democracy and core ideals of international society such as self-determination, human rights and sovereignty, never mind their central role in the UN Charter. This cleavage was temporarily obscured by the apparent unity between USSR (later Russia) and 'the West' over first Iraq's invasion of Kuwait, and then events in the former Yugoslavia in the early 1990s. It is incredible to recall that in 1992 then Russian foreign minister Andrei Kozyrev spoke of Russia's priority as being 'to ensure all human rights and freedoms in their entirety [. . .] I believe that these questions are not an internal matter of states but rather their obligations under the UN Charter . . .'[15] Already by 1993, however, Russia was expressing doubt about support for action in Yugoslavia. Nevertheless it was suggested that the end of bipolarity would mean that states would be able to agree on new principles of humanitarian intervention in the 'society of states'. Some, however, such as Robert Jackson were more sceptical, preferring to stress the danger that humanitarian intervention might disturb the order between the great powers.[16]

Therefore to see 9/11 as the point when US unilateralism reasserted itself, and the period before that as a golden era of multilateral consensus would be a misperception.

It should be recalled that, while expressing very fundamental objections to the bombing of Serbia in 1999, Russia was more than eager to participate in the post-war arrangements. Russia was happy to use the G-8 as the forum for discussion of Kosovo, in particular as this did not include China; indeed a Russian official stated that 'an overly hard line on China's part could delay a solution to the Kosovo problem as much as NATO intransigience'.[17] For Russia, the chance to partici-pate in a 'great power condominium' was opportune – naturally this was in part to attempt to influence the outcome, i.e. to prevent Kosovo's detachment from Serbia. But one might construe this participation as 'tacit acceptance of NATO action: 'otherwise, by authorizing UN civil governance in Kosovo, states would be eating the fruit of a poisonous tree by partaking in the regime brought about by NATO's aggression.'[18] A certain cloak of legitimacy was therefore lent to the post-war accommodation. However, at the time it was made clear that there would be no independence for Kosovo. An argument could be made in international law, whereby self-determination is seen as an inclusive, rather than exclusive princi-ple, i.e. that all citizens have an equal right to participation within a polity, but: 'When such participation is denied, when a people . . . is "geographically separate and is distinct ethnically and/or culturally"' and has been put in a position of sub-ordination, 'a secession option may re-emerge as an international legal entitle-ment'.[19] However, this suggests a rather low threshold; instead, Allen Buchanan's argument regarding a right to 'remedial secession' may be more pertinent in the Kosovo case, although it remains problematic: 'international law should confer legitimacy on and support for groups for whom secession is a remedy of last resort against persistent patterns of large-scale violations of basic human rights'.[20]

In the wake of Kosovo, and a few months after 9/11, the International Commission on Intervention and State Sovereignty produced a report. Their report argued that:

> Where a population is suffering serious harm, as a result of internal war, insurgency, repression or state failure, and the state in question is unwilling or unable to halt or avert it, the principle of non-intervention yields to the international responsibility to protect.[21]

Firstly, the 'just cause' threshold lists only two circumstances under which a mili-tary intervention for humanitarian purposes is justified. These are the large scale loss of life or large scale ethnic cleansing, actual or imminent, described as 'serious and irreparable harm occurring to human beings, or imminently likely to occur'.[22] Furthermore action must be guided by 'right intentions', with the primary purpose to halt or avert human suffering. It must be the last resort. It must be proportional with the scale, duration and intensity limited to the minimum necessary. It must have 'reasonable prospects' of success, with consequences not worse than inac-tion. It must be authorised by the 'right authority' which in the first instance is the UN Security Council, but can be the UN General Assembly under the 'Uniting for Peace' procedure, or regional and sub-regional organisations under Chapter VIII of the Charter and with Security Council authorisation, or finally, if all else fails, action may be taken by 'concerned states'. Finally, the conduct of the intervention must be suitable for the task at hand, and thus must be proportional and adhere to international humanitarian law.[23]

In the case of Iraq, notoriously, none of these criteria were fulfilled. The debate regarding the legality and legitimacy of the intervention is well-documented: as with Kosovo, the intervention took place without the authorisation of the UNSC. One might argue that this was no different from Kosovo: but those who suggest that one can find law 'outside the Charter' would retort that the legitimacy sprang from the multilateral nature of the intervention and the broad support among the UN General Assembly, as well as publics in many countries. The argument that these member states were merely seeking to 'uphold the UN Charter', by remaining true to its purposes and principles, in the face of a veto from Russia and China was perhaps the suggestion that some lawyers in particular had difficulty with, although Fernando Teson argues that 'the promotion of human rights is as important a purpose in the Charter as is the control of international conflict'.[24]

This permissive reading of the Charter over Kosovo arguably made it far easier for the US to interpret the Charter as it saw fit, thus leading to the US action in Iraq, whereby the US and UK sought to 'enforce' previous UN resolutions, on the basis of their own understandings and interpretations of these resolutions. The idea arose that if the UNSC was not 'doing its job' of maintaining international peace and security, then one of the member states could step in. This could entail finding law outside the Charter that could legitimise action (usually by relying on the Just War Tradition). Alternatively, one could argue that the prominent place allocated to human rights in the UN Charter shows evidence of a strong commitment to this agenda. Moreover, the UNSC has a very broad scope for determining threats to international peace and security and had in fact determined the situation in Kosovo to be a threat to IPS under Chapter VII. The UNSC should not be prevented from acting merely because of the threat of veto, so the argument ran.

Regarding Kosovo, as Mary Kaldor suggests, states such as the UK framed the intervention in terms of the Just War Doctrine, a legitimacy framework which, while of some merit, tends traditionally to be about justifying state action rather than emphasising the individual.[25]

Regarding Iraq 2003 it was precisely the perceived unilateral nature of the intervention as much as anything else which undermined its legitimacy, not only the lack of clarity regarding the motives for intervention. The war in Iraq was criticised by both international lawyers and security analysts: the attitude of lawyers was generally either to ignore it as an aberration not worthy of discussion or to vehemently deride the action as bringing the UN into disrepute. Elizabeth Wilsmhurst, the Foreign Office lawyer, was a famous exception who described the use of force as not only unlawful but tantamount to 'the crime of aggression' and duly resigned.[26]

There was a lack of conviction as to the link between Iraq, WMD and terrorism. Some humanitarian arguments were advanced but these were not the most memorable (WMD was probably the argument that stood out most, given the 'dodgy dossier' and Colin Powell's presentation on WMD to the UN). Indeed one analyst has concluded, on the basis of textual analysis, that humanitarian arguments were least used, so the level of rhetoric was quite low.[27] In any case, mere rhetoric does not contribute to the establishment of a norm in international legal terms: there must be evidence of *opinio juris* as well as state practice.

But the most controversial aspect of the Iraq war was the juxtaposition of the WMD arguments with the Bush Doctrine of preventive war which, allied to humanitarian arguments, appeared to be making a case for a new type of preventive humanitarian war. Matthew Evangelista suggests that the expansion of a norm (the responsibility to protect) has contributed to a state practice (preventive war) that makes many of the original norm entrepreneurs uneasy.[28] This may be going too far, as the norm was far from established; however, it certainly seemed as if security interests were fusing with humanitarian concerns to create a new doctrine of prevention. Preventative humanitarian intervention may be justified, but only if there is evidence that mass slaughter is imminent, which in the case of Iraq it was not.[29] Lord Goldsmith, the UK Attorney-General, suggested that while humanitarian intervention had been emerging 'as a further and exceptional basis for the use of force . . . *The doctrine remains controversial, however. I know of no reason why it would be an appropriate basis for action in present circumstances*'.[30] Arguably in the cases of both Iraq and Kosovo, these were cases of 'unfinished business': regarding Kosovo, it was suggested that this was a crisis that the international community should have addressed at an earlier stage. Regarding Iraq, in fact the US and UK had continued to use the no-fly zones to enforce UN resolutions against Iraq almost right up until the intervention in 2003, with little real opposition from other Security Council members. In the case of Afghanistan, this too had been on the UN Agenda for some time, with a series of UNSC Chapter VII resolutions demanding that the Taliban close down training camps and hand over al-Qaeda commanders for prosecution.

The doubt cast on the humanitarian motives of the war in Iraq also cast doubt on the humanitarian nature of the occupation. The constant shift in justifications for the war confused people as to the real motives, further undermining public support, and thus legitimacy. A debate ensued, focused around whether an 'unjust' war could possibly promote a 'just peace'. Some, like Fernando Teson, believed the motives to be immaterial: the outcome was the main thing, i.e. Iraq had been liberated from a cruel dictator, and Iraqis were therefore better off. As Teson put it, even if Bush 'intentionally lied about WMD, we can deride him, but that is not a reason to devalue the act of liberating Iraq'.[31] Wheeler also argued that while motives are important, they should not be the threshold consideration: actions which produce 'humanitarian good' should be lauded, irrespective of whether they are motivated by humanitarianism in the first place. One must however bear in mind that if one takes success to be the test for legitimacy, then legitimacy could only be judged 'with the benefit of hindsight'.[32] For Kenneth Roth, director of Human Rights Watch, the fact that the primary motive was not humanitarian affected the entire conduct of the war (both the *jus in bello* and the *jus post bellum*): too few combat troops; the use of cluster bombs in populated areas; lack of police, etc.[33] Richard Falk suggests that because the US troops were not perceived as 'liberators' by the Iraqi population, this was a further reason to condemn the intervention as 'illegal and illegitimate'.[34] It is unclear whether the consequences of the invasion are worse than the consequences of inaction would have been for the people of Iraq.

The humanitarian arguments advanced by the US and the UK brought a sigh of relief from some that the R2P had not in fact been formalised; as Gareth Evans suggests, 'any formalisation of the principle would, in the long tradition of *missions civilisatrices*, only encourage those who were all too inclined to misuse it'.[35] Still others were concerned that invoking humanitarian concerns as justifications for the Iraq action would make it less likely for states to undertake humanitarian interventions, the US in particular.[36] The lack of determination to intervene in Darfur has been cited as a good example of this; however, one cannot necessarily assume a direct linkage between the two. We only can speculate as to whether the US might have spearheaded an intervention in Darfur, had the Iraq War not taken place. However, there was in any case no clear evidence before the Iraq War that the US was poised to conduct a raft of humanitarian interventions. One might suggest though that the establishment of the International Criminal Court in 2002 provides an alternative avenue for bringing perpetrators of human rights abuses to justice, and indeed perpetrators of crimes against humanity in Darfur have been indicted by the Court. Moreover, there is some comfort to be taken from the fact that China, a notorious abstainer on issues of human rights abuses, persuaded the Sudanese government to accept an African Union peacekeeping mission.

Post-conflict peacebuilding

One trend which has received more attention in recent years than the debate over whether or not there is an emerging norm of humanitarian intervention as such, is the trend towards a prolonged outside presence in countries riven by conflict: in Just War Tradition known as the *jus post bellum*. While the Iraq War could reasonably be seen as leading to greater cynicism regarding humanitarian interventions, the occupation of Iraq may inadvertently have caused greater harm to the human security agenda. Add to this the doubts regarding the continuing legitimacy of the international presence in Afghanistan (increasingly seen as a joint UK–US venture), and the whole peacebuilding enterprise is brought into disrepute. The democratic governance thesis too seemed to be undermined, in particular due to its linkage to 'regime change'. The humanitarian argument was mainly employed as an ex-post facto legitimation of the invasion. Perhaps understanding that promotion of the idea of regime change would be unacceptable, Tony Blair said he accepted that 'however abhorrent and foul the regime and however relevant that was . . . regime change alone could not be and was not our justification for war'.[37]

Nevertheless the question arises as to whether a state which has violated human rights then forfeits its right not only to non-intervention, but should also be replaced completely, i.e. regime change. President Bush did claim that humanitarian goals could be accomplished in Iraq simultaneously with the defeat of al-Qaeda and the Taliban: the concept of regime change is an outgrowth of this idea. While Bush was initially opposed to the whole idea of so-called 'nationbuilding', this policy later 'became central to the US policy of regime change in Iraq'.[38]

One of the principal reasons for the doubt regarding the peacebuilding agenda is certainly due to the Bush administration's fondness for democracy promotion, the idea that cultivating democracy in Iraq would lead to its spread throughout the Middle East. Clearly, the fact that in Iraq this was, in effect, to be achieved via regime change undermined the legitimacy of the reconstruction exercise. Further, the questionable legal basis for the Iraq intervention called into question the legitimacy of the occupation. While post-conflict statebuilding operations in Germany and Japan were based on unconditional surrender, the aggressive nature of these regimes meant that the legitimacy of the occupations was undisputed. (This is not to gainsay the fact that if one is convinced by the *legal* arguments put forward by the US and UK, that Saddam's violation of SCR 687 'revived' the use of force under SCR 678, which was a resolution designed to counter his invasion of Kuwait, then logically, the occupation would have been quite within the bounds of legitimacy.) Importantly, however, there are some like Kaldor who, while taking issue with the US intervention in Iraq, see the continuing presence of outside powers as essential for promoting human security: she calls for an 'expanded international presence in areas of insecurity'.[39] Still, one should issue the caveat that the *jus post bellum* must not be used to mask an imperfect *jus ad bellum.*

One of the central questions in the practice of peacebuilding is whether the aim should be to return to the *status quo ante*, or as Michael Walzer prescribes, 'more secure than the *status quo ante bellum*, less vulnerable to territorial expansion, safer for ordinary men and women and for their domestic self-determinations'.[40] Bellamy has termed this a choice between the 'minimalist' or the 'maximalist' approach. Bellamy is rather more circumspect than some other commentators about the emergence of a *jus post bellum*, suggesting that it is 'premature' to claim that it represents a third component of Just War tradition.[41] Debates have also continued in the background regarding the issue of a state's right to choose its own path to government, and whether certain peacebuilding efforts (at least those more akin to statebuilding) by their very nature assume a certain type of government, usually a 'liberal' one. Certainly Russia and China would argue that self-determination entails the entitlement of each sovereign state to choose its own path to development. This clashes with Franck's notion that there is a 'right to democratic governance', implying that *democratic* governance is the only correct form. As Franck himself notes, one cannot assume that 'the people will choose free institutions if given a choice'.[42] Moreover the liberal idea of governance has been called into question by the conduct of the so-called War on Terror, with the use of unlawful and illegal practices such as extraordinary rendition and the treatment of detainees at Guantanamo Bay. One could argue, however, that this makes it even more imperative to ensure that peacebuilding efforts in countries such as Iraq and Afghanistan are conducted to the highest moral standards. As has been advocated with regard to the Afghan endeavour, the coalition needs to accept 'its responsibility to protect people rather than engage in ideologically motivated warfare against them'.[43] While one might agree that initially the Afghan operation was based on creating 'security for other countries', the new strategy has focused far more on the protection of civilians, fusing the humanitarian and the security imperatives.

Within the UN, however, there is a very definite norm emerging that peacebuilding is an essential part of the conception of 'positive peace'. The UN definition is that 'peacebuilding is aimed at preventing the outbreak, recurrence of continuation of armed conflict and therefore encompasses a wide range of political, developmental, humanitarian and human rights programmes and mechanism. This requires short and long term actions tailored to address the particular needs of societies sliding into conflict or emerging from it'.[44] In theory this peacebuilding agenda can be aimed at addressing the 'root causes' of terrorism by promoting certain types of development, although the 'root causes' approach some might think too empathetic with terrorists.

Andrew Rathmell suggests that there is increasing overlap between development agendas and those of the security community.[45] This can be viewed in negative or positive terms, depending on whether one views the 'co-option' of NGOs and donor agencies in the peacebuilding exercise as essential partners or if one sees their co-option as part of a dangerous merging of human security and national security concerns. There is a clear problem of human security being viewed as a liberal Western agenda. For example the EU has now taken on the human security agenda to some extent. There is a related problem noted by Edward Newman which is that human security tends to want to be 'policy relevant', which necessarily implies a state-centric approach. On the other hand this means that it can 'be a conduit for promoting human-centred security thinking in the policy world'.[46]

Failed states, intervention and terrorism

A further problem is the nexus of failed states and threats from terrorism: Robert Keohane discusses 'good' and 'bad' neighbourhoods; his idea is that we may soon see a new phenomenon, 'the constructive phase of humanitarian intervention *following* traditional military intervention in self-defence', i.e. in order to tackle states that 'harbour terrorists' then something must be put in their place.[47] Keohane was writing before the Iraq intervention, and it does indeed appear to be the case that an expectation is emerging that after intervention, whether humanitarian in nature, or to address terrorism, a long-term presence is required by the interveners in order to prevent the recurrence of the original problem. But in the context of the fight against terrorism there is a danger that post-conflict peacebuilding becomes a kind of extended deterrence to meet a 'continuing threat'. The problem arises when these 'bad neighbourhoods' provide a safe haven or a breeding ground for terrorists. Therefore a state which allows terrorists to operate freely from its territory, whether knowingly or unknowingly, is complicit and forfeits its right to sovereignty/non-intervention. Attempting to put a more humanitarian gloss on this type of argumentation, Wheeler has previously suggested that military interventions could be used to promote both counterterrorist and humanitarian objectives, asking if military intervention aimed at wiping out terrorist groups in failed states could not also contribute to protecting their endangered populations.[48] The two objectives may well converge almost coincidentally: but we need to be clear about distinguishing threats, in particular as otherwise our motives may be questioned. Moreover, conflating threats in this way may make it harder to define them, and thus to deal with them. That there is a direct link between state failure or collapse and the development of terrorism is also contested, although some failed states have certainly provided safe havens for terrorists.

The third pillar of the Responsibility to Protect

The 2004 UN Secretary-General's 'High-Level Panel Report on Threats, Challenges and Change' endorsed:

> the emerging norm that there is a collective international responsibility to protect, exercisable by the Security Council authorizing military intervention as a last resort, in the event of genocide and other large-scale killing, ethnic killings or serious violations of international humanitarian law which sovereign Governments have proved powerless or unwilling to prevent.[49]

The responsibility to protect is an attempt to reconcile the imperative of humanitarian intervention with the persistent reality of state sovereignty. The centrality of this state discourse is striking. The High-Level Panel Report of 2004 similarly demonstrates this trend. It stresses considerable concern regarding the trend to an erosion of state capacity and cites as a threat to international peace and security anything that 'undermines States as the basic unit of the international system', advocating further that state capacity for intervention should be increased, specifically at the regional level.[50] This demonstrates that R2P remains located in the sovereign state paradigm. This would appear to suggest that the R2P is not based on a paradigm which necessarily prioritises individual over state security, although Kaldor makes the point that one should differentiate between the approach of the Canadian government which adopted the R2P concept and promoted the idea of individual security, and the other approach, that of the UN, which was to emphasise development 'as a security strategy'.[51]

Nevertheless the R2P appeared to crystallise a consensus on 'sovereignty as responsibility', a positive duty to protect its citizens, rather than the negative formulation of a state's right to intervene. The endorsement of the core principles of the R2P at the World Summit in 2005 was a seminal moment in the history of the UN, but unfortunately it has not been operationalised. The High-Level Panel, drawing on the criteria set out in the ICISS report, had drafted a framework for intervention in cases of large-scale human abuses which would be based on the responsibility to protect. At the World Summit, however, the list of criteria were conspicuous by their absence. While states acknowledged a responsibility to protect, they preferred not to codify this responsibility, leading to the charge that the concept had been 'watered down'. However, the great difficulty encountered in achieving consensus on the R2P in the first place, which entailed a series of concessions, including a strong reaffirmation of state sovereignty, means that we should hardly be surprised by this. The continuing resistance of China and Russia, as well as India and a host of developing countries, are evidence of a division which may become more dangerous as and when China has finally completed its 'peaceful rise', depending on the nature of the regime in China.

However, a small victory for the drafters of the High-Level Panel was that its proposal for a Peacebuilding Commission (PBC) was approved at the 2005 World Summit. It should be remembered that the three pillars of the R2P are: 'prevention', 'reaction' and 'responsibility to rebuild'. By focusing on rebuilding societies after conflict, one can prevent the crises from occurring in the first place. As Louise Arbour reminds us: '[P]ost-conflict engagement represents an integral part of protection, rather than an afterthought . . .'.[52] While the PBC has a small budget and can only focus on a couple of countries at any one time, its remit, to draw the attention of the international community to conflict-ridden areas which have been forgotten, is evidence of continued commitment to the human security agenda on the part of those UNSC members who approved it. Bellamy suggests that the UN, rather than disassociating itself from 'unjust wars', should take on the responsibility of post-war reconstruction and peacebuilding.[53] The legitimacy of any peacebuilding enterprise is increasingly linked to its ability to deliver justice in the form of a 'just peace'.

Conclusion

It might be suggested that the new agenda, including non-traditional security threats, should have brought actors together and moved power away from state to non-state actors. However, the 'Global War on Terror' brings the state to the fore once again, in the preoccupation with national security, although ironically the 'enemy' is primarily a non-state based actor. As Newman points out a human security agenda 'raises important implications for the evolution of state sovereignty, due to its focus on the security of the individual'.[54]

Paul Roe suggests there has been little involvement from those engaged in peace research in the area of conflict[55]: a positive peace could be complemented by a search for more positive security. While human security might appear to provide a basis for this, its very breadth is also its limitation, as the agenda can seem to be stretched so far as to become meaningless. If, as Roe suggests, positive security is the maintenance of 'just, core values', then clearly the UN Charter still provides a solid foundation for this. What is needed is for greater dialogue between those pursuing hard security agendas, and those pursuing softer security goals: if the occupiers of Iraq can learn lessons from the UN's experience in Kosovo and Bosnia; and UN peacebuilding efforts learn from the NATO experience in Afghanistan then lessons learned might form a valuable bank of knowledge. The UN PBC whose mission statement is to prevent states 'falling off the radar' is a good place to start. In many of the countries where peacebuilding efforts are taking place one might argue that these operations are evidence of failures to tackle problems at a much earlier stage: for example Somalia, Kosovo, Haiti.

Although one could argue that core state values of 'liberal Western' states are culturally specific to them, one should remember that the UN Charter, which espouses the same values, was the product of a consensus, however fragile. While two of the P5, Russia and China, appear to subscribe to a different set of values, there have been some small signs of China attempting to behave in a manner more appropriate for a future great power by taking on greater responsibility in peace-keeping missions, for example. Precisely due to this fragility, any shards of the fragmented original consensus need to be preserved with great care: the human security agenda of the UN and the national security agendas of its member states need not be mutually exclusive. Through seeking to construct a just peace, and take on the 'responsibilities of victory', a common space could be found. However, the continuing lack of clarity regarding the use of force means that, as Georg Nolte suggests, 'general international law is in danger of becoming either blurred or ossified'.[56]

Part III
Self-defence

8 Principles of pre-emption

A commentary on issues and scenarios for self-defence in the 21st century

James Gow

Discussion surrounding the US approach to Iraq, prior to the 2003 launch of military operations, raised pre-emptive self-defence prominently and in potentially new ways, continuing a theme already begun in the wake of the September 11 attacks on the United States, in 2001, focused on the changing character of the right to self-defence and widening of its scope.[1] The US National Security Strategy of 2002 both sparked and fuelled debate, as it set out an agenda that appeared to claim for the Pentagon rights, more or less, to act whenever, wherever and in whichever way it chose around the world.[2] That document introduced formally an unformed notion of forcible 'preventive' action, allied to a grand declaration concerning the need to act pre-emptively in the new era, curiously underlining this declaration with the sweeping rhetoric that this was a long-held position, widely accepted by lawyers. While the proto-concept of preventive defence was radical, undeveloped and without any grounding in existing law, the fuzzy association with pre-emptive self-defence was achieved through the impressionistic swirl of bravado that the fallacy of claiming longstanding acceptance of this approach was at least embedded in recognised debate on the law of armed conflict. The Pentagon's claim was a clear fallacy, as the US, in one of its rare moments of clear condemnation of Israel, had joined UN Security Council 487 (1981) in condemning Tel Aviv's destruction of the Osirak nuclear reactor in Iraq, a putative act of pre-emptive self-defence. This official rejection of a radical interpretation of the right to self-defence did not necessarily preclude interpretation of that right by the US, including some possibility of some element of anticipatory, or pre-emptive action – indeed the US could be said to lead the way, often, in this context.[3] None the less, the crucial element in the Pentagon's approach was its attempt to sell something entirely new, extreme and deeply contentious as established and traditional.

The strongly contestable, and contested, character of the concept of pre-emptive self-defence, especially spiced by the notion of 'preventive' self-defence, spurred widespread debate, which sometimes tended to obscure the genuine need for new interpretation of the right to self-defence and, in particular, for a conceptualisation that might, at times, require pre-emption.[4] While much of the debate was hostile to the notion of pre-emptive self-defence, particularly as this was infused with hazy impressions of 'prevention', even attempts to address this issue positively could be confused and limited, focused on certain, key aspects of the traditional right to self-defence – that is, the principles of immediacy, necessity and proportionality – but did not investigate the changing nature of armed attack, as such – an equally, or perhaps more, important aspect of the subject.[5] That issue was addressed, to some extent, however, in the context of a project at Chatham House in London, instigated by Elizabeth Wilmshurst, director of the international law programme there. While it seems fair to characterise this project as an open attempt to engage with the issues from an initial perspective inclined to reject the ideas of preventive self-defence emerging from the Pentagon (Wilmshurst had resigned as a legal advisor in the UK Foreign and Commonwealth Office over London's approach to Iraq), an issue central to the discussion of pre-emptive self-defence, at the time, even if the formal basis for the US-UK action, when it came, was not pre-emptive self-defence, but rather enforcing compliance with binding Security Council demands, under Chapter VII of the UN Charter.

The prospect of pre-emptive self-defence raises serious dilemmas. As long as these remain contested issues (which will be a long time, undoubtedly), they will generate contests over legitimacy. Some of these – by no means exhaustively – can be discussed by reference to specific issues and scenarios. In this context, *Draft Principles* on the use of self-defence, produced by Chatham House, based on discussions between various informed individuals, including leading authorities (though not, inevitably, reflecting the precise views of all of them), offers useful cues for discussion, followed in the present analysis.[6] To do this, the remainder of this analysis reviews the concept of pre-emptive self-defence, then explores relevant aspects of the *Draft Principles*, as published – first, in relation to notions of prevention, pre-emption and immediacy, then, focusing on necessity, proportionality and the nature of armed attack – and, finally, explores three specific, hypothetical scenarios, derived from the context of the Chatham House project, but not included in the final output, and so used, here, for illustration of issues and critical appraisal of them.[7] In each case, it is evident that no issue is clear and straightforward, and that each point is a matter of interpretation, which, in a time of change, is even more contested than might be the case otherwise.

Pre-emptive self-defence

At the beginning of the 1990s, with Cold War division between the Soviet Union and the West melted into a cooperative approach, at least temporarily, the UN Security Council began to deal with problems it would not have previously touched, or been thought able to touch. It did so in ways that until they emerged would have been unthinkable, starting with sanctions against the territories of the Yugoslav federation as it dissolved in war and then Somalia as it collapsed in lawless mayhem and conflict. Later this included the effective identification of individuals as threats to international peace and security by the creation of *ad hoc* international tribunals to try individuals as war criminals, as well as authorising the deployment and employment of armed forces in a variety of places in order to generate or foster conditions of security.[8] Along the way, and at the heart of this process, the Security Council redefined the meaning of 'threat' to international peace and security, in January 1992.[9] This radical shift removed the complete protection offered to states by the traditional sovereignty regime. Under that scheme, the mutual recognition of sovereign status means agreement not to interfere in the internal affairs of other sovereigns, nor use armed force against them, in return for recognition of exclusive rights to decide on arrangements and issues within the boundaries of one's own state. In the new era, there was recognition that, while the sovereignty regime continued in normal circumstances, where there was a threat to international peace and security, whether the traditional threat of one state's attacking another, or the more radical interpretations that emerged in the 1990s, then the protection offered by sovereignty could be overridden.

The Security Council's altered definition of international peace and security confirmed a shift in attitudes towards ending the absolute protection provided by state sovereignty. In line with this, Chapter VII resolutions were passed by the Security Council, concerning a wide range of problems, all essential departures in terms of sovereignty in international relations and the management of international peace and security. This created a conceptual gap. The authority of the UN Security Council to address 'threats to international peace and security' was only one pillar regarding the use of armed force in the international system. The other was self-defence, which fell to the states in the system themselves. If a threat was a threat when the Security Council could act, it was also a threat for individual states when, for whatever reason, the Security Council could not do so. There was a new environment that required new thinking. In that context, the thorny issue of pre-emptive self-defence conceptually became a major issue, complemented by the public and practical brandishing of the need for such an approach by the United States in its 2002 National Security Strategy document. Pre-emption became a legal-political marker of the changes affecting the conceptual boundaries of war, albeit one highly contested.[10] If the right to pre-emptive self-defence were accepted, this would change the definition of that which was acceptable: actions covered by pre-emption would previously clearly have been unlawful aggression; now there was an emerging, but deeply contested case, that such actions could be legitimate war.

The traditional concept of self-defence, international law, is derived from the *Caroline* case, dating back to 1837, which assumed an armed attack by a state actor (as did the UN Charter implicitly), and that any response would be absolutely necessary, proportionate and immediate. The *Caroline* case involved an eponymous private steamship, which was carrying arms across the Niagara River to assist anti-British rebels in Canada. British forces attacked and captured the boat, then set it ablaze and pushed it over the Niagara Falls. This was an act of self-defence for the British. However, this was not accepted by the US side and in the subsequent diplomatic exchanges, US Secretary of State Daniel Webster laid out what have since been taken to be the classical terms of the right to self-defence: immediacy, necessity and proportionality.

In Webster's formula, iterated in a letter in 1841 that was accepted by the British, the test was 'necessity of self-defence, instant and overwhelming, leaving no choice of means, and no moment for deliberation'. Traditionally states and international lawyers have read this as meaning an equivalent to the domestic self-defence provisions in which, say, the aggressor's hands would have to be around the victim's throat before forceful self-defence would be permissible. However, given the time involved in mobilising armed forces to respond to an armed attack in the international system, as well as the complexities of taking decisions and making judgements, this does not mean that all non-forceful action must have been taken prior to a use of force. Armed force is the 'last resort' not only in a sequential and chronological sense, where other alternatives have been tried in practice, but it is also relevant where other means would be futile.

The domestic right to self-defence applies for the duration of the assault, meaning that once the assault has been stopped, any right to use force ceases. However, the international version of the right applies only to the commencement of an act of self-defence, meaning that once force has started to be used defensively, it is then permissible to continue its use beyond immediate defence, translating it potentially (at some point) into offence. Thus, once the decision to act forcefully in self-defence has been taken, stopping an attack is not the limit of the right. Rather, a state is entitled to take war to the aggressor state, even to the point of unconditional surrender (as did the Allies in the Second World War), to ensure that a repeat attack is not possible.

The difference between the domestic and the international contexts lies in the time and complexity that a response to an attack might take, which can include gathering intelligence and undertaking necessary diplomacy to build support. Thus, although conceptually, the terms of immediacy imply a clear and simple formula – too soon, unacceptable anticipatory action, too late, unacceptable reprisal – the relevance of context makes this impossible to render quite so sharply or straightforwardly. However, in terms of any conventional interpretation, there could be no justification for reprisals after the event, nor excessive use of force, nor, crucially, anticipatory action. The September 11 attacks, revealing trends already recognised regarding threats to peace and security, did not easily fit this bill. Al Qaeda was a transnational, non-state actor. The attacks were launched from the territory of the US itself. The weapons were civilian commercial aircraft. And the response required an extensive action initially focused on Afghanistan, but needing to address the transnational and international character of the aggressor, and its links to allies. This constituted radical, overnight change in the conceptualisation of self-defence.

The shift was supported by America's NATO Allies and by the majority of states around the world. But those rushing to give backing did not generally grasp the degree to which it represented change. With a group like Al Qaeda involved, very few governments, in the context, were thinking through what they were doing. They were meeting the needs of the moment. As perhaps unconscious Constructivist Realists, they were doing that which was necessary legally and conceptually to confront the problem with which they were faced. Alongside this, the UN Security Council, still (formally at least) unaware of the perpetrators of the attacks on New York and Virginia, appeared to confirm the relevance and currency of the right to self-defence in Resolutions 1368 and 1373, at least absent further

Security Council action. Such further action would have to include identification of any aggressor against whom action might be authorised. Further Security Council action is relevant to the reservations of commentators suggesting that Security Council Resolution 1373 did not confer or confirm the right to self-defence because the references to that right were contained only in the preamble to the Resolution. However, as Rein Müllerson correctly observes, when Resolution 1368 was passed on 12 September 2001, the Security Council was not in a position to use more specific language, at the same time as which it explicitly recognised a case for self-defence in a resolution entirely concerned with terrorist acts.[11] This resolution was later confirmed in Resolution 1373 on 28 September, although no greater definition was apparently thought necessary at that stage. In terms of international law and custom the support of NATO and others for American-led action over Afghanistan in response to the September attacks clearly constituted a widening of the right to self-defence.

This transformation does not have clearly delineated boundaries. More important, it is not enough. It does not address the real needs of the 21st-century environment, which might well require pre-emptive action. This imperative can be explained hypothetically, by reference to the September 11 attacks and understanding of the pressures, including those of accountability and responsibility, on Western leaders in a democratic system with essential hostile news media standing ready to damn them at any point.

If it is assumed that preventing September 11 might hypothetically have required armed action against targets, say, in Afghanistan or Yemen, in that situation, it would seem unreasonable, in and of itself, to suppose that the US Administration, or others, should not have used force to protect its territorial integrity, its people and its property, but instead should have waited and allowed the attacks to take place. It would also be unthinkable politically that a president, apprised of an imminent attack, would not seek to prevent it. And the same would be true for any leader of any country, especially a democracy.

Pre-emption, prevention and immediacy

It is clear that pre-emptive self-defence, always accepted by some lawyers, at some level, has gained considerable relevance in the 21st century. In this context, the Chatham House *Draft Principles* represent an attempt to collate and distil the views of numerous well-informed individuals on the issue. The *Draft Principles*, as published, represent the project convenor's interpretation of the various voices involved in the project. The following section introduces and critically explores the principles, as published.

First, there is a statement that pre-emptive self-defence might apply 'if there is requisite intent and capability'. As it stands, this is a perfectly defensible statement. However, the real issue is the scope of 'requisite'. Different schools of thought might diverge on this. Certainly in the contemporary situation, it is perfectly imaginable that there could be very different interpretations of that which met the 'requisite' test. Given the diverse possibilities for an 'armed attack' beyond those with conventional weapons, especially where dual-use technologies are in play, this is likely to be a fuzzy area, at best. In addition to considerations of the class of attack, interpretation over specifics might be at issue – Iran's having a nuclear weapons capability coupled with long-term hostile intent and relationship to Hizbollah might be 'requisite' for some, but not at all for others. And even where there might be agreement on what constitutes the 'requisite' threshold, *pace* Iraq, there might be enormous divergences regarding the available evidence.

Secondly, the *Draft Principles* address the problematic – and incorrect – introduction of the term 'prevention' by the *US National Security Strategy 2002* and by various US scholars and others seeking to justify precautionary action. The *Draft Principles* address this by stating: 'It is clear that the requirement for a threatened attack to be "imminent" precludes any claim to use force to *prevent* a threat emerging'. Once more the interpretation here is crucial, however. Some would regard Iran's being on the threshold of a nuclear weapon as a threat, in and of itself (and the pursuit of this weapon, backed by previous intent, could constitute an 'armed attack', in this case). Others would argue that this should be seen as seeking to prevent a threat emerging, rather than a threat per se. Here, imminence, as a function of necessity (as noted below), means 'before it is too late'. But that is also bound to be subject to considerable debate in most imaginable cases. What is clear – correctly – is that any claim to be taking action as a preventive measure – rather than dealing with something deemed to be a threat in itself – would be entirely unacceptable. The *Oil Platforms* case is interesting in this context:[12] the assertion that something should leave no room for any 'measure of discretion' and is therefore a strict and objective matter is not so straightforward. Whether or not something leaves space for a measure of discretion is essentially a matter of interpretation and perception. Person A is 154 cm and 46 kg and female. Person B is 184 cm, 90 kg and male. Person A judges that there is no measure of discretion either to allow Person C, a 180 cm, 100 kg male suspected both of carrying a fatal communicable disease and being prepared to conduct sexual assaults in their house. From this perspective, the threat is imminent as Person C approaches the house, there is no time to call for authorised assistance and Person A deems the use of force to be the only reasonable course of action, with no reasonable alternative available to prevent the threat, which is already regarded, in this view, as an attack. Person B, however, takes a different view, judging that it is possible to adopt some protective measures, such as clothing and a mask, to keep the physical entrances to the house locked and to engage in dialogue, either to persuade Person C not to seek to enter the house, or in the process of doing so, to gain time in which authorised assistance might arrive. Persons A and B make assessments on the basis of what and when would be too late, but the assessments are different. Is one objective and the other not? Do the different approaches confirm as a matter of objective fact that there is room for discretion? The real problem here is that perception is an essential part of whichever equation operates.

Following from this, there is a difficulty with another reference to 'prevention' in the *Draft Principles*, which suggests that there is something that could be called prevention, hypothetically, but would not be self-defence and would have no legal basis: 'To the extent that a doctrine of "pre-emption" encompasses a right to respond to threats which have not yet crystallised but which might materialise at some time in the future, such a doctrine (more properly called "prevention") has no basis in international law.' Prevention, however, is not more proper – and should be rejected adamantly as a term for anything of the kind described. It gives 'prevention' a bad name. There are good, useful and necessary diplomatic and other steps that can (and are) rightly called 'preventive'; these are concerned with avoiding the use of force. To suggest 'preventive' use of armed force (rather than preventive use of armed forces for peacekeeping, for example, where the strategic assumption is that force will not be used) as a label, irrespective of basis in international law, would corrupt the potential for, and scope of, 'prevention' properly construed.

Following from this, pre-emption and self-defence are far more appropriate terms for dealing with those situations deemed to be threats, where recourse to the UN Security Council does not offer appropriate responses to those threats. The issue here should be straightforward, conceptually, though, of course, would not be so in practice: the threats in question are deemed by those who perceive them to exist, they are not aiming to deal, in advance, with ones that have not yet come into existence, in their judgement. The dispute is one of interpretation over whether a particular emergency constitutes a 'threat' or not – or rather whether it constitutes an 'armed attack'.

In this context, the *Draft Principles* correctly point out that claims to pre-emptive self-defence could be 'inherently self-justifying' but, however much it might be desired, it is wrong to continue to declare that they 'can have no place in an ordered system of law'. Any act of self-defence is self-justifying – or at least relies on self-judgement. There is a heavy presumption here, therefore, regarding 'self-justifying', which might not necessarily be sustainable and which seems a little overwrought. There are things which could be covered by pre-emptive self-defence, based on significantly extended interpretation of imminence, necessity and armed attack, which deserve to have a place in an ordered system of law, even if we can take it that they certainly do not have an agreed place in the context of early 21st-century change. Because of the degree to which actors invoking pre-emptive self-defence are inevitably self-judging, a condition of any resort to pre-emptive self-defence should require *inter alia* an attempt to treat the matter via the UN Security Council, or if this is not possible in the circumstances, then any action and interpretation must be reported immediately to the UN Security Council; the state taking avowedly self-defensive action must demonstrate preparedness to take responsibility for the situation resulting from its use of destructive armed force, or armed forces (all the more so if it is unable *ex post facto* to support the rationale for its action). There would inevitably have to be threshold tests on the detail of situations, which would be specific to cases – including evidence of active hostility, behaviour that contributes to a high-level of suspicion about the alleged threat and so on. The suggestion that action would have to be justified against information 'perhaps sometime in the future' is problematic, however, given that it would be unreasonable to expect everything to be knowable, and that judgement will on occasion be necessary. Therefore, the burden of showing that actions were justifiable would also be an important factor – though one also complemented by issues of 'good faith'.

Immediacy, necessity, proportionality and the nature of an 'armed attack'

At the core of notions of legality, underpinned by traditions of thought on notions of 'Just War', lie the core concepts of necessity and proportionality, to which the category of immediacy is added, as noted above, in conventional interpretation of the right to self-defence. Quite rightly, some of these aspects relate to the others. 'Necessity is a threshold and as such can be seen to an aspect of imminence', the *Draft Principles* correctly state – and the same applies (perhaps even more so) vice versa, as the *Draft Principles* later note, 'necessity will determine imminence'.

This is all perfectly right. It means certainly that 'imminence cannot be construed by reference to a temporal criterion only'. Thus, when commentators speak of a 'last resort', for example, in opting to use armed force, this cannot be restricted to a chronological understanding – it is not the last in a sequence of actions, but in a series of issues to be considered and rejected if deemed inappropriate. In this, as in other matters, therefore, it is essential to recognise that 'each case will necessarily turn on its own facts'. However, there might well be disputes over what information constitutes the 'facts' in question, given a swiftly changing environment. Thus, while stating that force 'may be used only on a proper factual basis and after a good faith assessment of the facts' is right, in itself, it is not adequate to circumstances where different perceptions will give different readings of the 'factual basis' and of 'good faith'. As the *Draft Principles* suggest, there will be demands for a 'high level of justification' regarding pre-emptive claims to imminence and necessity. That said, however, it is hard to challenge the suggestion that, in the end, 'the requirement of necessity is only that there is no "practical" alternative to the proposed use of force that is likely to be effective.'

The assertion in the *Draft Principles* that proportionality 'means some kind of parity or similarity in scale between an actual or threatened attack and the response to it' is problematic in significant ways, and does not really or necessarily hold. There are radically different interpretations of proportionality. The one used in the *Draft Principles* appears akin to the UN peacekeeping approach – although not quite as restrictively 'tit-for-tat' ('if you are absolutely clear about the source of attack and can respond without causing harm to others'): traditional UN peacekeeping permits proportional use of force to the extent that if one shot is incoming, the source of it can be identified and a response issued without harm to third parties, then 'proportionate' self-defence can occur. By contrast, at the other extreme, the US military interpretation of proportionality entails such force as might be required to render the opponent helpless and incapable of constituting a further threat, whatsoever. And in the middle, the UK military approach has been whatever it takes to secure the desired goal – to be effective – but no more. From these three sketches, a sense of the variety that exists realistically on interpretation of proportionality among the military can be suggested.

Perhaps the most significant issue to emerge from the *Draft Principles* is consideration of what constitutes an armed attack. Discussion of the right to self-defence has focused on the triangulation of immediacy, necessity and proportionality, generally, in this context of change, but has not addressed significantly the issue of what constitutes an armed attack, beyond noting that the use of commercial airliners is a possible issue or innovation in this respect. Yet, this is perhaps where the core issues lie for debate and contest regarding pre-emptive self-defence, or other issues of threat and response. To begin with, there can be little dissent with respects to the *Draft Principles* regarding the absence of restriction based on the source an attack in applying the right to self-defence: 'The source of the attack, whether a state or non-state actor, is irrelevant to the existence of the right. There is nothing in the text of Article 51 to demand or even to suggest such a limitation and logic would be decisively against it.' Quite clearly, the letter of Article 51 does not insist on a state's attacking; and it would be illogical to preclude exercise of the right in the event of an attack by a non-state actor. Moreover, as noted later in the *Draft Principles*, as a matter of fact, this is widely accepted now. However, it is reasonable to note that Article 51, and so too Article 39 and its immediate successors, were drafted by those who took war and peace to be matters of state practice and that the 'threats' to international peace they had in mind were generally those of one state's attacking another, and in parallel, the same should be understood for the right to self-defence – it was assumed to refer to states as the only actors in international law, international politics, war and peace, even though the wording does not explicitly name states.

The *Draft Principles* also discuss the nature of the issue – an 'armed attack . . . whether threatened or actual'. The use of armed force is the issue. Therefore, distinctions between armed force and, say, political, cultural or economic 'forceful' measures should be recognised (sanctions are an 'enforcement' measure under Chapter VII of the UN Charter), as different versions of 'force'. This distinction between destructive armed force versus other uses of force is underlined – repeatedly – in the document: 'An armed attack consists of the threat or use of force and not mere economic coercion.' This is a well-established principle in the canon of international law.[13] However, such distinctions might be increasingly hard to maintain with clarity, in a world where the UN Security Council has already widened the notion of 'threat' and where, increasingly, non-traditional uses of armed force might be identified, for example, in the domain of so-called 'cyberwarfare'. 'Actual threat' of attack, this means, is therefore subject to the same issues of interpretation as other matters already discussed: what constitutes 'actual'? The litmus test of Iran and nuclear weapons could be seen either as indicating that only once Iran had pressed the buttons to launch a weapon would there be an 'actual' attack, or, alternatively, that the attempt to acquire a weapon of this kind itself constitutes an 'actual' attack.

Here, an extremely interesting point, worth further exploration and development, is relevant: 'There must exist circumstances of irreversible emergency.' It is precisely the identification of a point of irreversible emergency that is troublesome, and subject to the perceptions of the actors involved – as in the treatment of the nexus of imminence and necessity offered above. International approaches to the prospects of Iran's, or, hypothetically, a non-state actor's, acquiring a nuclear weapons capability, in this context, is indicative of the issues. The issue of 'irreversible emergency', or imminence and immanence, might turn on 'whether the relevant state or terrorist organisation is in possession of WMD or merely of material or component parts to be used in its manufacture; and the nature of the attack – such as whether the attack is likely to come without warning'. This is core to analysis and a significant point of discussion. Possession of a usable weapon where evident hostility could already be demonstrated would certainly be 'too late' under the 'imminence' and 'necessity' tests, meaning that hard issues of interpretation would be required over the 'not too late' issue regarding components and materials.

A hostile actor who works in breach of, or technically outside, the law to acquire components or materials, or to develop capabilities with them, must be regarded as a 'threat', and probably their actions should be seen as coming to constitute an 'armed attack' conceptually, even though there is no physical launch of an attack.

This is evidently a difficult and sensitive area – one that was set to invite and need significant development and discussion, as the first decade of the 21st century played itself out, and the discrete and conjoined issues of 'rogue states' and non-state actors in relation to WMD, notably, nuclear weapons – with North Korea and, especially, Iran prominent at the nexus of these issues.

Scenarios of self-defence

The Chatham House project devised hypothetical scenarios of potential self-defence, with the purpose of generating discussion both of interpretation and the empirical, factual demands that might determine judgements in practical cases. In the nature of such scenarios, as noted in the course of the commentary, further information than that provided is ultimately needed. But this does not preclude critical reflection and engagement, using the heuristic potential of the scenarios. This is my purpose in this final section of the present analysis, where individual critical appreciation of the scenarios is used to further understanding of the issues potentially involved – most notably, the changing character of armed attacks.

Scenario No. 1

State A, already rich in natural energy resources, has openly declared a policy of developing nuclear energy for peaceful purposes and has embarked on a large-scale development of nuclear infrastructure which is within months of completion. Regional neighbour, State B, and Security Council member, State C, have voiced their suspicions, based on intelligence information, that State A is secretly developing nuclear weapons and is within months of being able to manufacture nuclear weapons. The IAEA has also raised concerns after inspectors discover that State A has kept secret a number of dual use nuclear developments and materials, which it has acquired. Under international pressure, State A has agreed to halt temporarily certain uranium-enrichment processes, and to open its facilities to further inspections.

State A is hostile to the international political stance of both State B and State C; its position in the UN and in its domestic statements is particularly hostile to State C. States B and C wish to use military measures to remove the nuclear capabilities of State A.

In this case, the intention seems clear at face value, although in practice more would probably have to be known about the detail of the situation. In this context, a threat certainly exists. The issue would be whether this could or should be equated to an armed attack. The conditions for deciding this would be: the availability of reasonable alternative courses of action; the existence of an irreversible emergency, which would appear likely to be the case; and the interpretation that, given the first two conditions here and the hostile profile of State A, then its continuing efforts to generate a usable weapon and its defiance of international inspectors and other diplomatic manoeuvres, as well as a rejection of suggestions that it should transparently go beyond existing international standards to 'clear its name', could be interpreted as constituting an 'armed attack' in the sense that it concerns armaments capability and rejection of peaceful paths.

On a conservative, initial reading, this scenario would not necessarily involve an armed attack, and, so, the right to self-defence would not apply. In practice, it is likely, in any real case along these lines, that there would be a collective international attempt to tie State A into an organisational framework, demanding co-operation, and to encourage A to allow further inspections. However, given A's history and the reality that its activity likely constitutes a threat to international peace and security, a case could be made for self-defence, drawing on the notion of 'irreversible emergency' introduced in the *Draft Principles*. The crux of this would rely on actionable information (recognising that such information might inevitably be bounded by elements of uncertainty, as was evident in the case of Iraq and Weapons of Mass Destruction/Impact, in 2003). If such information indicated that State A was at the point of acquiring a qualitatively new level of capability, after which there could be no return to an earlier position, making the acquisition of that capability both hostile and irreversible, then self-defence, probably (though not necessarily) seen as a pre-emptive action, would be necessary and justifiable.

Scenario No. 2

State H is run by an effective, though dictatorial, regime, which often produces anti-Western propaganda. Western State I has been the target of attacks by the terrorist organisation ('TO') which is operating from numerous locations outside State I's territory, including in State H. In recent years, TO's attacks against State I have involved a low level of force and have been sporadic in nature, but have been highly symbolic. In their most recent attack, a TO agent shot at a government minister, slightly injuring him. Prior to that, TO acts involved a number of hit-and-run attacks with vehicles on people in State I waiting at bus stops and train stations.

Under pressure from the international community, State H has stated its opposition to, and intention to destroy, the TO group operating from within its territory. While State H has a powerful police force, a large proportion of its officers either belong to a faction of this international terrorist organisation or are sympathetic to its activities and objectives.

Despite recent offers of assistance from State I to send its troops to assist in the elimination of the resident terrorist group, State H has rejected and stated vociferous opposition to the direct intervention of foreign forces on its sovereign territory. State I wishes to bomb the terrorist encampments of the terrorist group in State H, and are considering using military means to change the regime in State H on the ground that only thus will the terrorist group be rendered powerless.

Both TO's intention and the relevant facts regarding it appear to be established in this case. The challenge is to relate that empirical data to the law. Judgement will rest, to start with, in significant part, on whether the right to self-defence against a non-state actor is recognised. There is a school of thought that views only international subjects – states – as relevant to international law.[14] In this view, the right to self-defence could not be applied to action against a non-state actor because the law could only be invoked in a case where the other actor was an equal subject of international law. So, because the non-state actor, without status in international law, could not itself invoke the right to self-defence, the state subject to attack by a non-state actor would not be able to call on the law of self-defence.

To some extent, this view could be said to have informed the US approach to action over Afghanistan in 2001, where the relationship between Al Qaeda and the Taliban regime is notionally taken as the state authorities in the country, for this purpose. The US, in invoking the right to self-defence, initially declared both to be the objects of its self-defensive action and, formally, gave the Taliban authority the opportunity first to dismantle Al Qaeda camps in Afghanistan (which, under the doctrine of objective state responsibility, might also have extended to accepting assistance to achieve the dismantling, if the relevant authority were unable to achieve it). Under an interpretation of this kind, TO needs to be seen as a proxy, or de facto organ of State H, for the right to self-defence to apply. A similar situation also applied when the US responded to Al Qaeda attacks on US embassies in Nairobi and Dar-es-Salam by exercising an 'extended' right to self-defence in 1998, striking targets in Afghanistan and Sudan, alleged to be Al Qaeda facilities. While the US action could be said to have been accepted, in principle (or theory), as there was little objection to it by states and, significantly, where there was objection – led by the League of Arab states – this only concerned Sudan and was based not on principle, but on the lack of factual basis.[15] It emerged that (as at least some parts of the American policy and information community had known) the government of Sudan had apparently evicted Al Qaeda two years previously, under US pressure. Thus, the objection was not to Washington's invoking the right to self-defence, *a priori*; rather, the objection concerned the evidentiary justification of the action. This view of the factual position is probably underpinned by the subsequent adoption of a UN Security Council resolution, at the end of August (making no reference to the US action), demanding an end to support for terrorists within Afghanistan,[16] thus confirming to some extent the US view on the facts, regarding the latter, but no reference to Sudan, suggesting, at a minimum, absence of agreement on the facts, concerning that country.

These situations invite significant difficulties, however, given that action on this basis against a non-state actor in a country could be judged to be an abusive and potentially unlawful use of force, infringing the sovereignty of the state on whose territory the targets are found, such as state H, in the scenario, or, arguably, Sudan, in practice. In effect, the putative act of self-defence against the non-state actor might also be an act of aggression against the state in question. To some extent the murky zone here is evident in the 1998 cases. Whether as a matter of self-defence, or forcible action as a matter of state necessity (an alternative approach, available in international law, but arguably blocked by the UN Charter's prohibition on the use of force other than in self-defence, or under the authority of the UN Security Council), State H could be regarded as objectively responsible for TO, if this were demonstrated as a matter of fact.

However, against the state subjectivity approach, three elements might be noted. First, while prevailing assumptions, prior to the end of the Cold War, were that the UN Charter and other provisions of international law referred to states alone, these assumptions do not necessarily hold. First, if it were not previously the case in the 1990s, the development of international criminal law, manifest in the creation under the UN Security Council of the ad hoc tribunals for Yugoslavia and Rwanda, as well as the qualitatively different subsequent creation of the International Criminal Law, made individuals, in restricted circumstances, subjects of international law, not merely matters of state responsibility.[17] It might be pointed out too that certain international organisations, albeit as the result of state action, also have subjectivity in international law. Beyond this, on one reading, for example, it is to be noted that the provision for the right to self-defence in Chapter VII of the UN charter makes no reference to the need for an armed attack to have been made by a state: the wording of Article 51 is bluntly 'if an armed attack occurs'.[18] There is no explicit reference to a state in the reference, a factor that was perhaps influential in the widespread support for the initial US response to Al Qaeda attacks, backed by the additional authority of the UN Security Council in resolutions 1368 and 1373. The key elements in addressing an armed attack by a non-state actor – aside from the factual link to, and responsibility of, any state on whose territory the actor might be found and be operating – would be the extent to which a pattern of hostile action could be established and the degree to which those responsible for this accumulation of events could be established as having recognisable structures and social basis, approximating that of a state.[19] Against traditional readings, therefore, it may be accepted that there can be a right to self-defence against a non-state actor carrying out a pattern of violent attacks.

If it is accepted that the right to self-defence against a non-state actor is permitted in a pure form (which both the logic established in the commentary and practice following UN Security Council Resolution 1373 suggest is the case) then aerial action against the camps would be permitted. However, even in this case, there would need to be consideration of prudence in taking such action. Absent a pure interpretation, the right to self-defence regarding non-state actors, and without additional factual material, the putative act of self-defence against a non-state actor could, at the same time, be seen as an act of aggression against State H. In this case, more factual evidence would be needed to support the case. As it stands, State H's anti-Western propaganda is not necessarily against State I (this would need to be established at a minimum) and that propaganda in and of itself is not necessarily sufficient indication of intention to carry out an armed attack (on the basis of information provided, it must be presumed that there is nothing verbal that could be construed as constituting or contributing to an armed attack in the 'propaganda' as this has not be mentioned). The key factual evidence, as presented, therefore, is the actual membership of TO by a proportion of State H's officers and their sympathy otherwise. One or both of these would need to be established clearly, preferably with publicly available evidence. In addition, the reluctance of State H to deal with the issue would be a factor. Rejection of offers to assist from State I might constitute some evidence of reluctance, but without a rich and detailed record would not be a sufficient indication of reluctance per se, given that the issue might be State I – assistance from other states might theoretically be acceptable to State H. Without this, although a case for self-defensive action could be warranted in practice, justified as a pure action against TO, while recognising complications regarding State H, this could be awkward prudentially. A broader case for self-defensive action against State H would need further and clearer specific detail that is not available here.

Scenario No. 3

States X and Y are neighbouring states, which have both acquired nuclear weapons. The two states have a history of minor hostilities, principally related to an intractable and long-running border dispute. The armed forces of both states are permanently at a state of alert. Members of the government of State X have stated in media interviews that they 'will always be ready to destroy the warmongers of State Y'. State X begins a programme of testing of missiles capable of carrying nuclear warheads directly to some of the major population centres of State Y.

State Y is suddenly the subject of a mysterious computer virus attack on the information technology systems used by its armed forces and central ministries of government, leaving it incapable of anticipating or mounting an effective defence to any attack which might be launched on it. State Y fears that any attack from State X would be catastrophic to its chances of survival and considers that its only means of guaranteeing its safety is to use nuclear weapons against State X immediately.

This scenario raises four key issues: the nature of an armed attack and application of the right to self-defence; information regarding State X's intentions and identifying the source of attack; practicability; and proportionality. The scenario, inevitably, leaves gaps concerning relevant matter, as noted below. However, it does provide a basis on which to explore some acutely important issues concerning the application of the right to self-defence in a rapidly changing world, of which the most important aspect concerns the nature of armed attack.

There are two ways in which the right to self-defence might be approached in this scenario. One, perhaps more conservative, would focus on anticipatory, or pre-emptive self-defence (assuming that the evidence available was strong and supported this approach). Under a reading of this kind, the cyber action would be taken as a clear and major step preparatory to a conventional armed attack and so providing justification for pre-emptive self-defence, in principle. While the anticipatory character of self-defence, in this case, would likely be contested, with suitable firm information, this case could be made. However, the second approach that might be taken is, at once, more interesting, difficult, and relevant: interpreting the cyber attack as an armed attack itself.

In an age of rapidly changing capabilities and with a wide range of dual capability technologies available, the potential nature of an armed attack has changed, and is changing, significantly. To some extent, it should be evident that the nature of a 'weapon' has always been a constructed notion, as seen in many a murder mystery book, or film, where, for example, the murder weapon is a candelabra, for example – that is, an implement that is usually not regarded as a weapon, but in the context and given its use, clearly has become such.[20] The centrality of computer processes to the more advanced armed forces in the contemporary world makes them major targets within a military's arsenal and, conversely, on the key weapons for prosecuting warfare. While clearly not a weapon in the conventional sense of a sword or gun, computers are key armaments in the attempt to overwhelm and 'beat' an opponent. In principle, therefore, a cyber attack, especially when targeting military capabilities, would need to be recognised as constituting an armed attack for the purposes of the law – and not a version of an economic measure, such as sanctions, which would conventionally be treated in a separate category from the use of armed force.[21] If cyber action as armed attack is accepted in principle, as logic suggests it must, then the real questions are those of 'fact'. These may be taken to determine judgement on the three remaining key elements to interpretation of Scenario C.

In the scenario, the virus attack has no source. It would therefore have to be presumed that before taking action, State Y would have established in good faith that State X was responsible for the attack. In addition (and perhaps contributing to a conclusion that State X was the source of the attack), State Y would need to have persuasive evidence that State X's hostile intentions are such that there is no room for discretion, doubt or waiting to see before carrying out the act of self-defence described. In one actual example, the Estonian defence system was subject to an apparent cyber attack in 2007. While Estonia's allies in NATO responded collectively by contributing to cyber defence in Estonia, this did not lead to any form of armed action in self-defence. Aside from questions of practicability and power politics, while it was clear that the source of these assaults was inside the Russia Federation, there was officially no definitive evidence concerning involvement of Russian state organs – although this possibility certainly cannot be ruled out – and, given that the attacks ceased, Russia could not be deemed to be acting irresponsibly, through intention or negligence. However, this incident put the issue of cyber self-defence firmly on the international agenda. On the basis of this case, and given the gravity of the situation and the response envisaged in the scenario, it would seem incumbent on State Y to have very high quality, firm and actionable intelligence before responding against State X, per the scenario.

Even assuming that there was incontrovertible evidence of State X's responsibility for the cyber attack, on a simple equation, jumping to the nuclear option in response to a viral attack would, initially, seem to be a disproportionate action, which could only be justified by the necessity of being the only available option, assuming that it is indeed available. While the use of nuclear weapons might generally be regarded as unimaginable, it is fairly clear that such a use would not necessarily be unlawful. In contrast to the complete prohibition on the use of other types of weapon considered to be of 'mass destruction' or 'impact', such as chemical weapons (embedded in the Chemical Weapons Convention[22] and the International Criminal Court Statute[23]), there is no clear and general prohibition on the use of nuclear weapons. This view is corroborated by the International Court of Justice's nuclear weapons advisory opinion.[24] That opinion found that there was no absolute prohibition on the use of nuclear weapons, although this was heavily qualified by the majority view that using, or even threatening to use, these devices would be difficult to justify under international humanitarian law, particularly in terms of proportionality. However, proportionality meant that there might, theoretically at least, be a situation that could justify using such weapons – for example, in circumstances where the very existence of the state was in question. Use of nuclear weapons might be possible, in principle, if undesirable and hard to justify, in practice. If there were any use, or threat to use, its lawfulness would be predicated on interpretation of proportionality in an acute and extreme circumstance. Proportionality, however, would require an effectiveness test.

In this context, it seems to be a major and curious assumption that the nuclear option could be available technically under Scenario 3 but that neither further information nor any lesser alternative would not. Further evidence of State X's intentions would be important. If available means, prior to the viral attack, had already established, for example, a major build up of armed forces in apparent attack formations, then this would contribute significantly to the interpretation. Similarly, if other means of communication and operation remain available – as would seem to be likely, if the nuclear option remained – then there might be evidence of State X's having begun operations, of whatever scale, which would contribute significantly, and perhaps decisively, to any decision. If one or both of these were the case, and State Y could see no alternative way of protecting itself, then self-defensive action would be justifiable, and if use of nuclear weapons were the most practicable response in order to defend the country, then the proportionality issue would swing in its favour. It would be using the one available means that it deemed would give it a chance of defending itself against State X's attack (and presumably would have made the practical calculation that its use would be able to neutralise State X's nuclear weapons capability – which would probably not be possible, in reality, if the information technology systems had been put out of action), ensuring, as a matter of prudence, that a nuclear counter-attack would not happen. Of course, even if there remained a risk of nuclear counter-attack the resort to self-defensive action in the face of evidence that State X was the source of the viral attack, that it had the intention to undertake further operations or, in practice, was carrying out further aspects of an armed attack, and absent any other practical means available to State Y, could be proportionate, on the grounds that, in a situation of immediate and irreversible emergency and necessity, it was the only means that might be effective. However, the additional qualifications and factual elements here are not contained in the original scenario, which, at face value, would not make recourse to nuclear weapons proportionate. But, it is hard to conceive of that scenario as being realistic, given that some of the other material here would have to be available in practice.

The foregoing factors contribute to interpretation of proportionality. That interpretation would be dependent on assessments of capacity, practicality and effectiveness. Assuming a nuclear response were available to State Y, it must then also be assumed that further information could be attained and that other, albeit limited and incoherent, forms of action might be available. If the virus attack has been so successful as to render State Y incapable of anticipating an attack or *mounting an effective defence* to one, then there must be a question over whether it could actually take the action suggested in the scenario. If it could take this action, at the higher end of the technical spectrum, it must be presumed that other possibilities would be in play too, including the ability to identify whether or not State X is taking aggressive action to exploit State Y's incapacity.

Conclusion

Self-defence has entered a new era. While many of the issues traditionally associated with the concept – including its core tenets of immediacy, necessity and proportionality – remain eternally relevant, the parameters on the interpretation of these tenets have changed and will change further. In the context of that process of change, the nature of that which constitutes an armed attack will also meet situations requiring new interpretation and subsequent re-visiting. Indeed, it is the question of what constitutes an armed attack that emerges as the most important aspect of change. Other shifts are, in many respects, contingent on the evolution of means for conducting hostile, armed action.

The Chatham House *Draft Principles* and scenarios from that project provide interesting and useful vehicles for the exploration and examination of the issues involved. The scenarios, while not used in the published part of the Chatham House project, and while also limited in their development, offer considerable scope critically to reflect on hypothetical situations that contain elements of some situations that might emerge as real policy and legal questions in the 21st-century security environment. While the *Draft Principles*, themselves, remain limited, in several respects, they clearly provide a platform for further discussion. And in identifying the issue of 'irreversible emergency', albeit in a conservative context, Wilmshurst's principles also offer the key to re-examination and, indeed, revision, of each aspect of self-defence – immediacy, necessity, proportionality and, crucially, the character of that which is judged to be an armed attack. Whichever aspect of self-defence is in question, the central issue is whether there is an irreversible emergency that makes defensive action necessary. And the character of armed attacks will increasingly be the core question in delineating the lawful and legitimate boundaries for applying the right to self-defence.

9   Who killed the right to self-defence?

Thomas Jones

The United Nations Charter today bears little more resemblance to the modern world than does a Magellan map.[1]

In the past decade, several events have provided the backdrop for a great public debate about the legality of the use of force by states in international relations. Military actions in Kosovo, Afghanistan, Iraq and Lebanon have increased public awareness of, and thus the political consequences of, the legal arguments for and against the use of force by states. Meanwhile ongoing conflicts in Africa and the Caucasus region have served as a reminder that the use of armed force by irregular and guerrilla forces are still as much a part of conflict today as the proxy wars that occurred during the Cold War. Notwithstanding the prohibition on the threat or use of force contained in Article 2(4) of the Charter of the United Nations, the UN itself has observed that military force has been used hundreds of times since 1945.[2] So clearly, the use of force by states to resolve problems and conflicts is alive and well. Does this mean conversely that Article 2(4) is dead as Thomas Franck controversially suggested almost 40 years ago?[3] It is doubtful that any state would claim that it still possesses a nineteenth-century style legal right to go to war when it considers it in its national interests. It is also not a stretch to claim that the vast majority of states and most academics would agree that the use of armed force for aggressive purposes is illegal.[4] However, force is still being used with regularity. Certainly, not all uses of force since 1945 have been legal given any reasonable interpretation of the post-Charter state of the law regarding the use of armed force. At the same time, it is also difficult to see how they could all be illegal. The legal tension is not to be found in the general prohibition on the use of force, but rather is located in the primary exception thereto, namely, self-defence.[5] Article 2(4) is not dead, but Article 51 is struggling.

Article 51 provides an exception to the prohibition in Article 2(4) based on the inherent right of a state to use force for individual and collective self-defence. The interpretation and scope of Article 51 has been hotly debated almost since the Charter was drafted and, given the importance of the exception in international law, it is neither surprising nor unfortunate that the legitimate application of the rule is a subject of debate. However, in the last two decades, the

International Court of Justice has developed a jurisprudence of self-defence under both the Charter and customary international law that is highly restrictive.[6] In particular, the Court's interpretation that self-defence is only available to counter uses of force that are grave enough to constitute an 'armed attack', and its apparent requirement that an illegal use of force be imputed to a state actor, set standards that would make the use of force in self-defence a very limited right, even in the face of the use of armed force against the victim state. The nature of armed conflict in the modern world and the clear willingness of states to resort to force when they feel threatened raises the question of whether the ICJ's conception of self-defence should be rejected in favour of a simpler and more practical, but no less effective, interpretation of Article 51.

It is often contended that the nature of warfare has changed but the related legal rules, in particular *jus ad bello*, have not. The basic argument is that the legal regime regarding the use of force was not designed for a world where industrialised, inter-state wars have been replaced by terrorism and low intensity conflicts often waged by non-state actors. This chapter seeks to turn that thinking on its head. Terrorism, guerrilla warfare and non-state actors have been around for centuries. The destructive potential of terrorism has increased in the modern age, but it is certainly not a technique that is unique to the post-WWII era. What has changed is not so much the form of war but the legal regime surrounding it. In particular, the jurisprudence that has developed around the right of self-defence included in Article 51 of the UN Charter has created an overly restrictive and unworkable legal regime for states to defend themselves against these uses of force.

The problems with Article 51

There are several problems with Article 51 that arise out of the historical circumstances surrounding its drafting, the drafting history itself, textual ambiguities that appear within the article and interpretive debates concerning its application. At the time at which the clause was drafted, the drafters either did not foresee the changes to armed conflict that were going to take place in the next several decades or they did contemplate such changes but still wished to construct a narrow, restrictive regime that would advance the goals of international peace and security. The need for an exception for self-defence within the text of the Charter was debatable and it is unclear whether Article 51 was designed to replace and restrict or merely reiterate customary international law. The text of Article 51 that was finally agreed uses undefined terms that make the scope and application of the clause unclear and its terms do not match up with the other provisions of the Charter dealing with the use of force. These issues have led to a long-standing debate about the interpretation and scope of the article.

At the close of World War II, recognising that the League of Nations had failed in its task, delegates of 49 nations met at the San Francisco Conference to draft the Charter of the United Nations.[7] The Charter was designed to govern the international behaviour of states in the post-war era, and in particular to set new norms and rules governing the use of force by states.[8] The theory behind the Charter rules regarding the use of force was to favour peace over justice. While justice was to be sought, in forms such as the pursuit of humanitarian values, self-determination, and the righting of a variety of wrongs, it was not to be pursued at the expense of peace.[9] States were exhausted from fighting the two world wars and peace was to be the ultimate goal of the Charter. As a result, the rules governing the use of force were going to be drafted in a very restrictive manner such that in the future most uses of force would be deemed illegal.[10]

It is important to also consider the technology and practice of warfare that existed at the time of the San Francisco conference. Although atomic bombs had been developed and used at the end of World War II, the type of warfare that was being considered at the conference was the large-scale industrial warfare prevalent in the last two world wars. These types of wars involved attacks that took place only after the build up and deployment of large forces and where the concept of what was an armed attack was reasonably clear. So the drafters did not appreciate how the technological developments evidenced at the end of the war, i.e. nuclear weapons and rockets, would change the strategic landscape and compress the timing of a potentially devastating attack to a matter of minutes.[11] In addition, the drafters' conception of the use of force failed to contemplate the rise in guerrilla and revolutionary warfare, including terrorist activity, that was already taking place in the world.[12] The drafters could not even agree on a definition of aggression, the primary activity that was to be banned by the Charter. For example, the Chinese proposed a definition of aggression that included harbouring and supporting insurgent and terrorist groups that were committing armed attacks against another state.[13] Neither the Chinese definition nor any other definition of aggression or armed force or even just force was accepted though and the definitions of these terms were just left open.

When drafting the Charter, an issue arose as to the relationship between the Security Council and regional arrangements that also provided collective security measures for their members.[14] Regional defence arrangements that had already been agreed such as the Act of Chapultepec were able to do what the Charter was not to make the defence of its members a legal obligation of all members.[15] Affected member states of the United Nations did not want to see their regional defence pacts undermined by the Charter and wanted a clause to expressly allow for these arrangements for collective self-defence.[16] A proposal to exempt these arrangements from the Security Council veto was proposed but rejected.[17] Instead, a new paragraph was proposed that was essentially identical to what ended up in Article 51 but was actually intended to clarify the collective security rights of members under these regional arrangements rather than codify the right of self-defence.[18] However, this text was also not intended to vary the rights of self-defence that were otherwise permitted by the Charter (by implication or otherwise) and it was generally believed that the text represented the scope of the customary right to self-defence at the time.[19]

The text of Article 51 that was finally agreed upon is as follows:

> Nothing in the present Charter shall impair the inherent right of individual or collective self-defence if an armed attack occurs against a Member of the

United Nations, until the Security Council has taken measures necessary to maintain international peace and security. Measures taken by Members in the exercise of this right of self-defence shall be immediately reported to the Security Council and shall not in any way affect the authority and responsibility of the Security Council under the present Charter to take at any time such action as it deems necessary in order to maintain or restore international peace and security.

The operative elements of the article are either undefined or raise additional questions that are left unanswered by any other provisions of the Charter. There is no definition of 'armed attack'. It is not clear what 'the inherent right' of self-defence means or what that concept embodies. Questions of interpretation have been raised regarding the relationship of the Article with customary international law, in particular whether Article 51 acts as a 'trump' on self-defence under customary international law or whether it just represents one distinct version of the right. Should the text be interpreted in a narrow and restrictive manner or is it more appropriate to use a broad and purposive interpretation? What constitutes a legal use of self-defence within Article 51 is highly dependent on the answers to these questions.

Describing self-defence as an inherent right has led to a lot of confusion about the meaning of the term. One argument is that it refers to the rights attached to the sovereignty of a state and as such takes on an almost *jus cogens* status such that a treaty could not impair the right in the first place. While there is some support for this approach in the background to Article 51, the view of sovereignty it espouses seems to contradict the prohibition in Article 2(4). If a sovereign state has been viewed in the past as possessed of an inviolable right to wage war when it deems fit, then presumably Article 2(4) would not be a valid restriction on that right.[20] The variable content of state sovereignty over time leads to the rejection of this approach.[21] A better approach is to view the reference to inherent as being to the right as it existed in international law at the time.[22]

Notwithstanding the first sentence of Article 51, the text of the Article attempts to impair the inherent right of self-defence in several ways. First, the right appears to be available only if an armed attack occurs. Second, the right appears to only exist up to the point that the Security Council takes action to maintain international peace and security. At that point, presumably, the inherent right is inherent no more. Third, the state that exercises its right of self-defence must report it to the Security Council. It is not clear from the text whether failing to meet the reporting obligation impairs the inherent right of self-defence or whether it is simply a procedural rule and a failure of compliance is not intended to affect the basic right set out in the first sentence.[23] Finally, the end of the second sentence makes it clear that the authority of the Security Council to take action is not itself to be impaired by the exercise of this inherent right, though the end of the first sentence presumably implies this authority.

There are two basic ways of reading Article 51. The first is to use a narrow reading that would restrict the use of self-defence to those situations specifically covered by the clear language of the text. This approach discounts the meaning of the words 'inherent right' by suggesting that a state is not intended to retain a broad customary legal right to self-defence, unrestricted by the Charter, but rather that such an interpretation would nullify the rest of Article 51 by retaining such a broad right notwithstanding the restrictions contained therein.[24] Under this method of interpretation, the right to self-defence is highly restricted. The other way to read Article 51 is instead to place much importance on the inherent nature of the right and look to a broad customary international legal right that purportedly existed at the time of the drafting of the Charter for the scope of self-defence as retained by the Article.[25] Under this methodology, the right is not limited by reference to armed attack. Rather those words are there to make it clear that certain scenarios are definitely, but not exclusively, covered by Article 51.[26] Self-defence under this interpretive methodology is a broader, more flexible right that is mostly defined by customary international law. The meaning of the inherent right and the choice of interpretive method can therefore have significant impact on the elements of self-defence under Article 51.

Probably the greatest difficulty with applying Article 51 to the modern forms of conflict has been the qualification that self-defence is only allowed 'if an armed attack occurs'. This language raises a host of questions about when states may use force in self-defence. First of all, there is no definition of armed attack in the Charter and the drafting history does not clarify what states meant by the term.[27] However, when discussing the draft proposals the US delegation did not conceive of armed attack as anything more than an attack using force.[28] In drawing the distinction with propaganda, the delegation considered the use of propaganda as possibly being an 'attack', but only an attack using force would be an 'armed attack'.[29] There was no indication that 'armed attack' was a particularly serious use of force that needed to be distinguished from other uses of armed force.[30] It is especially confusing when compared to other provisions of the Charter that use different terms to refer to the use of force. For example, the fact that the prohibition in Article 2(4) is against 'the threat or use of force' has led to a presumption that that is a broader concept than armed attack and therefore armed attack can only be a particular sub-set of uses of force. It is argued that the result of this is that there is a gap between Article 51 and Article 2(4) in which the aggressor can use force but the victim state cannot respond in kind and the size of that gap is itself the subject of further argument.[31] There is also the question of timing, i.e. when a state can use armed force in self-defence. Questions of timing have received a lot of attention recently with scholarly debates focused on the reasons for and against anticipatory or pre-emptive uses of force. Does a state have to wait for an attack to be launched before it can use self-defence? The text of Article 51 seems to require that it does by stating that the right exists once an armed attack occurs. However, this does not seem to be a practical requirement given the nature of warfare in the modern world nor is it clear that it was a requirement of the customary right of self-defence at the time the Charter was drafted. Many commentators argue that some form of anticipatory right exists, though the existence and the parameters of such a right are hotly debated.[32] Finally there is the question of whether the attacker must be a state. Article 51 does not seem to require it, though the customary right of self-defence presumed that a state was the target given that self-defence, as opposed to other self-help measures, required some state wrongdoing, i.e. an illegal use force, for its application. In sum, the text of Article 51 has caused a fair number of interpretive problems. In particular, the reference to self-defence as an inherent right of a state coupled with interpretive ambiguities and express restrictions have made Article 51 an opaque legal standard.

The pre-Charter law of self-defence

If the reference to an inherent right is to a legal standard that existed under customary international law at the time the Charter was drafted, then what is the substance of such a right? Brownlie's thorough examination of state practice and other diplomatic correspondence of the time though makes it reasonably clear what were the basic rights of states to resort to war or armed force prior to the Charter.[33] All attempts to restrict the use of force by law appeared to be themselves restricted by at least two exceptions: when exercising a right of self-defence and, where relevant, with authorisation from a competent international body.[34] The right of self-defence was considered to be an inherent, sovereign right of a state derived from customary international law. It was available as an exception to the prohibition of the use of force only in response to the threat or use of force against the state claiming the right. It is unclear whether anticipatory uses of force in self-defence were allowed or not, and the academic world is clearly divided on this subject.[35] It is certainly not clear though that anticipatory action was always considered illegal and defining the circumstances under which it would be allowed would appear to be part and parcel of the condition of necessity.[36] While force was generally considered to mean armed force, there was no requirement that the amount of force used be especially grave nor were there two tiers of force, a greater form to which self-defence applied and a lesser form to which it did not.[37] However, the right to use force to redress other legal violations (i.e. a broader right of self-help) was no longer legally available to states.[38] Assuming the force threshold was crossed, the use of force in self-defence was allowed as long as the conditions of necessity and proportionality were met.

The two primary conditions that need to be satisfied for an act of self-defence to be considered legal under customary international law are necessity and proportionality.[39] A third requirement, immediacy, is often referred to and will be discussed briefly below, but the timing requirement of that condition overlaps with the elements of necessity. Although most famously formulated by Daniel Webster in the *Caroline* case, the requirements of necessity and proportionality have been further developed over the years.

Necessity

The two primary elements of necessity as originally set out by Webster are: (i) the availability of other methods of redress and (ii) that the action in self-defence is contemporaneous with the provocation.[40] For example, self-defence should not be used for retaliation or reprisals but rather to halt and repel an attack.[41] This formulation appears somewhat restrictive however, perhaps because it is unclear whether it is supposed to apply to self-defence in the limited sense or rather to a broader right of self-help.[42] For example, a state could always resort to peaceful means of redress even if it has been subject to a full-scale invasion, though in most instances it would be unreasonable to expect a state to do so. The difficulty with Webster's narrow formulation becomes more obvious when the timing element is brought into play. If an attack succeeds in capturing territory and the attacker stops the attack to consolidate or just hold onto its gains, is the victim state no longer entitled to use force to regain the territory unless all peaceful means of negotiation or coercion have been exhausted?[43] Since it would be difficult to devise a universal answer to this question across all conceivable fact patterns, the key to the answer lies in Webster's statement that, 'the extent of this right is a question to be judged of by the circumstances of each particular case'.[44] Oskar Schachter has accurately captured both the fact-specific nature of necessity and the reasonableness of such an approach:

> The difficulty in proposing a general rule does not mean that a reasonable answer cannot be given in particular cases. In a case involving imminent danger to the lives of captured persons, as in Entebbe or arguably in Tehran, it would be unreasonable to maintain the continued pursuit of peaceful measures must preclude armed rescue action. In contrast, the 'necessity' of armed action to recover long lost territory (as in the Malvinas-Falklands case) does not have a similar justification. In such cases, there is no emergency (as evidenced by the danger of irreparable injury), nor can it be said that all reasonable avenues of settlement have been exhausted.[45]

The requirement of necessity under customary international law is now considered to encompass the following elements. First, the state being attacked must not have had any means of recourse to halt the attack other than its own use of force.[46] This needs to be considered in the light of the particular circumstances of the case and should be subject to a reasonability standard as to when recourse to means other than force would be considered to be ineffective or to have failed.[47] Second, the force used must be designed to halt the attack or prevent an imminent attack.[48] This is where the timing element comes into play. If an attack is completed and it does not appear to be part of a series of attacks or the precursor to another attack, then it typically would not be considered necessary to respond with force to the attack and such an action would most likely be classified as an illegal reprisal rather than a justifiable use of self-defence.[49]

Proportionality

Webster's approach is also the starting point for the elements of proportionality. For an act of self-defence to be proportionate according to Webster, it must not be excessive or unreasonable, but rather it should be limited in scope and manner to the act that created the necessity for self-defence in the first place, and never beyond those limits.[50] As with necessity, this basic formulation leaves room for differences of opinion as to what is proportionate under any particular circumstances. But, again as with necessity, that does not invalidate the principle or make its application impractical or impossible in differing scenarios.[51]

The standard approach to proportionality is to link it closely with necessity and to allow for all the force necessary to halt the attack or, if preventive self-defence is allowed, to prevent it from occurring.[52] Under this approach, the use of force in self-defence may actually be disproportionate to that used in the attack. What is important is the result; a state can use all the force it needs to provide for its own defence under the circumstances and no more.[53] When the use of force in self-defence must stop should also be linked to ending the attack on the victim state, though it has also been suggested that in the case of actual war, self-defence would allow the victim state to invade and force the complete collapse of the aggressor state.[54] As with necessity, proportionality is a fact-specific test and notwithstanding the general principle, it will always need to be judged in light of the facts and circumstances of a particular case.

Immediacy

Immediacy is sometimes referred to as being a third requirement for self-defence under customary international law. Immediacy is the requirement that self-defence be exercised while an attack is happening, not after it has ended.[55] As noted above, it is intrinsically tied to the concept of necessity and some authors treat it as part of necessity rather than a separate requirement.[56] This approach makes sense given two of the main difficulties with this requirement. First is the question of when an attack has ended. Does each attack have to be viewed in isolation or can successive attacks be aggregated to be considered an ongoing attack?[57] The answer to this is relevant to analysing both the necessity of an armed response in the first place and the proportionality of such a response. Once again, it is a very fact-specific question and both scholars and the ICJ have struggled with formulating a general rule. The second problem is determining whether a gap in between the attack and the response is justifiable. If necessity requires that states only used armed force in the absence of any other method of recourse, surely a state would be excused for attempting to use peaceful means to resolve an armed conflict before it resorts to force in self-defence.[58] Again, this seems to be almost inextricably tied up with the requirement of necessity. If necessity is considered to have both a timing and a means element to it, then the conditions to the use of force in self-defence can be boiled down to just necessity and proportionality.

ICJ jurisprudence regarding the law of self-defence

Given that most incidents involving the use of force are either dealt with at the political levels of the United Nations, i.e. the Security Council and the

General Assembly, or are not formally submitted to any international organisation for action or adjudication, the International Court of Justice has had relatively few opportunities to address the issue of what constitutes a valid use of force in self-defence under Article 51 or customary international law. This has been compounded by jurisdictional disputes that have further limited the ability of the Court to rule on Article 51 issues. In the last two decades though there have been some important cases decided and advisory opinions delivered by the ICJ that have examined both the interpretation of Charter provisions and the customary international law regarding these topics. These precedents have significantly informed the thinking of legal scholars on the scope of the exception. However, in an apparent attempt to further the norm regarding the non-use of force, the Court has created a jurisprudence that lacks sufficient clarity and would force states to make unreasonable decisions about when they are legally allowed to use force in self-defence. The benchmark case in this respect is the *Case Concerning Military Activities and Paramilitary Activities in and Against Nicaragua* (referred to herein as the *Nicaragua* case). This case set forth the Court's thinking on the relationship between Article 51 and customary international law and laid the groundwork for all of the Court's subsequent decisions on self-defence. It also set a precedent for interpreting the armed attack requirement that would be compounded by the following cases and is largely responsible for making Article 51 a restrictive and unrealistic exception.

The Nicaragua case

In 1984, Nicaragua instituted proceedings at the ICJ against the United States alleging that by supplying and supporting the Contra insurgents in Nicaragua and by mining Nicaraguan harbours, it had, among other things, violated Nicaraguan sovereignty, breached its treaty obligations under the Charter and the Charter of the Organisation of American States, and violated the customary international law obligations to not use or threaten force and to not intervene in the affairs of Nicaragua.[59] The United States rejected the allegations on the basis that its use of force was an exercise in collective self-defence of El Salvador (as well as Honduras and Costa Rico) and therefore justified. However, although the United States participated in the preliminary proceedings to contest the jurisdiction of the court to hear the case, it withdrew from the proceedings and did not participate in further hearings or arguments when the court decided that it did have jurisdiction under the circumstances. The court found in favour of Nicaragua on the merits and in particular that the United States' claim of self-defence was unjustified because the Nicaraguan activities in support of the Sandinista guerrillas in El Salvador did not amount to an armed attack.[60]

In examining the law of self-defence, the Court first concluded that the multilateral treaties, such as the Charter, referred to by Nicaragua did not apply.[61] Notwithstanding that conclusion, the Court determined that customary international law did apply. In order to reach that conclusion, the Court determined that customary international law stands separate and distinct to treaty obligations, even if the content of the two are identical.[62] The Court went even further though and specifically equated the 'inherent right' text from Article 51 with customary international law and appeared to argue for a right of self-defence under customary international law that exists separate from the Charter and that could have additional elements. It is worth quoting the opinion on this point at length:

> The Court therefore finds that Article 51 of the Charter is only meaningful on the basis that there is a 'natural' or 'inherent' right of self-defence, and it is hard to see how this can be other than of a customary nature, even if its present content has been confirmed and influenced by the Charter. Moreover the Charter, having itself recognized the existence of this right, does not go on to regulate directly all aspects of its content. For example, it does not contain any specific rule whereby self-defence would warrant only measures which are proportional to the armed attack and necessary to respond to it, a rule well established in customary international law. Moreover, a definition of the 'armed attack' which, if found to exist, authorizes the exercise of the 'inherent right' of self-defence, is not provided in the Charter, and is not part of treaty law. It cannot therefore be held that Article 51 is a provision which 'subsumes and supervenes' customary international law. It rather demonstrates that in the field in question, the importance of which for the present dispute need hardly be stressed, customary international law continues to exist alongside treaty law. The areas governed by the two sources of law thus do not overlap exactly, and the rules do not have the same content.[63]

Arguably, the Court's logic means that an action in self-defence could be legal under customary international law but not under the Charter and vice versa. Most likely though, it means that the Court can use customary international law when it is technically barred from adjudicating in relation to Article 51.

Having determined that customary international law was the appropriate body of law for the analysis, the Court proceeded to conclude the following provisions as a matter of law. First, that an armed attack is a necessary precursor to self-defence under customary international law but only grave uses of armed force will be armed attacks.[64] Second, after deciding that the *Definition of Aggression* passed by the General Assembly reflected customary international law, that action by irregular forces may constitute an armed attack, 'if such an operation, because of its scale and effects, would have been classified as an armed attack rather than as a mere frontier incident had it been carried out by armed forces'.[65] However, the provision of assistance in the form of logistical or financial support does not constitute an armed attack, even though such action may constitute a use of force or intervention in the affairs of another State.[66] So an action that is a use of force may not be resisted with self-defence unless that action is serious enough to also be an armed attack. While the victim state itself may have the right to use 'proportionate counter-measures' (which may or may not include some measure of force, it is not clear from the opinion), such counter-measures presumably do not equate to self-defence and, in particular, there is no right of collective self-defence for uses of force that do not rise to the level of armed attack.[67] A 'mere frontier incident', even one that involves the use of armed force, will either restrict the victim state from using force in response, or allow it to do so but without any assistance from a third-party state (that itself would equate to using force).[68]

The Court was clear in its view that, as a matter of customary international law, for an action in self-defence to be legal it must also be necessary and proportionate.[69] However, given that it had already decided that the actions by Nicaragua in relation to El Salvador did not amount to an armed attack, it was unnecessary to determine whether the United States' response complied with these conditions.[70] Nevertheless, the Court decided to analyse whether the actions of the United States were necessary and proportionate. It found that they were not. Given the timing and nature of the actions of Nicaragua compared with those of the United States, the Court found that the United States failed both conditions.[71]

Several criticisms have been raised with respect to the Court's legal analysis and application of the facts in the *Nicaragua* case.[72] For present purposes, two will be considered here. First, regarding the distinction between an armed attack and a use of force that is not an armed attack, the Court did not provide much clarity of what constitutes 'the most grave forms of the use of force' that would constitute an armed attack as opposed to a lesser form that is merely a use of force.[73] Given the importance of this distinction in *Nicaragua* and in the cases and advisory opinions of the Court that followed *Nicaragua*, it is worth examining in detail the Court's reasoning on this point, in particular as it appears in paragraphs 191 and 195.

In paragraph 191 of *Nicaragua*, the Court attempts to use the Declaration on Principles of International Law Concerning Friendly Relations and Cooperation among States (the Declaration) as an 'indication' of the *opinio juris* of customary international law regarding what forms of force are grave (and thus armed attacks) as opposed to less grave uses of force that would not be an armed attack.[74] In doing so, the Court appears to equate examples of prohibited force in the text of the Declaration that use the word 'aggression' with grave forms of force that presumably are armed attacks. Logically following from this, the Court concludes that the principles in the Declaration that do not refer to the word aggression are examples of lesser forms of force that presumably are not armed attacks.[75] The Court also refers to similar language regarding non-intervention that does not refer to aggression as further support for this distinction.[76] The Court thus begins to hang its hat on the distinction between aggression and other forms of force as being dispositive of whether an armed attack has occurred.

In paragraph 195, the Court continues its approach of equating acts of aggression with armed attacks by referring to the Definition of Aggression (the Definition) as reflecting customary international law, presumably to give content to the 'general agreement on the nature of the acts which can be treated as constituting armed attacks'.[77] However, apparently in an attempt to give some meaning to armed attack that would be qualitatively different than that applied to uses of force, the Court engages in some interesting sleight of hand. To illustrate this point, it is helpful to quote extensively from para 195:

In particular, it may be considered to be agreed that an armed attack must be understood as including not merely action by regular armed forces across an international border, but also 'the sending by or on behalf of a State of armed bands, groups, irregulars or mercenaries, which carry out acts of armed force against another State of such gravity as to amount to' (*inter alia*) an actual armed attack conducted by regular forces, 'or its substantial involvement therein'. This description, contained in Article 3, paragraph (g), of the Definition of Aggression annexed to General Assembly resolution 3314 (XXIX), may be taken to reflect customary international law. The Court sees no reason to deny that, in customary law, the prohibition of armed attacks may apply to the sending by a State of armed bands to the territory of another State, if such an operation, because of its scale and effects, would have been classified as an armed attack rather than as a mere frontier incident had it been carried out by regular armed forces.[78]

The Court starts with the general proposition that it is agreed that the activities described in Article 3, paragraph (g) of the Definition amount to an armed attack. In order to assist the reader, the Court quotes directly from paragraph (g). But note that the quote is truncated in the middle, with the Court stepping out of the text of paragraph (g) to imply that it states that it only covers acts of armed force of such gravity that they amount to '(*inter alia*) an actual armed attack conducted by regular forces', before returning to the actual text to include substantial involvement in such acts. This is not what the Definition says though. Nowhere in the Definition is the phrase 'armed attack' used. The actual text of paragraph (g) is, '[t]he sending by or on behalf of a State of armed bands, groups, irregulars or mercenaries, which carry out acts of armed force against another State of such gravity *as to amount to the acts listed above*, or its substantial involvement therein'.[79] The 'acts listed above' include actions such as a blockade, *any* attack by the armed forces of a state, bombardment of the territory of one State by the armed forces of another State, and the use of *any* weapons by a State against the territory of another State.[80] In addition, if aggression is to be considered tantamount to armed attack, then the other provisions of the Definition should be relevant as well.[81] Article 1 of the Definition states quite simply that, '[a]ggression is the use of armed force by a State against the sovereignty, territorial integrity or political independence of another State, or in any other manner inconsistent with the Charter of the United Nations, as set out in this Definition'.[82] Taking the Court's reasoning to its logical conclusion (an act which the Court failed to do) this should mean that any use of armed force in violation of Article 2(4) of the Charter should be an act of aggression, equivalent to an armed attack, triggering a right of self-defence.[83] The Court strains even further to work armed attack into the analysis by referring to the customary international law rule prohibiting armed attacks. The rule, as reflected in the Charter, is a rule against the unlawful use of force or aggression, which encompasses acts that would be armed attacks according to the Court but clearly would also include the lesser forms that the Court tried so hard to enumerate as not being armed attacks. Finally the Court further twists the language in paragraph

(g) by requiring that these effects have the 'scale and effects' equivalent to an armed attack, whereas as noted above, paragraph (g) only requires that the act have 'such gravity as to amount to the acts listed above'.[84]

The Court's analysis in paragraph 195 is also inconsistent with its analysis in paragraph 191. In paragraph 191, the Court had already drawn a distinction between acts labelled as aggression under the Declaration as equating to armed attacks and those that are not being the less grave forms of force that do not equate to armed attack. On this point, the Definition and Declaration conflict with each other. For example, the Declaration states that '[e]very State has the duty to refrain from organizing or encouraging the organization of irregular forces or armed bands, including mercenaries, for incursion into the territory of another State' and also that, '[e]very State has the duty to refrain from organizing, instigating, assisting or participating in acts of civil strife or terrorist acts in another State or acquiescing in organized activities within its territory directed towards the commission of such acts, when the acts referred to in the present paragraph involve a threat or use of force'.[85] These are cited by the Court as examples of the less grave use of force that would not be an armed attack.[86] However, as previously noted, Article 3, paragraph (g) of the Definition includes in its non-exclusive list of actions deemed to be aggression, '[t]he sending by or on behalf of a State of armed bands, groups, irregulars or mercenaries, which carry out acts of armed force against another State of such gravity as to amount to the acts listed above, or its substantial involvement therein'.[87] Clearly the former cannot be a use of force that is not an armed attack while the latter can. The Court makes no attempt to clarify the supposed distinctions between these acts.

In addition, the Court did not give any examples of state practice that would confirm that this is a distinction that states actually make. While vague references to 'established and substantial practice' are made to support the legality of the principle of non-intervention, there is a complete lack of evidence that in practice states treat uses of force against them on a two-tier plane and will only respond with force to actions that can somehow be additionally defined as an armed attack.[88] All the court offers up is the statement that '[t]here appears now to be a general agreement on the nature of the acts which can be treated as armed attacks'.[89] If this general agreement is supposed to refer to the full and un-edited version of aggression as laid out in the Definition, as opposed to the Court's restricted version, then perhaps this is defensible. In fact, it is interesting to note that both Nicaragua and the United States agreed that the use of force as alleged in the case (assistance to irregulars that engage in cross-border attacks), if proven, would be a use of force against which a right of self-defence could be asserted.[90] They agreed on the law but not the facts. The Court, however, did not agree on this crucial point and, as a consequence, maintained its distinction between armed attack and lesser uses of force.

The second criticism is that, given that the Court has set the bar for what constitutes an armed attack quite high, it is unclear what the need is for an additional test of necessity. It is unlikely that a state suffering a use of armed force equating to the Court's version of armed attack would feel that a response in self-defence was not necessary. Conversely, if there is a need to consider the necessity of the use of force in self-defence, then what is the purpose of the armed attack threshold?[91] If it is necessary to defend against a use of force, then that necessity is present regardless of the categorisation of the initial use of force. It is unclear why the Court on the one hand confirms the importance of the condition of necessity to the customary international law of self-defence but on the other hand robs it of its customary meaning by imposing a supposedly customary and *sine qua non* condition that the attack in question be significantly grave before it will constitute an armed attack.[92] Unfortunately, these problems with the judgment and the difficulties they raise for a practical and state-practice supported rule of self-defence would be repeated in subsequent cases.

The Nuclear Weapons opinion

In 1994, the General Assembly of the United Nations asked the Court to deliver an advisory opinion on whether the threat or use of nuclear weapons could ever be permitted under international law.[93] Noting that states possess a right of self-defence and that Article 51 does not limit that right to any specific weapons, the Court reiterated its view that the requirements of necessity and proportionality are, however, conditions to the exercise of self-defence.[94] The Court noted that proportionality would not exclude the use of nuclear weapons under all circumstances, but given the similar but separate considerations of proportionality that arise under international humanitarian law, the use of nuclear weapons might possibly be lawful, 'in the extreme circumstances of self-defence, in which the very survival of a State would be at stake'.[95] Besides confirming the relevance of customary international law to an Article 51 analysis, the Court also confirmed that armed reprisals in a time of peace are unlawful.[96] Presumably this refers to armed force that does not meet either the armed attack threshold or the requirement of necessity.

The Oil Platforms case

In the *Case Concerning Oil Platforms (Islamic Republic of Iran v. United States of America)*, the court once again reviewed the law of self-defence under customary international law (as well as Article 51 of the Charter) and applied it to a dispute between Iran and the United States.[97] The dispute arose out of the Iran-Iraq war of 1980–1988 and in particular the so-called Tanker War that was fought in the Persian Gulf. The Tanker War arose when Iraq began to attack tankers carrying Iranian oil in the Persian Gulf and Iran responded in kind.[98] In order to protect its vessels, Kuwait called on several states, including the United States, to re-flag its vessels. In the case of US-flagged vessels, the United States also provided a naval escort to ensure the safety of the ships.[99] In the course of the conflict, several ships were attacked or were hit by mines. In particular, a US-flagged vessel, the *Sea Isle City*, suffered a missile attack on 16 October 1987 and the USS *Samuel B. Roberts* struck a mine on 14 April 1988.[100] The United States attributed these attacks to Iran and attacked several Iranian oil platforms on 19 October 1987 and 18 April

1988, in each case claiming it was acting in self-defence.[101] The ICJ ruled against the United States in relation to both of these incidents finding that (i) the evidence offered by the United States was insufficient to prove that the missile and mine attacks were the result of an Iranian armed attack and (ii) even if they were, that the United States response was neither necessary nor, in the case of the action on 18 April, proportionate.[102]

In its judgment on the merits delivered on 6 November 2003, the Court based its analysis of the US claims of self-defence on the factors it had set out in *Nicaragua* as further refined in the *Nuclear Weapons* opinion. As before, the action in self-defence must be in response to a use of force that is serious enough to also qualify as an armed attack.[103] The Court also confirmed that measures taken in self-defence must be both necessary and proportionate, though in this case the Court did recognise that the necessity of a measure 'overlaps with the question of validity as acts of self-defence'.[104] Regarding acts that qualify as armed attacks, the Court continued its reasoning that only acts that constitute grave forms of use of force will be considered armed attacks for the purposes of self-defence. However, once again the Court was unable to provide any bright line, or even dim line, test of when the line is crossed between lesser uses of force and armed attack nor did it give any compelling reasons for this distinction as a requirement of customary international law.[105] The Court did say that the mining of a single military vessel might constitute a grave use of force sufficient to trigger self-defence, but it was unable to do so under the circumstances.[106] What was absent from this decision was the reference to 'proportionate counter-measures' referred to in *Nicaragua* that are somehow less than self-defence and that should have been available to the United States as the actual victim of the use of force. The absence of such a discussion could be read as confirmation that such measures do not extend to uses of force.

A slightly expansive addition to the Court's jurisprudence on self-defence arising from the case was a suggestion that several attacks could be accumulated together in determining whether an armed attack has occurred and also the proportionality of any response thereto.[107] On the other hand, the Court also seemed to add to its restrictive jurisprudence on self-defence that the attack must be intended to hit a specific target for self-defence to be available.[108] Altogether, though, the Court's reasoning in this case served to only muddy the waters further regarding what constitutes a valid exercise of self-defence by a state.

The Wall opinion

The ICJ next considered the concept of self-defence when it was requested by the General Assembly to deliver an advisory opinion on the legality of the wall being constructed by Israel in areas of the West Bank.[109] In one short paragraph in its opinion, the Court managed to further restrict the right of self-defence in a way that cannot even be supported by the text of Article 51. Having first recited the first sentence of Article 51 verbatim, the Court then summarises the exception as applying when one state attacks another state.[110] It then declares that since Israel did not claim that the attacks were imputable to a foreign state, Article 51 has no relevance to the case.[111] Nothing in the text of Article 51 requires the armed attack to come from another state. Although the drafters of Article 51 certainly had state-to-state conflict in mind, and the Court in *Nicaragua* implied that imputation of action to a state was necessary. It is certainly arguable that the Court's approach in this opinion was not in accordance with either *opinio juris* and state practice at that time, particularly given the Security Council resolutions following 9/11 that recognised a right of self-defence against terrorist attacks.[112] However, this was no accident or one-off decision, as was to be evident the next time the matter came before the Court.

DRC v. Uganda

The facts of the case before the ICJ in the *Case Concerning Armed Activities on the Territory of the Congo (Democratic Republic of the Congo v. Uganda)* were extremely complicated and the Court had to grapple with significant evidentiary issues before it could even begin to apply the law to the facts. With respect to the Ugandan claims of self-defence, in summary the Court had to decide whether the activities of the Ugandan armed forces in the DRC ostensibly undertaken to repel and prevent attacks against Uganda by irregular forces that were allegedly supplied and supported by the DRC and its allies could be classified as self-defence. The Court did not accept many of the factual allegations of Uganda and rejected its claim in respect of self-defence.

In this case, the Court seems to be more clearly deciding the issue by reference to Article 51 rather than to customary international law.[113] It does note that the customary law requirements of necessity and proportionality would be relevant to the case if the 'preconditions' to the exercise of force in self-defence had been met, but in its judgement that was not the case.[114] The precondition referred to in this case does not appear to be the requirement that the use of force provoking self-defence meet a level sufficient to qualify as an armed attack; instead the Court reaches its decision based on its opinion that the attacks were not attributable to the DRC.[115] The Court also took the view that the use of force by Uganda was mostly preventive or anticipatory in nature with the implication that this is not sufficient as a timing issue for a state to rely on self-defence.[116] Finally, the Court implicitly continued its line of reasoning from *Nicaragua* that failure to report to the Security Council was a factor in assessing the legality of a claim of self-defence.[117]

Following its reasoning in the *Wall opinion*, the Court appears to solidify its view that self-defence is not available to a state to counter-attacks that are not attributable to another state. In their separate opinions, Judges Kooijmans and Simma both sharply criticise the majority opinion on its narrow reading of Article 51 in this respect. Notwithstanding the fact that nothing in the text of Article 51 restricts self-defence to responses to armed attacks only by states, both dissenting judges point to a combination of state practice and *opinio juris* (including Security Council resolutions) that show that states do not believe Article 51 to be restricted in this way.[118] The Court's reasoning also suffers from a lack of common sense. If state A is being attacked by forces in state B, there should be little doubt that state B will respond (or at the very least think that it has the legal right to respond if it can) with armed force in self-defence regardless of whether it can satisfy the ICJ's test for imputation of the acts to state A. Kooijmans' separate opinion suggests that this example may still be legal under ICJ jurisprudence as long as the action taken by state B was directed at the actual attackers and not at state A and he laments the fact that the majority opinion was silent on this point.[119] But this distinction is not particularly helpful, especially since state B's response would most likely involve a cross-border use of armed force in state A, violating state A's sovereignty and territorial integrity even if its use of force is technically directed at the actual attackers. What is more helpful is the more practical formulation of self-defence articulated by Judge Kooijmans, specifically whether 'the armed action by the irregulars amount to an armed attack and, if so, is the armed action by the attacked State in conformity with the requirements of necessity and proportionality'.[120] However, this formulation leaves open the question of whether the armed attack threshold is only met by grave uses of armed force and, if so, the relevance of necessity to the equation. By addressing these questions in light of principles of customary international law, a more effective formulation can be crafted.

Conclusion: A return to necessity and proportionality

In *Nicaragua*, the Court started on the right foot in holding that Article 51 was not exclusive of customary international law and that Article 51 needed to be interpreted through the lens of customary international law. However, the Court should have stayed focused on that point and on the requirements of necessity and proportionality rather than engaging in a convoluted argument on the definition of armed attack. In principle, those are the only two things that are needed to determine whether a use of force in self-defence is legal. In order to keep the rule consistent with the text of the Article, the pre-condition of armed attack should be retained, but the interpretation of this pre-condition should be 'downgraded' to a use of armed force in contravention of Article 2(4). The definition of armed force should also be defined in terms of effects, such that any threat or use of force that has or would have the same effect as that with a weapon would be armed force. For example, a cyber attack that disrupted power stations and hospital infrastructure in a way that caused injury and property damage would be an armed attack. A spam attack on a web site that did not cause damage or injury would not be an armed attack. Diverting a river upstream in way that makes downstream farmers incur extra irrigation expenses would not be armed force, but poisoning the river and killing people downstream would. Granted, even this broader definition of armed attack could be subsumed within necessity, but it is more internally consistent with the Charter to define rather than ignore armed attack.

Once it is confirmed that the threat or attack involves armed force, necessity and proportionality are all that is needed to determine the legality of self-defence. The legality of anticipatory or even preventive forms of self-defence is really a matter of necessity. The claimant must make the case that there was no other reasonable alternative to armed force both in terms of the timing for alternatives and in terms of the effectiveness of armed force to defend against the threat claimed. The actual use of force would need to be only that required to neutralise this threat. What is necessary and proportionate will be different under each set of facts and circumstances and it is this natural flexibility that makes the simpler interpretation so powerful. Granted, this will be a difficult analysis under most cases and will entail some of the difficulties of the current interpretation; the argument will be about what is necessary rather than what is an armed attack. However, at least it will be one test, rather than the current two-step approach (armed attack first, then necessity and proportionality second). Also, by making customary principles the meat of the test, the test is more removed from the confusing text of the Article and is returned to the more flexible regime of customary law. As threats evolve and attitudes change towards acceptable uses of force, the customary law principles can evolve too and stay current without the constant need to engage in a modern day 'angels on the head of a pin' discussion about what is or is not an armed attack or any other parsing of the language of the treaty.

Finally, any plea for a re-interpretation of the rule along the lines of the approach above is bound to be countered with the argument that a more flexible rule will just make it easier for states to use force illegally by giving them an easier argument with which to justify their actions. This is a weak argument. First of all, if necessity was already part of the test then by retaining it the rule should not be opened up to rampant abuse. Second, by putting a renewed emphasis on proportionality and recognising its overlapping nature with necessity, the test under Article 51 will retain the normative function of ensuring that force is not used for aggressive purposes but only to redress serious wrongs. Of course, the legality of using force in self-defence will not be the only (or even primary) factor that determines whether a state uses or refrains from using force. But by putting reasonable and flexible, but still robust, legal restrictions on the use of force in self-defence, states should feel compelled to argue for the legality, and therefore the legitimacy, of their uses of force within a construct where the parameters are clear and the requirements are difficult to discount. The judgement of a state's arguments will still remain in the hands of the ICJ, the Security Council or even the public, but by using a more simple and logical test that is grounded in customary international law, assessing the legality of a state's use of force in self-defence will be a more sensible and transparent task.

10 Computer network attacks, self-defence and international law

Elaine Korzak

In April and May 2007 Estonia experienced a number of cyber attacks that came close to shutting down the country's digital infrastructure.[1] Although the attacks were suspected to have originated from Russia, no direct link could be proven.[2] The attacks turned out to be a watershed event for raising awareness in the cyber security domain. They illustrated the potential utilization of cyberspace as a new battlespace and raised a number of important political, strategic and legal questions.

Within the context of legal questions, the attacks reinvigorated existing debates as to the characterization of cyber attacks, specifically computer network attacks, as a use of force or armed attack. Using non-kinetic force, computer network attacks promise to fundamentally challenge the existing legal framework regulating the use of force and the conduct of hostilities in international relations. In doing so, they may push the capacity of international law to adapt to new technology to its limits indicating the need for a new regulatory framework.

This chapter will assess these claims by reviewing three debates, the categorization of computer network attacks as: a (1) use of force under Article 2(4) of the UN Charter, as an (2) armed attack under Article 51 of the UN Charter; as well as (3) the applicability and implementation of international humanitarian norms. To this end, the first part of the chapter sets the scene for the legal analysis by introducing computer network attacks and their key characteristics. The last part of the article will then identify three problems – ambiguities, uncertainties and insufficiencies – that are created when applying the current legal framework to computer network attacks. Whether these three difficulties warrant the creation of a new regulatory framework, however, is ultimately not a function of the capability of international law to incorporate computer network attacks per se but a question of how states – as the major shapers of international law – tackle these three difficulties.

Computer network attacks in context

The ascendancy of cyber warfare

The information age has come to fundamentally transform the way the world operates.[3] The invention of the internet has facilitated the exchange of digital information, which has become the new 'lifeblood of today's economic and political world'.[4] More and more computer networks and telecommunications systems are being interlinked around the world to form what has come to be regarded as the fourth dimension – cyberspace.[5] Modern societies have become increasingly reliant upon this fourth dimension for the control and operation of key infrastructures with large segments of economic, social, political as well as military activities depending to varying degrees upon information and telecommunications technology.[6]

Just as the information revolution has changed the way modern societies operate, it has begun to revolutionize the way military operations are conducted. Already during the Gulf War in 1991 the US military utilized over 100 satellite units that provided for up to 700,000 telephone calls and 152,000 messages per day.[7] Additionally, there were more than 3,000 computers in the war zone that were actually linked to computers in the US.[8] If the Gulf War was an indicator for the developments that were to come in the 1990s, then it has become apparent that the utilization of information and information technology by the military has become a reality. Advances in information technology have started to fundamentally transform the military arguably ushering in another Revolution in Military Affairs (RMA).[9]

As capabilities and doctrines in this field are still evolving,[10] the strategic significance of what has commonly been described as 'cyber attacks' or 'cyber warfare' will be a subject of debate for years to come. Be that as it may, the features of 'cyber warfare' present states, terrorist groups and individuals with unique opportunities for asymmetrical warfare that have prompted a comparison to 'eWMDs'.[11] The entry costs to conduct 'cyber attacks' are comparatively insignificant. All it takes is a computer, easily obtainable software and a connection to the internet.[12] As a result, warfare conducted by virtual means is no longer the prerogative of the nation state – organized non-state actors as well as individuals enjoy virtually the same access as government agents.[13]

Cyber warfare defined

As the impact of the information revolution on the conduct of warfare is still evolving, definitions and concepts of 'cyber warfare' abound with no common ground in sight.[14] Existing concepts and definitions are fairly broad and based on the premise that the ultimate goal is to achieve and maintain information superiority of one's own forces while denying the same to adversarial forces.[15] Arguably, the control of information has always been key to military strategy.[16] Yet, information is no longer exploited to make existing weaponry and methods of combat more effective.[17] Information and information infrastructure is being turned into a target rather than a means to achieving other military objectives.[18]

This doctrinal development is best captured by the novel technique of computer network attacks (CNAs) that describe 'actions taken through the use of computer networks to disrupt, deny, degrade, or destroy information resident in computers and computer networks, or the computers and networks themselves'.[19] CNAs specifically focus on electronic information and infrastructure. The defining element – the computer network – might be the actual target or used as a means to affect information or related processes.[20] CNAs can effectuate a range of results from mere inconvenience to physical destruction.[21] In doing so, they exhibit a number of unique characteristics that promise to challenge fundamental concepts of international law.

Key characteristics of computer network attacks

a) The non-kinetic nature of computer network attacks

The defining feature of CNAs is that they do not utilize kinetic force. They can cause physical destruction or harm without the traditional elements of impact, blast and fragmentation that transfer kinetic energy. Instead CNAs comprise different modes of attack that aim at either computer systems, at the information stored or administered by them or at both. Syntactic attacks encompass the first category seeking to compromise a computer system by introducing malicious code, conducting denial of service attacks or hacking.[22] The goal is to cause delays or otherwise make the system unpredictable. Computers can be turned into 'zombies' without the owner's knowledge and can be used to run malicious programs under the command of an external computer – a bot herder.[23] These zombie computers can then be directed to flood a target's server, router or internet connection with requests in order to overload it and make it unavailable.[24] If such a denial-of-service attack (DoS) is executed by a large number of computers, it is called a distributed denial-of-service attack (DDoS).[25] The DDoS attack on Estonia in 2007, for example, involved 90 megabits of data per second being pumped at Estonia's networks for ten hours at a time using a million computers located in over 100 countries.[26]

The second category of attacks target the information stored or administered by a computer system and not primarily the system itself. If these so-called semantic attacks occur, the computer system is perceived to operate correctly; yet, it will generate information that is at variance with the supposed result.[27] Semantic attacks target information, substituting correct information for inaccurate or misleading data. Providing false data to an air traffic control system, for example, including changed flight paths and non-existent planes would cause significant disruption if not even destruction.[28]

Finally, mixed attacks combine both syntactic and semantic attacks in order to target a computer system and the information resident within it resulting in a variety of techniques to disrupt information systems.[29]

b) The anonymity of computer network attacks

Another key feature of CNAs with significant ramifications results from the structure of cyberspace which renders it increasingly difficult to establish the identity and location of an attacker. First, the identification of a 'place' in cyberspace is more ambiguous and less conclusive than in the real world.[30] Attackers can use so-called stepping stones – computers owned by innocent parties but controlled by the attackers or hackers in their activities.[31] Stepping stones can be located anywhere in cyberspace and are not restricted by territorial boundaries since the internet consists of a hierarchy of networks that interconnect individual computers across physical boundaries.[32] Thus, activities routed through internet servers of one country do not necessarily emanate from that country. Computer network attacks are unique because technology enables attackers to conceal the true point of origin of their activities. This creates fundamental problems since responsibility for attacks can no longer be inferred from the location where the attack was launched.

Second, even if it was technologically possible to trace an attack to a single computer or a number of computers from which the attack originated,[33] ambiguity still abounds with regard to the identity of the attacker. An attack could be perpetrated by an individual, a group or a state.[34] As Barnett puts it, 'Actors may perform their activities in singular privacy, without personal mentoring and a modicum of instruction. Alternatively, they may be organized and scripted by anti-government groups, or as part of a government or industrial team.'[35] Since the financial and intellectual barriers have been significantly lowered in cyberspace, the pool of potential perpetrators has increased dramatically while the internet and cyberspace offer criminals, terrorists or government agents a veil creating such a degree of anonymity that identifying actors and locations of attacks becomes a very difficult endeavour. Closely related, the resulting anonymity of the perpetrators also significantly hampers the determination of the question whether an attack is a mere act of crime, related to cyberterrorism or perpetrated by a state or sponsored by it.

Categorizing computer network attacks under international law

The prohibition on the use of force under Article 2(4) of the UN Charter

With the ascendancy of CNAs as a potent tool of warfare fundamental questions arise as to the characterization of CNAs in relation to Article 2(4) of the UN Charter. Do computer network attacks per se constitute a use of force under international law? If only certain computer network attacks would fall under the prohibition of the use of force, then what would be the determining criteria?

At the heart of the collective security regime of the United Nations lies Article 2(4) which codifies the prohibition on the use of force:

> All Members shall refrain in their international relations from the threat or use of force against the territorial integrity or political independence of any state, or in any other manner inconsistent with the Purposes of the United Nations.[36]

In order to analyze whether CNAs could qualify as 'force', the scope of the term in Article 2(4) needs to be ascertained. So far, scholarly opinion has asserted that Article 2(4) prohibits armed or military force excluding political and economic coercion from its purview.[37] Indicating that Article 2(4) should be construed narrowly 'this fundamental proscription against the use of interstate force is traditionally regarded as being confined to the use or threat of "armed" force, meaning the possible resort to a violent weapon that inflicts human injury'.[38]

The features of CNAs have prompted a questioning of this majority view in two respects. First, it has been argued that CNAs exhibit unique characteristics, particularly their non-kinetic nature coupled with the ability to immediately inflict a wide-ranging spectrum of damages, so that the earlier debates over economic and political coercion are not relevant and should consequently not be applied to a determination of the status of CNAs.[39] Traditionally, economic coercion involved external and gradual pressure.[40] CNAs, in contrast, enable economic pressure to be swifter and more devastating while targeting internal economic structures directly.[41] Consequently, Sharp argues that 'any computer network attack that intentionally causes any destructive effect within the sovereign territory of another state is an unlawful use of force within the meaning of Article 2(4) . . .'.[42] According to this interpretation a computer network attack could be considered a use of 'force' under Article 2(4) if its effects could be characterized as 'destructive'. Such reasoning, however, would reopen established categories of armed force on the one hand and economic and political pressure, on the other hand. It would also be difficult to implement since a subjective determination of the 'destructive' effects of economic or political measures would be required[43] (a circumstance that the traditional view of excluding economic and political coercion from the purview of Article 2(4) avoids). Although CNAs might differ from earlier forms of economic and political pressure this does not necessarily mean that they should not be viewed as another form of economic and political coercion which the international community has not acknowledged as falling under the meaning of 'force' in Article 2(4).[44]

Second, if the separation of 'armed' force and economic or political coercion is maintained, then the question arises, whether computer network attacks could qualify as armed or military force in the sense of a 'violent weapon that inflicts human injury'.[45] Consequently, it is unclear whether instruments or techniques such as Trojan horses, viruses or denial of service attacks could qualify as violent weapons. The non-kinetic nature of computer network attacks poses significant challenges in this regard. Silver, however, points out that the concept of armed or military force carries a certain degree of flexibility especially with regard to technological advancements of weaponry.[46] Yet, it remains unclear whether CNAs could be qualified as weapons in all or some circumstances.

One interpretation seeks to qualify computer network attacks as weapons on the basis of their destructive effects. Accordingly, computer network attacks could be considered as force on the basis that 'physical injury or property damage must arise as a direct and foreseeable consequence of the CNA and must resemble the injury or damage associated with what, at the time, are generally recognized as military weapons'.[47] This approach shifts attention from the weapons employed – the instruments of military or armed force – to the characteristic consequences of their employment, primarily physical destruction and injury. As a result, computer network attacks whose consequences encompass injury or damage could be characterized as force under Article 2(4). Joyner and Lotrionte likewise argue that, 'the real possibility that computer-based information operations in one state could destroy lives and damage property in other states points up the legal rationale for concluding that such activities should be prohibited as a "use of force" under UN Charter law'.[48] Similarly, Silver asserts that a computer network attack can be considered a use of force if 'it causes physical injury or property damage that is recognizably similar to that produced by instruments generally identified as weapons'.[49] The problem however lies in the wide range of consequences that can be effectuated with computer network attacks, from mere inconvenience of not accessing certain websites to widespread destruction and injury. A consequence-oriented interpretation of armed force would be able to capture the most extreme or severe instances of CNA. Definitional problems, however, will arise in the majority of cases that lie between the extremes of consequences. It has been suggested, however, that the majority of these computer network attacks would be captured by the prohibition on non-intervention.[50]

As a result, computer network attacks need to be considered on a case-by-case basis in order to assess whether they could be classified as a use of force prohibited under Article 2(4) of the UN Charter.[51] The non-kinetic nature of computer network attacks, however, does not easily fit within established categories, particularly the understanding of 'armed' force as it has been interpreted since the adoption of the UN Charter. A consequence-based analysis has been advanced that could capture those computer network attacks that effectuate physical destruction and injury. In practical terms, however, a characterization of computer network attacks as an 'armed attack' might be more pressing since only an 'armed attack' can trigger a state's right to respond forcefully.

The right to self-defence under Article 51 of the UN Charter

Not surprisingly, debate has been spurred as to the ramifications of computer network attacks (CNAs) on the right to self-defence.[52] Two sets of questions will be analyzed in this context. First, questions relating to the characterization of CNAs as an 'armed attack' mirror the debate regarding Article 2(4) of the UN Charter. Second, assuming a computer network attack can be categorized as an 'armed attack' a number of important questions arise with regard to the exercise of the right to self-defence.

The first set of questions pertains to the debate whether computer network attacks can qualify as an 'armed attack' triggering the right to self-defence. Article 51 of the UN Charter provides that:

> Nothing in the present Charter shall impair the inherent right of individual or collective self-defence if an armed attack occurs against a Member of the

United Nations, until the Security Council has taken measures necessary to maintain international peace and security.

Debate as to the interpretation of the term 'armed attack' continues.[53] Nonetheless, it is now established that an illegal use of force has to cross a certain threshold to qualify as an 'armed attack'.[54] Thus, 'when the use of force is trivial – say, a few stray bullets are fired across a frontier – no armed attack can be alleged to have occurred'.[55] This opinion was expressed by the International Court of Justice in its famous Nicaragua judgment saying, 'It is necessary to distinguish the most grave forms of the use of force (those constituting armed attack) from other less grave forms.'[56] Although this pronouncement has not passed without criticism, the question arises whether a computer network attack could qualify as a grave form of the use of force – an armed attack.

Similar to the discussion of computer network attacks as a use of 'force' the qualification of CNAs as an armed attack has produced a number of conceptual problems. The adjective 'armed' even more obviously collides with the way CNAs operate; 'Obviously, computers are neither troops nor tanks.'[57] Techniques such as syntactic and semantic attacks thus challenge traditional conceptions of armed attacks involving the use of armed force. Armed force has been distinguished from economic and political coercion by the instrument used – military weapons or the actions of armed forces. The difficulties in equating bits and bytes with troops and tanks illustrate the inherent limits of this instrument-based approach when it comes to computer network attacks. Consequently, and in line with arguments advanced in the previous section, several authors have extended a consequence-based approach to qualify certain computer network attacks as an 'armed attack'. Accordingly, Michael Schmitt argues that,

> To constitute an armed attack, the CNA must be intended to directly cause physical damage to tangible objects or injury to human beings . . . States, acting individually or collectively, may respond to a CNA amounting to armed attack with the use of force pursuant to Article 51 and the inherent right of self-defense.[58]

Joyner and Lotrionte state that, 'it seems reasonable to qualify cyber-assaults that are sufficiently destructive as "armed attacks", regardless of the level of intrusion'[59] because 'the consequences of the cyber-attack on the targeted programs may be more important than the means used to implement it'.[60]

Lastly, Dinstein gives a number of examples that in his opinion qualify as armed attacks which likewise entail loss of life and property damage as consequences:

> Fatalities caused by loss of computer-controlled life-support systems; . . . a shutdown of computers controlling waterworks and dams, generating thereby floods of inhabited areas; deadly crashes deliberately engineered (e.g. through misinformation fed into aircraft computers), etc. The most egregious case is the wanton instigation of a core-meltdown of a reactor in a nuclear power

plant, leading to the release of radioactive materials that can result in count-less casualties if the neighboring areas are densely populated. In all these cases, the CNA would be deemed an armed attack.[61]

As with the definition of 'force' under Article 2(4) of the UN Charter, however, the uses of computer network attacks that fall short of fatalities and property damage as a direct result are the most difficult to categorize even using a consequence-based approach. Consider the following example:

> Suppose a state is the targeted victim of a computer network attack from . . . another country. The IW [information warfare] attack takes the form of sophisticated intrusions into top-secret military databases of the victim state. Classified military information is stolen, destroyed and altered. When the victim state's intrusion-detection mechanisms fail to give warning of these intrusions, the victim state erroneously relies on false data in making foreign policy and military decisions. The goal of the attack is successful. The result is the death of 20 servicemen who perish when a military unit conducting training operations launches a missile into their military unit, rather than the vacant training grounds because they relied on the compromised data.[62]

This case illustrates the problems posed by computer network attacks. Does the computer network attack amount to an armed attack? Is the victim state empow-ered to respond in self-defence? Does the computer network attack qualify as a prohibited use of force under Article 2(4) of the UN Charter? Did the compu-ter network attack '*directly* cause physical damage to tangible objects or injury to human beings'?[63] The above-described case would probably not qualify as an armed attack triggering the right to self-defence even under a consequence-based interpretation since the results are not a 'direct or foreseeable'[64] result of the attack. The time delay allows a number of intervening variables to enter the picture which could have equally contributed to the death of the servicemen.

The example illustrates that the consequence-based approach is not a panacea for the problems encountered by computer network attacks. As Schmitt admits, 'it would prove extraordinarily difficult to quantify or qualify consequences in a normatively practical manner'.[65] The long-held interpretations of Articles 2(4) and 51 requiring the involvement of military or armed force (and in the case of an armed attack the sufficient gravity criterion) offer a relatively simple framework. 'It eases the evaluative process by simply asking whether force has been used, rather than requiring a far more difficult assessment of the consequences that have resulted.'[66] In the case of computer network attacks, the subjective evaluation of consequences is compounded by the range of effects that can be achieved by using CNAs. Because the effects of computer network attacks cut across the entire spec-trum of consequences affecting the economic, social, and physical well-being of individuals or entire societies, an evaluation of consequences becomes increas-ingly difficult.[67] The existing framework rests on the assumption that 'armed coercion usually results in some form of physical destruction or injury'.[68] Thus, computer network attacks challenge the existing framework fundamentally as they show that armed coercion is no longer necessary to effect physical destruction or injury.

As a result, CNAs that result in mass casualties and widespread damage can be absorbed by the existing framework by resorting to a consequence-based interpretation – the consequences of extreme cases of CNA sufficiently resemble established categories. Such an approach, however, becomes ever more challenging, the less destructive or more subtle results of computer network attacks become.[69] Consequently, the current framework seems unfit to absorb the entire spectrum of possible CNAs. Similar to the considerations earlier with regard to the prohibition on the use of force, computer network attacks do not easily fit in established categories. Analyzing the consequences effectuated by CNAs is an inherently subjective process that tends to blur already established categories. The question then is whether it is possible to draw a 'line' between armed force and other forms of coercion with regard to computer network attacks. What would relevant criteria be? And more importantly, is it possible to draw such a 'line' without fundamentally disturbing the balance that has been calibrated over the last sixty years?

The second set of questions relates to aspects of an exercise of the right to self-defence if it is assumed that a computer network attack can amount to an armed attack. Within this context one of the major questions would be who a victim state would or could respond against. Conceptually this depends upon an interpretation of who could launch an armed attack under Article 51 of the UN Charter. At the time that the provision for the right of self-defence was written, it was assumed that only states had the capabilities to do so. Nevertheless, Article 51 does not specify the potential perpetrators of an 'armed attack' and thus leaves room for interpretation. In its Nicaragua judgment the International Court of Justice asserted that armed attacks could be carried out by regular forces as well as through 'the sending by or on behalf of a State of armed bands, groups, irregulars or mercenaries, which carry out acts of armed force against another State of such gravity as to amount to an actual armed attack conducted by regular forces, or its substantial involvement therein'.[70] Thus, states do not dispute the assertion that irregular and regular troops can carry out an armed attack; controversy rather centres on the degree of state involvement and questions of attribution and state responsibility.[71] Moreover, following the terrorist attacks of 11 September 2001 this debate has gained momentum illustrating that the question whether non-state actors could carry out armed attacks is still not conclusively resolved.[72] Likewise, it remains legally disputed whether non-state actors can launch an armed attack provoking the exercise of the right to self-defence in the absence of any state involvement.[73]

With the use of computer network attacks the aforementioned controversies will not be easily dispensed with. On the contrary, computer network attacks will significantly compound the problems encountered so far due to their unique features. Firstly, the low technological and financial entry requirements significantly enlarge the pool of potential 'cyber attackers'. Worst-case scenario CNAs could hypothetically be conducted by individuals or small groups of individuals.

Coupled with the large degree of anonymity described earlier, finding out where the attack originated from and who actually attacked you – whether an individual, a criminal organization, a terrorist group, state agents or state-sponsored entities – might prove futile. The 'attack' on Estonia in 2007, for example, resulted in only one conviction – on January 24, 2008 an ethnic Russian student living in Tallinn was found guilty of posting a fake letter of apology for removing the symbolic Soviet statue on the Reform Party's website of Prime Minister Andrus Ansip. He was fined 1,642 US-Dollars.[74] Technological progress, however, might make it easier in the future to identify the source of the attack.[75] Nevertheless, computer network attacks will significantly reinvigorate existing controversies as to whether non-state actors can launch an armed attack granting a victim state the right to self-defence. As a consequence, the question whether states, state-sponsored groups or even groups without any state sponsorship can be the target of the self-defence exercise will be equally revisited. The power asymmetry afforded by the anonymity and the potentially disastrous effects of CNAs might also prompt individuals to enter the picture.

Secondly and closely related, the anonymity and potential individualization of CNAs pose a number of obstacles to existing concepts of state involvement and attribution. In times where the internet is the 'perfect platform for plausible deniability'[76] proving state involvement becomes a real challenge. As Susan Brenner points out, 'Physical attacks involve detectable staging efforts that can be difficult to conceal, which can make it challenging for a nation-state to disavow knowledge of (and at least tacit complicity in) activity within its borders'.[77] Whereas in the case of CNAs, 'We have only the virtual "presence" of signals, bits and bytes, which traveled through cyberspace by routine means, the same means used by civilian and government traffic every second of every day. The signals bear neither state insignia nor other markers of military allegiance or intent.'[78] Thus, in the case of state-sponsored computer network attacks, establishing a link between the state and group in question with irrefutable evidence will be fraught with great difficulties. Attributing terrorist activities to a state has proved difficult enough; and these activities inadvertently involve 'physical' elements – the presence or movement of equipment and personnel or the provision of a sanctuary. Cyberspace, on the other hand, does not correlate with territorial boundaries and as a result states might theoretically sponsor CNAs all across the world and not only in the territory under their jurisdiction.[79] This also means that an attack does not necessarily have to come from outside the attacked state; it could also originate within its own borders. Furthermore, computer network attacks are usually spun through a number of servers in different countries. As a result, state involvement and sponsorship are increasingly difficult to establish. Furthermore, questions arise as to the responsibility of those states through which the attacks are being routed. Do these states provide the attackers with something analogous to a staging ground for their attacks? Or even a sanctuary?

In summary, computer network attacks will pose significant difficulties for countries wanting to exercise their right to self-defence even if it can be established that an 'armed attack' has taken place. Existing interpretational limits will be revisited and the individualization and anonymity granted by computer network attacks has the potential to fundamentally challenge a legal paradigm that is centred on the exclusive ability of states to use force in international relations. In a way computer network attacks promise to take the problems posed by international terrorism – the ability of non-state actors to inflict wide-ranging damage and questions of state responsibility – a step further.

The applicability of international humanitarian law

Another major debate with regard to computer network attacks revolves around the applicability of international humanitarian law.[80] The most pressing concern has been whether isolated CNAs that are not accompanied by conventional attacks would be subject to rules and regulations of international humanitarian law.[81] This question revolves around an interpretation of common Article 2 of the Geneva Conventions that provides for the application of the Conventions in 'all cases of declared war or of any other armed conflict which may arise between two or more of the High Contracting Parties, even if the state of war is not recognized by one of them'.[82] The question whether CNAs could give rise to an 'armed conflict' is similar but not identical to the debates reviewed earlier whether CNAs constitute a use of 'force' or an 'armed attack'. It is important to note that international humanitarian law and law pertaining to the use of force in international relations are normatively distinct.[83] Yet, the interpretation of the 'armed conflict' threshold for purposes of *jus in bello* applicability mirrors a number of aspects described earlier in the sections on Article 2(4) and 51 of the UN Charter.

The term 'armed conflict' obviously clashes with the non-kinetic nature of computer network attacks. Since the purpose of international humanitarian law is to limit damage resulting from hostilities and to protect civilians, it can be argued that an expansive interpretation of 'armed conflict' could be supported. Thus, as in the cases of Articles 2(4) and 51 of the UN Charter, authors have argued in favor of a consequence-based interpretation. Contrary to the ICRC commentary to the Geneva Conventions which qualifies an 'armed conflict' as involving the intervention of 'members of the armed forces',[84] Schmitt asserts that,

> Humanitarian law principles apply whenever computer network attacks can be ascribed to a State, are more than merely sporadic and isolated incidents, and are either intended to cause injury, death, damage, or destruction (and analogous effects), or such consequences are foreseeable. This is so even though classic *armed* force is not being employed.[85]

Likewise Doswald-Beck opines,

> there is an argument to be made in favor of the implementation of IHL [international humanitarian law] when CNA is undertaken by official sources and is intended to, or does, result in physical damage to persons, or damage to objects that goes beyond the bit of computer program or data attacked.[86]

Thus, as in the debates analyzed earlier, a consequence-based interpretation is applied in order to incorporate CNAs into the existing legal framework.

A similar set of questions arises with regard to the applicability and implementation of specific humanitarian law norms, particularly the principles of distinction and proportionality. A fundamental question will be whether those principles apply to any or all computer network attacks conducted during an armed conflict. The relevant provisions of Additional Protocol I are triggered by 'attacks' which are defined as 'acts of violence against the adversary, whether in offence or in defence'.[87] The arguments analyzed earlier are revisited in this context. Authors similarly argue that violent consequences rather than violent acts should be determinative for subsuming computer network attacks under 'acts of violence'.[88] Thus, computer network attacks that are likely to result in injury, death, or damage qualify as 'attacks' triggering the application of the principle of distinction and related prohibitions that flow from it.[89] As has been the case in the context of Articles 2(4) and 51 of the UN Charter 'other effects remain open to debate (e.g., neutralizing a target, denying service to a system), or clearly fall outside the definition (e.g., [. . .] electronic embargoes)'.[90]

As a result, computer network attacks resulting in injury or physical destruction would have to comply with the requirements of the principle of distinction and its related norms. Computer network attacks that do not meet this threshold, however, would not be covered and could theoretically be employed regardless of the military advantage gained. It becomes, therefore, increasingly important whether a computer network attack can be characterized as an 'attack' under Article 49 (1) of Additional Protocol I or not.[91] The result is a mismatch between the purpose of humanitarian law, i.e. to protect civilians and civilian objects from attack, and the realities and possibilities created by computer network attacks. This 'grey' area can be interpreted in several ways. On the one hand, there is an expansion of possible non-military targets if computer network attacks are employed that do not result in injury or destruction and consequently do not trigger the principle of distinction. Schmitt asserts,

> For instance, if the Serbian State television station had been targeted by CNA rather than kinetic weapons during NATO strikes on Belgrade in April 1999, there might well have been no consequent injury, death, damage, or destruction; in that circumstance, criticism on the basis that a civilian target had been hit would likely have fallen on deaf ears, thereby probably avoiding the negative publicity that resulted . . .[92]

It is unclear, however, whether such a development would be normatively desirable or not. Schmitt argues that it does not weaken the existing framework; 'instead, it simply represents an expansion of permissible methods and means resulting from advances in technology; existing norms remain intact'.[93] Hollis, on the contrary, argues that,

> The irony of IO [Information Operation] is that the less likely it is that a particular IO [Information Operation] functions as an attack, the more likely it is

that its use against civilians and their objects is permissible. In other words, IO′s development may actually result in warfare having more impact on civilians by expanding militaries' ability to target (but not attack) them. In such circumstances, applying existing civilian distinction rules to IO challenges the notion that the law of war should protect civilians and their property as much as possible.[94]

On the other hand, an expansion in civilian targets might be tolerated because computer network attacks that do not rise to the level of 'attack' have less severe effects than traditional kinetic weapons.[95]

Be that as it may, the novelty of computer network attacks creates challenges with regard to the application of the principle of distinction. Again, the worst-case scenario computer network attacks can be integrated into the existing legal framework by resorting to a consequence-based interpretation of the term 'acts of violence'. Computer network attacks that do not meet this threshold, however, fall outside of established categories with the astonishing result that a range of CNAs can be employed without the legal restrictions of distinction and proportionality. Thus, a legal lacuna is created that leads to an actual expansion of civilian targets. Whether this is desirable from a humanitarian standpoint, particularly in light of the 'more humane'[96] effects of computer network attacks is not conclusively resolved. However, it illustrates the challenges posed by computer network attacks in the area of international humanitarian norms.

Computer network attacks as a challenge to international law

The adaptability of international law to technological progress

It is a common position that international law lags behind technological advancement.[97] As technological change cannot be comprehensively anticipated, a certain degree of uncertainty is brought into the efforts to regulate the relations between states through law. The development of the laws pertaining to the use of force and the conduct of hostilities has confirmed this position showing that experience and not logic have been the driving forces in shaping the legal regime that is in place today.[98] The First and Second World Wars were defining events for the UN Charter and the Geneva Conventions. Regulations regarding weaponry in particular have shown that time and again international law has not been able to keep up with path-breaking technology and as such has failed to regulate it effectively.[99]

The features of computer network attacks, particularly the non-kinetic nature of its operation as well as the anonymity granted by pervasively interconnected civilian and military networks, prompt the question whether and how far international law is capable of regulating computer network attacks under the existing framework. It also begs the question whether a new framework, such as a convention to regulate the use of computer network attacks, is necessary or desirable and what factors would have a bearing on such a development.

The extent to which international law is challenged by CNAs has to be assessed by examining how the concrete application of existing rules plays out. This depends upon the interpretation of relevant treaty language – in the context of this article predominantly the terms 'use of force', 'armed attack' and 'armed conflict'. This interpretation, in turn, is influenced by the novelty of the technology in question – in this case computer network attacks – and the limits provided by the rules of interpretation of treaties – the ordinary meaning of the relevant terms in light of the object and purpose of the treaty.[100] Part B of this chapter analyzed the interplay between the technological novelty presented by computer network attacks and the dynamic interpretation of existing legal norms with regard to three major debates. A number of conclusions can be drawn based on observations made in the previous sections.

Computer network attacks and the challenges of uncertainty, ambiguity and insufficiency

With regard to the categorization of computer network attacks as a 'use of force' under Article 2(4) of the UN Charter and as an 'armed attack' under Article 51 of the Charter it has been shown that CNAs do not easily fit within established categories of 'armed force' and 'armed attack'.[101] The non-kinetic operation of CNAs obviously collides with traditional notions of 'armed force' and 'armed attack'. Therefore, several authors have advanced an interpretation that would shift the focus of analysis from the instrument used – armed or military force – to the consequences of an attack. Such a consequence-based interpretation, however, can only capture some CNAs, namely the most extreme cases resulting in death and destruction. Other cases of CNAs would be significantly harder to characterize resulting in differing interpretations. As a consequence, integrating CNAs in the existing framework through the use of a consequence-based interpretation creates a number of problems.

First, a consequence-based interpretation of CNAs is more subjective than the instrument-based approach used so far. This is especially true for CNAs that are short of directly causing damage or injury. As a result, a computer network attack could be categorized differently by different states – meeting the 'use of force' (or 'armed attack') threshold for some but not for others. Differing interpretations illustrate the ambiguities that are created in trying to categorize the range of computer network attacks under the existing framework. It can be argued that some CNAs will qualify as 'use of force' or maybe even as an 'armed attack' whereas other uses might be captured by the principle on non-intervention. Thus, the existing framework might be capable of incorporating computer network attacks without fundamentally being challenged by them. This analysis is valid but it misses the point. The problem lies in the ambiguities created by trying to draw the line between computer network attacks that can be characterized as 'use of force' or as mere economic or political coercion prohibited by the principle of non-intervention. In the case of CNAs, this line can be drawn slightly differently by each state because of the subjectivity introduced by the consequence-based interpretation.

The results are ambiguities and uncertainties as to the status of CNAs under current law caused by differing interpretations.[102]

Second and closely related, the subjectivity introduced by a consequence-based interpretation also runs the risk of diluting established categories. The difficulty with computer network attacks is that 'computer warfare lies at the uncomfortable intersection between the use of force and nonforcible influence'.[103] A focus on consequences of an attack might reinvigorate past debates whether economic or political coercion could constitute a 'use of force' under Article 2(4) of the UN Charter. Thus, categories that have been delineated over the past sixty years might become a subject of debate again.[104]

Ambiguities and uncertainties are also created with regard to the exercise of the right to self-defence. Problems that have already been encountered with the phenomenon of transnational terrorism are going to be significantly compounded in the case of CNAs. The individualization of computer network attacks and the anonymity of the internet are major factors in exacerbating problems of attribution, state responsibility and the categorization of non-state actors. In this case, however, definitional problems and differing interpretations already exist in the context of international terrorism.

In the case of international humanitarian law similar considerations as described above arise with regard to the applicability of its rules. Again, computer network attacks with destructive or violent consequences can be accommodated through a consequence-based approach in order to trigger the applicability of international humanitarian law. Uncertainties and ambiguities, however, prevail with regard to CNAs that fall short of this standard. It has been pointed out earlier, though, that an isolated use of computer network attacks appears unlikely and thus, from a practical standpoint, the implementation of international humanitarian law to all potential uses of CNAs becomes relevant.[105] In this context, the implementation of the principles of distinction and proportionality also depends upon a consequence-based interpretation of the term 'acts of violence'. The result of the analysis showed that certain uses of CNAs will meet this threshold and will be subject to the rules of distinction and proportionality. More importantly, uses of CNAs that do not meet this threshold would currently not be regulated under the rules of international humanitarian law. Thus, a significant lacuna is created that could be exploited by states. Moreover, this legal grey area might question the effectiveness of international humanitarian rules which might not be able to protect against all potential damages caused by CNAs.[106] Consequently, CNAs challenge international humanitarian law by creating uncertainties, ambiguities and insufficiencies.[107]

Factors in establishing a new regulatory framework

The features displayed by computer network attacks are indicative of the fundamental challenge CNAs pose to the international legal framework. The analysis above has shown that international law is capable of incorporating the unique characteristics of CNAs to a certain extent. However, problems such as uncertainties, ambiguities and insufficiencies are created. As a result, many authors claim that CNAs are analytically different[108] and thus an international treaty is desirable and necessary in order to regulate computer network attacks.[109] Attempts to regulate information operations or computer network attacks have been unsuccessful so far.[110] In the end, it depends upon states as the main subjects of international law to determine whether an international treaty, code of conduct, etc. is going to be negotiated or not. This, in turn, depends upon the question whether they perceive an international regulatory framework (whatever its final shape is going to look like) to be in their interests or not. Existing and potential capabilities relating to computer network attacks are a major factor in this regard. Ultimately considerations of interests as a function of capabilities reflect concerns over the status quo and the position of individual states in the international system. Regulation through international law might be seen as a vehicle to maintain or change the status quo. Likewise, leaving international regulations ambiguous or uncertain might be seen as a way to preserve or alter the status quo. With an increasing number of states acquiring capabilities in the field of information operations it remains to be seen whether the majority of states will perceive it to be in their interest to negotiate specific rules.

However, three points can be highlighted that are likely to influence future developments. Firstly, the problems created by a consequence-based interpretation of relevant international legal terms, namely ambiguity, uncertainty and insufficiency, can be seen as vulnerabilities as well as opportunities by states. Different interpretations of the status of CNAs can be perceived negatively by some states, as more capable or powerful states can seek to exploit existing interpretational differences. Yet, it is important to note that particularly in the context of international humanitarian law, computer network attacks are viewed as potentially more humane and effective modes of operation.[111] Thus, there is no shared understanding as to the normative desirability of computer network attacks. Their use is associated with opportunities as well as disadvantages. This fact will have a bearing on the development of a common threat perception in the international community.

Secondly, computer network attacks offer unique asymmetric benefits that impact both technologically advanced and less advanced countries. For technologically advanced countries, such as the US, the sophistication of cyberspace capabilities correlates to its overall technological edge. Thus, technologically advanced countries are prone to acquire and extend cyber warfare capabilities to preserve their lead vis-à-vis other states. The inherently asymmetric nature of CNAs, however, disturbs this calculation because 'to the extent that an opponent is militarily and economically advantaged, it is probably technologically-dependent, and therefore, teeming with tempting CNA targets'.[112] Technologically advanced countries turn out to be the most vulnerable when it comes to CNAs. Hence, an ironic situation is created wherein technologically advanced countries are the prime targets of CNAs while they are the states with the most sophisticated capabilities and thus an interest to use them. For technologically less-advantaged countries, however, CNAs could prove 'a high gain, low risk option for a state outclassed militarily and economically'[113] while at the same time they are disproportionately less vulnerable to attacks against them. Important to note in this context is that the asymmetric character of CNAs will have numerous implications for the advantage-disadvantage calculus of states.

Thirdly, technology itself will have an impact on future developments as it introduces another layer of uncertainty. Technological progress and in this case the development of computer network attack capabilities is not 100% predictable and thus current technologies might become obsolete in a very short time span.[114] The newness of CNAs and uncertainties as to the consequences of their use might also lead to an inertia in their application. Reportedly, during the Kosovo conflict in 1999 plans were made to deplete Slobodan Milosevic's personal financial accounts via information operation means.[115] The plans, however, were never executed illustrating the potential inertia in the application of new technology – a circumstance that will also affect the way states will move forward in dealing with the ambiguities, uncertainties and insufficiencies created by the current legal framework.

Conclusion

The information age has fundamentally transformed societies. Likewise, it has started to revolutionize the way modern militaries operate. Emerging technologies have created new possibilities such as cyber attacks or cyber warfare. Computer network attacks, in particular, embody this technological progress and promise to fundamentally challenge existing legal norms on the use of force and the conduct of hostilities. This chapter examined whether and to what extent computer network attacks fit within established categories of international law by reviewing three major debates. It sought to examine the interpretations advanced so far in order to ascertain the adaptability of international law to technological progress.

The analysis showed that some CNAs can be accommodated within existing legal categories by resorting to a consequence-based interpretation. Other uses of computer network attacks, however, are less clearly categorized. As a result, problems such as ambiguity, uncertainty and insufficiency are created that led some commentators to advocate the need for an international treaty specifically addressing CNAs. Such a development, however, is open and is ultimately dependent upon the perception of states and their interests and capabilities in the field. There are three factors that flow from the unique characteristics of CNAs that could however significantly influence the interplay of interests, perceptions and capabilities of states. Firstly, CNAs represent both opportunities and dangers for states, i.e. their normative desirability is not established. Secondly, the asymmetric benefits afforded by CNAs render the most technologically advanced countries also the most vulnerable. Finally, the unpredictability of technological advancement adds a layer of uncertainty potentially resulting in inertia in applying CNAs.

11 Conclusion

War, law and ethics

Aidan Hehir

There is, it seems, widespread consensus that the war on terror has been a profound failure. As Andrew Mumford succinctly notes in his chapter, 'the direction of the American-led "War on Terror" since the invasion of Iraq in 2003 has led to a tangible increase in the threat posed by transnational networked Islamist insurgents' (p. 42). Indeed, the recent plethora of emotively titled books – such as *Fiasco, The End of Iraq, Winning the War Losing the Peace, Why We Are Losing the War on Terror* – is illustrative of this negative consensus. The big loser, it seems, is the US; indicatively, according to Paul Rogers, 'the first six years of war on terror have shown the idea of the New American Century boosted by the war on terror to be something of a lost cause'.[1] Whatever one's views on the moral rectitude of the US, the fact that the world's primary superpower has failed so spectacularly must be cause for concern. While the prospect of US imperialism is clearly unappealing to most, the alternatives – a return to a multi-polar world similar to that which existed at the beginning of the 20th century, or the spread of Islamic fundamentalism – are hardly palatable. This book has explored the issues exposed by the war on terror with a more general focus on navigating a way out of the present mire towards a more secure system regulated by an effective legal regime informed by universally agreed ethical principles. If this is ever to be realised we must be clear as to the nature of the threat posed by al Qaeda, the role and efficacy of law, and the ethics which guide both our actions and our aims.

The purpose of this concluding chapter is to reflect on some of the key themes explored in this book, namely war/terrorism, law and ethics. It is not the intention here to summarise each chapter or divine an overarching common narrative but rather to offer reflections which draw on the contestations and problems exposed in this book in the hope that these may stimulate further research.

War, law and ethics in a 'time of terror'

The uneasy confluence of 'war', 'law' and 'ethics' has been the catalyst for reflections on international relations for millennia and, as the preceding chapters have shown, we have yet to contrive a means of reconciling them. Ethics clearly influence our behaviour, laws (derived from ethical codes) constrain our behaviour and yet, neither ethics nor law have removed the scourge of war, negated the occurrence of terrorism or, it seems, attenuated the excesses of both.

War/terrorism

The events of 11th September 2001 graphically illustrated the existence of a well organised and extremely violent group determined to destroy the 'West'. While it is certainly conceivable that this group constituted the expression of genuine grievances – a form of 'blowback' caused by decades of nefarious Western foreign policy – few supported either the methods employed by al Qaeda or the ultimate aims of this group. The attacks quite naturally demanded a response but it is the nature of this response which has generated most controversy. Faced with a new 'foe', clearly the first issue was to establish the nature of this group before determining a strategy to tackle it. Mumford argues, however, that the strategy adopted – the so-called war on terror – was premised on a fundamental misreading of al Qaeda; rather than adopting a strategy to deal with a 'terrorist group' the US-led campaign should have operated on the basis that the group was an organisation involved in a global insurgency and thus traditional counter-terrorism methods were not likely to be effective. While there is, he argues, 'an obvious need for domestic counter-terrorism' this should have been, 'conjoined with a wider, transnational politico-military counter-insurgency strategy' (p. 3). The unilateralist rhetoric of the Bush administration and the bellicose 'you are either with us or against' ethos underpinning the Bush doctrine clearly undermined any efforts to fashion the collective international response so manifestly required. The threat posed by al Qaeda, though real, did not cohere with many of the more the fantastical claims made about the group by statesmen and, indeed, academics. Indicatively Christopher Coker has criticised 'many of my fellow academics who tend to hype up the threat posed by terrorism in the absence of any useful, solid data'.[2] The spike in terrorism studies within academia certainly fed the pervasive notion that al Qaeda was a new type of organisation with apocalyptic aims which demanded a particular type of robust response. This overlooked the fact that many of the grievances which compelled individuals to claim allegiance to al Qaeda were very much centred on traditional national liberation struggles, underdevelopment and domestic misrule.

This strategic failing was complicated further, Nigel White notes, by both the manifest lack of an agreed legal definition of terrorism and the tension within international law 'between the security imperative requiring coercive measures to tackle the terrorist threat and concern for protecting the human rights of those rightly or wrongly suspected of terrorism' (p. 9). The latter point in particular necessarily undermined the strategy employed to tackle al Qaeda as evidenced by the damage done by the Abu Ghraib revelations and the detention centres at Guantanamo Bay.

The war on terror has, therefore, unquestionably undermined the optimism which abounded at the end of the Cold War. The debates on intervention in the 1990s largely focused on humanitarian concerns and the idea that the spread of liberal values, while obviously good for the West, was a moral imperative that would reap universal benefits. The war on terror, however, has cast a shadow over this optimism; humanitarian intervention has been tainted by association with the invasion of Iraq; the rise of al Qaeda, and anti-western feeling more generally, has shattered the illusion that the spread of Western values would be welcomed across the globe; the duplicity, if not outright deceit, associated, rightly or wrongly, with Bush and Blair, compromised the idea that democracies were somehow inherently virtuous; and the military failures have clearly undermined faith in the capacity of the West's military preponderance to exercise muscular leverage when required.

Law

If we reflect on the nature of the divisive debate about the war on terror it should remind us that the idea of history as constituting a progressive trajectory is not as axiomatic as many suggest, given that the source of the majority of the contemporary controversy centres on the *response* of the so-called civilised world to barbaric attacks. That the 'civilised world' was attacked is not in itself necessarily grounds for questioning progress; such aberrant behaviour can be characterised as the violent expression of frustration felt by those aggrieved at their relative underdevelopment. It is the nature of the West's response to these attacks, however, which illustrates the limitations; if our civilisation cannot maintain its values in the face of brute force and its key members circumvent the legal architecture established to regulate behaviour, then there is evidently a profound problem. The test of a legal system's resilience occurs not when people obey the law and the system is not threatened, but rather when there is a fundamental challenge to the system.

Few would disagree that reform of the international legal system is a pressing requirement. It is quite easy to highlight certain elements of the Charter as evidence of its anachronistic character. The fact that, for example, the Military Staff Committee and Article 51 appear very outdated does not necessarily mean, however, that the entire system has to be altered. In the aftermath of the September 11th attacks the Bush administration advanced a view which essentially called for a revolutionary reordering of international law which was arguably unnecessary and born from expediency. Law, of course, *does* periodically change, but this is a process best catalysed by consensus rather than emotion. As Michael Byers noted, 'law . . . retains a specificity and resistance to short-term change that enables it to constrain sudden changes in relative power, and sudden changes in policy motivated by consequentially shifting perceptions of opportunity and self-interest'.[3] It is, therefore, on one level heartening that the core tenets of international law withstood the post-September 11th clamour for change, but also somewhat unfortunate that reform came to be associated with the Bush doctrine and hence viewed with suspicion. As White notes in his chapter, the failure to take advantage of the window of opportunity that briefly opened in the aftermath of the September 11th attacks is to be regretted given that this could have been an ideal chance to reorder certain aspects of international law. Likewise James Gow and

Rachel Kerr's chapter highlights the extent to which the current conflict blurs the lines between war fighting and policing and between combatant, and non-combatant but the fissures caused by the war on terror have militated against the implementation of the necessary reforms. Gow's analysis of the US's interpretation of self-defence clearly highlights the extent to which the traditional understanding of the term is no longer apposite. The question 'what constitutes an armed attack' he argues clearly remains outstanding. Thomas Jones also suggests that Article 51 is overly restrictive. He argues, however, that rather than this being a function of the emergence of 'new' threats – primarily terrorism – the legal regime established by the UN Charter altered the norm of self-defence rendering the relevant laws anachronistic. The contemporary confusion and contestation surrounding self-defence is not, therefore, due to al Qaeda but rather the provisions of the Charter itself. Korzak's chapter deals with an issue which was literally inconceivable in 1945 and thus further evidence of the need to be flexible, if not creative, when applying international law to certain exclusively modern phenomena. The war on terror has, therefore, highlighted many of the anachronisms and failings within the current legal system and, as many note, legal reform is manifestly required. Sadly, given the disrepute now associated with change these reforms appear unlikely to materialise.

Gow highlights the fact that the US sought to 'sell something entirely new, extreme and deeply contentious as established and traditional' in its efforts to jus-tify the doctrine of pre-emptive self-defence (p. 111). On first reading one may conclude that this is evidence of the US's negative view of international law but this is perhaps a misreading. If the US believed international law was essentially impotent and of minor importance then it would surely not have expended so much energy in justifying its actions as being in accordance with international law. This would seem to lend credence to Sir Arthur Watts's assertion, 'It is strik-ing that virtually without exception states seek always to offer a legal justification for their actions, even in extreme circumstances where the action is manifestly contrary to international law. . . [This] demonstrates the value attached by states to compliance with international law'.[4] This is of course, somewhat compromised by certain statements made by President Bush denigrating international law cited in Hehir's chapter. Nonetheless, the war on terror may not be as great a 'degrada-tion' of international law as some feared.[5] If one considers law, and the interna-tional institutions established to regulate it, to be what David Armstrong and Theo Farrell describe as 'a site of legitimation for state action . . . normatively bounded in the sense that state reasoning, deliberation and action is constituted and con-strained by pre-existing norms that shape social identities and situations' then the war on terror can be cited, to some extent, as evidence of the efficacy of interna-tional law.[6] In the midst of a crisis there was a challenge to the fundamental rules governing the use of force and this challenge was ultimately repelled.

It is additionally worth noting that, as Hilary Charlesworth and David Kennedy write, 'Normally, international lawyers specialize in crises. Our sense that we are living through a momentous period in history is permanent. We will always feel as though there is something peculiarly challenging and significant about this moment in international law and that the core of our discipline is somehow under threat'.[7] The pessimistic lamentations of many commentators decrying the war on terror's deleterious effect on international law, should, therefore, been seen in the context of this near perennial state of crises.

Ethics

For thousands of years thinkers have struggled with the ethics of war. The just war tradition is the most obvious manifestation of this historical predisposition and while the famous dictum 'war is hell' may well be an appropriate depiction of the realities of war and the limitations of ethical warfare, the search to contrive and implement the criteria of the just war tradition continues to the present day. The war on terror has been regularly criticised through the application of the just war criteria, both in terms of its initiation and conduct, and the dominant consensus appears to be that the endeavour has largely failed to adhere to these ethical guidelines.

Nonetheless, the utility of the just war theory, and the application of ethical judgements on war, has been called into question given the ease with which the intervening powers were able to justify their actions as 'just'. The primary architects of the war on terror continue to assert that while the fabled weapons of mass destruction did not materialise in Iraq and the conflict in Afghanistan has been more prolonged than envisaged, the war on terror still constitutes a just war. Indicatively, in 2004 Tony Blair stated, 'I can apologise for the information that turned out to be wrong, but I can't, sincerely at least, apologise for removing Saddam. The world is a better place with Saddam in prison not in power'.[8] The moral virtue of the intervention, therefore, remains compelling and, according to Blair, continues to constitute a sufficient justification for the intervention even though the other rationale advanced have been proved to have been flawed. The problem exposed here, of course, is the subjective nature of morality and ethics; while many reject Blair's moral justifications this contestation is not, in essence, resolvable given that it constitutes a clash between two different moral claims. The ethical justifications made by the US-led coalition, therefore, highlight the ease with which ethical claims can be made. As James Connelly and Don Carrick argue, however, the ethical claims made can be at least criticised and exposed as weak; 'moral reasoning', they argue, 'cannot be reduced to rules, tick boxes or codes' (p. 44). Moral contestation, therefore, may not culminate in a binding ruling to which all must adhere, but this does not mean the result is a neutral stand-off. While Bush and Blair's administrations may continue to articulate their ethical claims, this resilience is in effect negated by the fact that these claims are rejected by the majority of observers. Connelly and Carrick rightly note, 'reliance on law and its forms of reasoning narrowly conceived can never be sufficient' and thus our assessment of a particular use of force cannot be solely based on legality, hence moral contestation is inevitable. Given the extent to which the legality of many of the acts committed during the war on terror are themselves sources of keen dispute, moral judgements may well be a more useful means of determining legitimacy.

Conclusion

Coker, lamenting the methods employed during the war on terror, cautioned, 'if terrorism threatens us directly it can also make us so fearful that we destroy the liberal values we believe in'.[9] This echoes Nietzsche's famous axiom, 'He who fights with monsters might take care lest he thereby become a monster'. The war on terror, initiated to protect the West – if not the world – from the apocalyptic threat ostensibly posed by al Qaeda, and global terrorism more generally, has, it seems, been counter-productive. States have implemented often draconian domestic legislation to fight terrorism which has curtailed civil liberties, initiated foreign interventions which have catalysed an upsurge in global terrorism, diminished the legal architecture of the international system, and engaged in myriad acts which have gravely offended moral sensibilities throughout the world.

In the face of the mounting evidence that the war on terror has been a profound failure one can easily despair at the future of the international system. The contributors to this book, however, have avoided this, preferring to articulate, to varying degrees, prescriptions that may chart a way forward. Crises, in themselves, do not necessarily signal the imminent demise of a particular system or structure and the coming of a new dark age, but rather can highlight the pressing need for substantial change and act as the catalysts for this change; World War II being an obvious example. History is replete with instances of revolution, both literal and figurative; instances when constructive change occurs suddenly spearheading a new era of progress. The chapters in this book reflect a general consensus that the present system has reached the limits of its applicability. The new warfare, the anachronisms within international law and the changed contours of universal ethics have been dramatically highlighted by the war on terror and while we may forever lament the destruction and loss of life that accompanied this misadventure, the lasting legacy may well be a new and improved set of global institutions, norms and laws.

Notes

2 Terrorism, security and international law

1 The main non-UN sponsored treaties in force are: Convention on Offences and Certain Other Acts Committed on Board Aircraft (Tokyo Convention) 1963; Convention for the Suppression of Unlawful Seizure of Aircraft (Hague Convention) 1970; Convention for the Suppression of Unlawful Acts against the Safety of Civil Aviation (Montreal Convention) 1971; Convention on the Physical Protection of Nuclear Material (Vienna Convention) 1980; Protocol on the Suppression of Unlawful Acts of Violence at Airports Serving International Civil Aviation (Montreal Protocol) 1988; Convention for the Suppression of Unlawful Acts against the Safety of Fixed Platforms Located on the Continental Shelf (Rome Convention) 1988. The main UN sponsored treaties are the Convention on the Prevention and Punishment of Crimes against Internationally Protected Persons, including Diplomatic Agents 1973; International Convention against the Taking of Hostages 1979; International Convention for the Suppression of Terrorist Bombing 1997; International Convention for the Suppression of the Financing of Terrorism 1999; International Convention for the Suppression of Acts of Nuclear Terrorism 2005.

2 For academic support see W.M. Reisman, 'In Defense of World Public Order', *American Journal of International Law* 95/833, 2001 where he states that 'the ambition, scope, and intended fallout of the acts of September 11 make them an aggression, initially targeting the United States but aimed, through these and subsequent acts, at destroying the social and economic structures and values of a system of world public order, along with the international law that sustains it. Not just the United States, but all peoples who value freedom and human rights have been forced into a war of self-defense'.

3 See Article 5, Third Geneva Convention Relative to the Treatment of Prisoners of War 1949; Art. 51 Geneva Protocol I Additional to the Geneva Conventions of 12 August 1949, and Relating to the Protection of Victims of International Armed Conflicts, 1977.

4 Art. 75, Additional Protocol I 1977; Common Article 3 to all Geneva Conventions of 1949.

5 On terrorist trials see generally D. Moeckli, *Human Rights and Non-Discrimination in the 'War on Terror'*, Oxford: Oxford University Press, 2008, pp. 128–62.

6 For seminal discussion see D. Kretzmer, 'Targeted Killing of Suspected Terrorists: Extra-Judicial Executions or Legitimate Means of Defence?', *European Journal of International Law* 16/171, 2005.

7 T.J. Farer, 'Beyond the Charter Frame: Unilateralism or Condominium', *American Journal of International Law* 96/ 359, 2002 at 364.

8 GA Res. 49/60, 9 Dec. 1994.

9 SC Res. 1368, 12 Sept. 2001.

10 Art.8 of the International Law Commission's Articles on the Responsibility of States for Internationally Wrongful Acts 2001, which reads: 'The conduct of a person or a group of persons shall be considered an act of a State under international law if the person or group of persons is in fact acting on the instructions of, or under the directions or control of, the State in carrying out the conduct'.

11 The 1970 GA Declaration on Friendly Relations in interpreting the principle of the non use of force states that 'every state has the duty to refrain from organizing, instigating assisting or participating in acts of civil strife or terrorist acts in another State or acquiescing in organized activities within its territory directed towards the commission of such acts, when the acts referred to . . . involve a threat or use of force'. The same Declaration when interpreting the principle of non-intervention states that 'no State shall organize, assist, foment, finance, incite or tolerate subversive, terrorist or armed activities directed towards the violent overthrow of the regime of another State, or interfere in the civil strife of another state'. GA Declaration on Principles of International Law concerning Friendly Relations and Cooperation among States in accordance with the Charter of the UN, GA Res. 2625, 24 Oct. 1970.

12 Arts. 49–54 Articles on State Responsibility 2001.

13 For example see Art. 51(2) Additional Protocol I of 1977, which prohibits 'acts of violence, the primary purpose of which is to spread terror among the civilian population'.

14 See Art. 4 International Covenant on Civil and Political Rights 1966. Human rights law, to the extent it has not been derogated from or qualified by international humanitarian law, continues to apply during armed conflict.

15 Judgment of the Nuremberg Military Tribunal, *American Journal of International Law* 41/172, 1947.

16 See Art. 40 of the Articles on State Responsibility 2001.

17 GA Res. 60/1, 24 Oct. 2005, which in part states: 'We are prepared to take collective action, in a timely and decisive manner, through the Security Council, in accordance with the UN Charter, including Chapter VII, on a case by case basis in co-operation with relevant regional organisations as appropriate, should peaceful means be inadequate and national authorities manifestly fail to protect their populations from genocide, war crimes, ethnic cleansing and crimes against humanity'.

18 Art. 1(c) of the Montreal Convention for the Suppression of Unlawful Acts Against the Safety of Civil Aviation, 1971.

19 B. Saul, *Defining Terrorism in International Law*, Oxford: Oxford University Press, 2006, pp. 134–5.

20 Ibid.,135.

21 Starting with SC Res. 1267, 15 Oct. 1999.

22 Starting with SC Res. 1373, 28 Sept. 2001.

23 SC Res. 748, 31 March 1992.

24 Article 25 provides: 'The Members of the United Nations agree to accept and carry out the decisions of the Security Council in accordance with the present Charter'.

25 Art. 103 of the UN Charter provides: 'In the event of a conflict between the obligations of Members of the United Nations under the present Charter and their obligations under any other international agreement, their obligations under the present Charter shall prevail'. In a judgment on provisional measures the International Court of Justice accepted that the combined effect of Articles 25 and 103 of the Charter meant that the obligations imposed on states by Resolution 748 prevailed over obligations in the Montreal Convention – *Lockerbie Cases*, 1992 ICJ Rep. 126.

26 F. Megret, 'Justice in Times of Violence', *European Journal of International Law* 14/327, 2003 at 327.

27 A. Bianchi, 'Assessing the Effectiveness of the UN Security Council's Anti-Terrorism Measures: The Quest for Legitimacy and Cohesion', *European Journal of International Law* 17/881, 2006 at 903–910; B. Fassbender, 'Targeted Sanctions Imposed by

the UN Security Council and Due Process Rights: A Study Commissioned by the UN Office of Legal Affairs and Follow-Up Action by the United Nations', *International Organisations Law Review* 3/437, 2006.

28 SC Res. 1730, 19 Dec. 2006.
29 SC Res. 1822, 30 June 2008.
30 *Reparation for Injuries Suffered in the Service of the United Nations*, 1949 ICJ Rep. 174.
31 Art 2(a) of the 1999 OIC Convention on Combating International Terrorism excludes from being terrorism – 'peoples struggle including armed struggle against foreign occupation, aggression, colonialism, hegemony, aimed at liberation and self-determination in accordance with international law'. The OIC has 56 member states.
32 See for example GA Res. 3034, 18 Dec. 1972.
33 Art. 2(1)(b).
34 Art. 2 Draft Comprehensive Convention 2005 UN Doc. A/59/894 (2005). For an earlier version see P.J. van Krieken, *Terrorism and the International Legal Order*, The Hague: TMC Asser Press, 2002, p. 290.
35 J. Friedrichs, 'Defining the International Public Enemy: The Political Struggle Behind the Legal Debate on International Terrorism', *Leiden Journal of International Law* 19/69, 2006 at 74–7.
36 Debates in the General Assembly's 6th Committee, 6 October 2009 (UN Press Release, GA/L/3362).
37 Friedrichs, op. cit., p. 80.
38 Ibid., 84.
39 Ibid., 84–5.
40 SC Res 1566, 8 Oct. 2004.
41 Friedrichs, op. cit., p. 70.
42 See also Saul's elements of a definition, op. cit., pp. 57–66.
43 GA Res. 49/60, 9 Dec. 1994.
44 Saul calls it a political not legal agreement – op. cit., p. 213.
45 International Bar Association, *International Terrorism: Legal Challenges and Responses*, New York: Transnational Publishers, 2003, p. 129.
46 Ibid., 136.
47 Van Krieken, op. cit., p. 65.
48 Ibid., 143.
49 www.un.org/sc/ctc
50 GA Res. 60/288, 9 Sept. 2006.
51 GA Res. 61/40, 18 Dec. 2006.
52 See N. Quenivet, 'You are the Weakest Link and We Will Help You! The Comprehensive Strategy of the United Nations to Fight Terrorism', *Journal of Conflict and Security Law* 11/317, 2006 at 389. See also the High Level Panel's Report, *A More Secure World: Our Shared Responsibility* (2004), para. 148(a).
53 Quenivet, op. cit., 390–1.
54 1970 Hague Convention (hijacking), 1971 Montreal Convention (acts against aircraft), 1973 Protected Persons Convention, 1979 Hostages Convention, 1988 Rome Convention (maritime navigation), and 1988 Rome Protocol (fixed platforms).
55 Saul, op. cit., p. 182.
56 Rome Statute on the International Criminal Court 1998, arts. 12–13.
57 Ibid., art. 17.
58 SC Res. 1757, 30 May 2007.
59 See for example SC Res. 579, 18 Dec. 1985; SC Res. 638, 31 July 1989.
60 SC Res. 1438, 14 Oct. 2002 (Bali); SC Res. 1530, 11 March 2004 (Madrid); SC Res. 1611, 7 July 2005 (London).
61 SC Res. 748, 31 March 1992.
62 SC Res. 1044, 31 Jan. 1996.

63 SC Res. 1636, 31 Oct. 2005.
64 SC Res. 1267, 15 Oct. 1999. See also SC Res. 1333, 19 Dec. 2000; SC Res. 1390, 16 Jan. 2002; SC Res. 1735, 22 Dec. 2006.
65 SC Res. 1566, 8 Oct. 2004. See also SC Res. 1540, 28 April 2004, which deals with the link between terrorism and WMD. States are obliged to stop non-state actors acquiring, manufacturing, possessing, transporting, transferring, or using nuclear, chemical or biological weapons 'in particular for terrorist purposes'. A supervisory committee was established.
66 UN Doc. 2007/775, 31 Dec. 2007.
67 See also the decision of the Human Rights Committee in *Sayadi and Vinck v Belgium* (2009) 16 IHRR 16. For discussion see H. Keller and A. Fischer, 'The UN Anti-terror Sanctions Regime under Pressure', *Human Rights Law Review* 9/257, 2009.
68 *Kadi and the Al Barakaat International Foundation* v *Council of the European Union*, Judgment of the Grand Chamber of the European Court of Justice, 3 Sept. 2008.
69 *R (Al-Jedda) v Secretary of State for Defence* [2007] UKHL 58.
70 Ibid., Lord Bingham, paras. 2 and 27.
71 Ibid., Lord Bingham, para. 39.
72 Ibid., Lord Carswell, para. 136.
73 Ibid., Lord Carswell, para. 130.
74 Saul, op. cit., p. 46.
75 C.A. Ward, 'Building Capacity to Combat International Terrorism: The Role of the United Nations Security Council', *Journal of Conflict and Security Law* 8/289, 2003.
76 SC Res. 1373, 28 Sept. 2001; SC Res. 1624, 14 Sept. 2005.
77 Available at http://www.un.org/sc/ctc/pdf/CTED_ED_briefing_to_MS_1209.pdf
78 UN Doc. S/2009/620, 3 Dec. 2009, 48–50.
79 M. Happold, 'Security Council Resolution 1373 and the Constitution of the United Nations', *Leiden Journal of International Law* 16/593, 2003. But see S. Talmon, 'The Security Council as World Legislature', *American Journal of International Law* 99/175, 2005.
80 See Art. 42 of the UN Charter. For the development of this option see N.D. White and O. Ulgen, 'The Security Council and the Decentralized Military Option: Constitutionality and Function', *Netherlands International Law Review* 44/378, 1997.
81 12 Sept. 2001.
82 E.P.J. Myjer and N.D. White, 'The Twin Towers: an Unlimited Right to Self-Defence', *Journal of Conflict and Security Law* 7/5, 2002.
83 SC Res. 1701, 11 Aug. 2006.
84 SC Res. 1860, 8 Jan. 2009.
85 But see the International Court's narrower view in *Legal Consequences of the Construction of a Wall in the Occupied Palestinian Territories*, 2004 ICJ Rep. paras. 138–41.
86 Even judicial precedents are notoriously hard to delineate – see K.N. Llwelleyn, *The Common Law Tradition*, Boston: Little, Brown, 1960, pp. 75–92.
87 M.E. O'Connell, 'Evidence of Terror', *Journal of Conflict and Security Law* 7/19, 2002.
88 Prime Minister Tony Blair, for example, declared: 'We will see this struggle through to the end and to the victory that would mark the victory not of revenge but of justice over the evil of terrorism', HC Deb. 8 Oct. 2001, Col. 814.
89 C. Henderson, 'The Bush Doctrine: From Theory to Practice', *Journal of Conflict and Security Law* 9/3, 2004.
90 IBA, 25; K. Trapp, 'Back to Basics: Necessity, Proportionality, and the Right of Self-Defence Against Non-State Terrorist Actors', *International and Comparative Law Quarterly* 56/141, 2007 at 146–7.
91 SC Res. 1386, 20 Dec. 2001; SC Res. 1510, 13 Oct. 2003.
92 International Bar Association, op. cit., p. 24.

93 See the UK Attorney General's opinion in *International and Comparative Law Quarterly* 52/811, 2003.
94 See N.D. White, 'The Will and Authority of the Security Council After Iraq', *Leiden Journal of International Law* 17/645, 2004 at 660 citing President Bush's statement that 'we don't really need the United Nations' approval to act . . . when it comes to our security'.
95 International Bar Association, op. cit., p. 58.
96 E.J. Flynn, 'The Security Council's Counter-Terrorism Committee and Human Rights', *Human Rights Law Review* 7/371, 2007.
97 SC Res. 1593, 31 March 2005.
98 S. von Schorlemer, 'Human Rights: Substantive and Institutional Implications of the War Against Terrorism', *European Journal of International Law* 14/265, 2003 at 271.

3 Al Qaeda and networked international insurgency

1 D. Omand, 'Countering International Terrorism: The Use of Strategy', *Survival* 47/7, 2005, p. 108.
2 J.P. Sullivan and R.J. Bunker, 'Multilateral Counter-Insurgency Networks' in R.J. Bunker (ed.) *Networks, Terrorism and Global Insurgency*, Abingdon: Routledge, 2005, p. 194.
3 See D. Kilcullen, 'Countering Global Insurgency', *Journal of Strategic Studies* 28/4, 2005, p. 603; B. O'Neill, *Insurgency and Terrorism: Inside Modern Revolutionary Warfare*, Washington DC: Brassey's, 1990, p. 13; I. Beckett, 'The Future of Insurgency', *Small Wars and Insurgencies* 16/1, 2005, p. 24.
4 For example see W. Laqueuer, *The New Terrorism: Fanaticism and the Arms of Mass Destruction*, Oxford: Oxford University Press, 1999.
5 For an insight into the debate see P. Neumann, *Old and New Terrorism*, Cambridge: Polity, 2009 and A. Field, 'The "New Terrorism": Revolution or Evolution?', *Political Studies Review* 7/2, 2009, pp. 195–207.
6 I. Beckett, *Modern Insurgencies and Counter-Insurgencies: Guerrillas and Their Opponents Since 1750*, London: Routledge, 2001, p. vii; J.A. Lynn, 'Patterns of Insurgency and Counter-Insurgency', *Military Review* July/August, 2005, p. 24.
7 T.X. Hammes, 'Countering Evolved Insurgency Networks', *Military Review*, July/August, 2006, p. 20.
8 A transcript of the declaration, announced as a means of establishing the 'World Front for Jihad Against the Jews and Crusaders', can be found in F. Halliday, *Two Hours That Shook the World – September 11, 2001: Causes and Consequences*, London: Saqi Books, 2002, Appendix 1, pp. 217–19.
9 T.X. Hammes, *The Sling and the Stone: On War in the Twenty-First Century*, St Paul, MN: Zenith Press, 2006, p. 140.
10 M. Sageman, *Understanding Terror Networks*, Philadelphia, PA: University of Pennsylvania Press, 2004, p. 18.
11 F. Gerges, *The Far Enemy: Why Jihad Went Global*, Cambridge: Cambridge University Press, 2005, p. 12.
12 Ibid, 24.
13 D. Kilcullen, 'Counter-Insurgency *Redux*', *Survival* 48/4, 2006, p. 117.
14 R. Smith, *The Utility of Force: The Art of War in the Modern World*, London: Penguin, 2006, p. 328.
15 To follow the series of exchanges begin with Hoffman's review of Sageman's book: 'The Myth of Grass-Roots Terrorism', *Foreign Affairs* 87/3, 2008, pp. 133–38; and then see Sageman's response 'The Reality of Grass-Roots Terrorism', 87/4, 2008, pp. 165–66.

16 K.L. Fishel, 'Challenging the Hegemon: Al Qaeda's Elevation of Asymmetric Insurgent Warfare on to the Global Arena' in Bunker (ed.), *Networks, Terrorism and Global Insurgency*, p. 122.

17 Sageman, *Understanding Terror Networks*, 48.

18 Kilcullen, 'Countering Global Insurgency', 598.

19 Ibid., 600.

20 For accounts of the interconnectivity of Islamist cells around the world see R. Gunaratna, *Inside Al Qaeda: Global Network of Terror*, New York: Columbia University Press, 2002, and L. Vidino, *Al Qaeda in Europe: The New Battleground of International Jihad*, New York: Prometheus Books, 2006.

21 B. Reed, 'A Social Network Approach to Understanding an Insurgency', *Parameters*, 37/2, 2007, p. 26.

22 Some good examples of the growing academic literature on the impact of globalisation on political violence include A. Kurth Cronin, 'Behind the Curve: Globalization and International Terrorism', *International Security* 27/3, 2002–03, pp. 30–58; and F.B Adamson, 'Globalisation, Transnational Political Mobilisation and Networks of Violence', *Cambridge Review of International Affairs* 18/1, 2005, pp. 31–49.

23 S. Sloan in Bunker (ed.), *Networks, Terrorism and Global Insurgency*, p. xxii.

24 R.M. Cassidy, *Counter-Insurgency and the Global War on Terror: Military Culture and Irregular War*, Westport, CT: Praeger, 2006, p. 11.

25 J. Sullivan and R. Bunker, 'Multilateral Counter-Insurgency Networks', in Bunker (ed.), *Networks, Terrorism and Global Insurgency*, pp. 196–97.

26 M.C. Fowler, *Amateur Soldiers, Global Wars: Insurgency and Modern Conflict*, Westport, CT: Praeger, 2005, p. 16.

27 R.M. Cassidy, 'Feeding Bread to the Luddites: The Radical Fundamentalist Islamic Revolution in Guerrilla Warfare', *Small Wars and Insurgencies* 16/3, 2005, p. 335.

28 A.N. Awan, 'Radicalisation on the Internet? The Virtual Propagation of Jihadist Media and its Effects', *Royal United Services Institute Journal* 152/3, 2007, p. 76.

29 Ibid., 76–77.

30 T. Hammes, *The Sling and the Stone*, 196.

31 R. Scruton, *The West and the Rest: Globalization and the Terrorist Threat*, London: Continuum, 2002, pp. 131–32 & 127.

32 D. Kilcullen, 'Countering Global Insurgency', p. 605.

33 P. Rich, 'Al Qaeda and the Radical Islamic Challenge to Western Strategy', *Small Wars and Insurgencies* 14/1, 2003, p. 39.

34 J. Mackinlay, 'Is UK Doctrine Relevant to Global Insurgency?', *Royal United Services Institute Journal* 152/2, 2007, p. 34.

35 For two of the best texts to emerge from the 'classical' era see R. Thompson, *Defeating Communist Insurgency*, St Petersburg, FL: Hailer Publishing, 2005 [1966], and D. Galula, *Counter-Insurgency Warfare: Theory and Practice*, Westport, CT: Praeger, 2006 [1964].

36 P. Wilkinson, *Terrorism Versus Democracy: The Liberal State Response*, 2nd edn, Abingdon: Routledge, 2006, p. xv.

37 Omand, 'Countering International Terrorism', p. 113.

38 For an indictment of American post-war planning in Iraq see P. Galbraith, *The End of Iraq: How American Incompetence Created a War Without End*, London: Pocket Books, 2006, and D. L. Phillips, *Losing Iraq: Inside the Post-War Reconstruction Fiasco*, New York: Basic Books, 2006.

39 B. Obama,'Remarks made by the President in address to the nation on the way forward in Afghanistan and Pakistan', 1 December 2009, http://www.whitehouse.gov/the-press-office/remarks-president-address-nation-way-forward-afghanistan-and-pakistan

40 B. Riedel, 'Al Qaeda Strikes Back', *Foreign Affairs* 86/3, 2007, p. 24.

41 Smith, *The Utility of Force*, p. 305.

4 Ethical and legal reasoning about war in a time of terror

1 G. Lucas, '"Methodological Anarchy": Arguing about Preventative War', in R. Wertheimer (ed.) *Empowering our Military Conscience*, Farnham: Ashgate, 2010, p. 43.
2 G.M. Reichberg, H. Syse, & E. Begbe (eds) *The Ethics of War: Classical and Contemporary Readings*, Malden, Mass: Blackwell, 2006, p. 47.
3 Lucas, 'Methodological Anarchy', pp. 41 & 53–54.
4 The term 'legalist paradigm was first coined by Michael Walzer.
5 A third category, justice after the war (*jus post bello*), has been neglected for some time, although recent events have produced a revival of interest in it. We return to this later in the text.
6 Briefly, the Athenians maintained what we now call a realist view of war – the more powerful side will always prevail. If the Melians didn't surrender, the Atheians said, their town would be sacked and all the male inhabitants slaughtered. The Melians, who were more concerned with justice, understandably complained that this was a most unjust way of looking at the situation and refused to surrender. The Athenians then carried out their threat (but ultimately lost the Pelaponnesian War itself – justice of the poetic kind, perhaps?).
7 In fact, the religious and secular origins of JWT cannot be separated from each other – the eminent JWT scholar James Turner Johnson calls JWT 'in its origins a synthesis of Graeco-Roman and Catholic values' (see J.T. Johnson, *The Quest for Peace: Three Moral Traditions in Western Cultural History*, Princeton: Princeton University Press, 1987, p. 45) – and the respective sets of values have continued to feed into each other right up to the present day.
8 One long-lasting consequence was that, for many centuries following the Reformation, reigning English monarchs bore the title 'Defender of the Faith'.
9 B. Orend, *The Morality of War*, Peterborough, Ontario: Broadview Press, 2006, p. 14.
10 Ibid., p. 17.
11 *Jus in bello*, by contrast, continued to be developed and refined, but we are not here greatly concerned with this aspect of the subject.
12 It is still a matter of debate as to whether the notorious Nazi-imposed Nuremberg Laws of the 1930s, which marginalised Jews and others and ultimately 'legitimised' the Holocaust, should have been unquestionably obeyed simply because they were laws, as most legal positivists did and still do maintain, or whether such laws were *morally so abhorrent* that their very status as laws was suspect in the first place.
13 D. Kennedy, *Of War and Law*, Princeton: Princeton University Press, 2006, p. 116.
14 Lucas, 'Methodological Anarchy', pp. 35–6.
15 M. Walzer, 'The Triumph of Just War Theory (and the Dangers of Success)', in R. Wertheimer (ed.) *Empowering our Military Conscience*, Farnham: Ashgate, 2010, p. 20.
16 Ibid., pp. 15 & 18.
17 General M. Krulak, 'The Strategic Corporal: Leadership in the Three Block War', *Marines Magazine*, January 1999.
18 G.E.M. Anscombe, 'The Justice of the Present War Examined', in *Ethics, Religion and Politics*, Oxford: Blackwell, 1981, pp. 78–9.
19 Walzer, 'The Triumph of Just War Theory', pp. 23–4.
20 See Chapter 9 of M. Walzer, *Just and Unjust Wars; A Moral Argument with Historical Illustrations*, New York: Basic Books, 1991.
21 T.M. Scanlon, 'The Proper Role of Intention in Military Decision Making', in R. Wertheimer (ed.) *Empowering our Military Conscience*, Farnham: Ashgate, 2010, p. 77.
22 Ibid., p. 79.

23 C.P.M. Waters, 'War Law and its Intersections', in D. Whetham (ed.) *Ethics, Law and Military Operations*, London: Palgrave, 2010, p. 104.
24 Ibid., p. 104.

5 Law and war in the global war on terror

1 This research essay is based in part on research conducted for a project funded by the Arts and Humanities Research Council's Beyond Text Programme, 'Pictures of Peace and Justice' (AHRC Award AH/H015566/1). The work also draws on research funded by the Economic and Social Research Council's New Security Challenges Programme (ESRC Award RES-223-25-0063 'Shifting Securities: Television News Cultures Before and After Iraq 2003' with Dr. M.L. Gillespie, Professor A.J.W. Gow and Dr. A.D. Hoskins).
2 James Gow, *Defending the West*, Cambridge: Polity, 2005. We owe particular thanks to Marilyn Croser, whose work was important in helping find the way around some of the issues involved in this study that led some readers to chastise it for being carelessly anti-American and others to see parts of the work as representing the Bush Administration. We should like to assert that neither of those judgements applies and we have endeavoured to avoid anything in the piece that could suggest anything of the kind.
3 See Rachel Kerr and Eirin Mobekk, *Peace and Justice: Seeking Accountability After War*, Cambridge: Polity, 2007.
4 Lord Bingham, formerly the most senior judge in the United Kingdom, suggested that these practices were wholly unacceptable and should be subject to an explicit and complete ban. *The Daily Telegraph*, 6 July 2009.
5 Amos Guiora, 'Targeted Killing as Active Self-Defense', *Case Western Research Journal International Law* 36, 2004, p. 319, http://articles.cnn.com/2001-08-01/world/mideast_1_nablus-hamas-israeli-attack-nablus-attack?_s=PM:WORLD
6 L. Feinstein and A.M. Slaughter, 'A Duty to Prevent', *Foreign Affairs* 83/1, 2004.
7 *Arutz Sheva*, 2 November 2005 available at http://www.israelnationalnews.com/news.php3?id+92336
8 Asaf Zussman and Noam Zussman, *Targeted Killings: Evaluating the Effectiveness of a Counterterrorism Policy*, Discussion Paper, Jerusalem: Bank of Israel, 2005.
9 *The Wall Street Journal*, 14 July 2009.
10 Interview with Emma Brown, Barrister, Chambers of David Etherington QC,18 Red Lion Court and Advisor to ARRC SHAPE. London, 20 October 2010.
11 Philip Bobbitt, *Terror and Consent*, New York: Knopff, 2009, pp. 250–85. John Yoo's books are particularly important in this context. Yoo was Deputy Assistant Attorney General in the Office of Legal Counsel at the US Department of Justice from 2001 to 2003. He was intimately involved in, and responsible for, much of the legal advice to President Bush, which proved to be controversial as both the 'grey area' and the Administration's preferences were negotiated. His *War by Other Means* sets out the justification for various legal interpretations and policies adopted, while the later *Crisis and Command* offers commentary on how the Obama Administration failed to find alternatives on issues, and made mistakes in its attempt to change others. Yoo, *The Powers of War and Peace: The Constitution and Foreign Affairs After 9/11*, Chicago: University Of Chicago Press, 2005; *War By Other Means: An Insider's Account of the War on Terror*, New York: Atlantic Monthly Press, 2006; *Crisis and Command: The History of Executive Power from George Washington to George W. Bush*, New York: Kaplan, 2009.
12 For an administration perspective on the detentions and the legal issues surrounding them, see John B. Bellinger, III, 'Legal Issues in the War on Terrorism', London School of Economics, 31 October 2006.
13 Charles Garraway, *The 'War on Terror': Do the Rules Need Changing?* Chatham House International Law Briefing Paper 6/2, 2006.

14 Marilyn Croser, *To What Extent do the Obama Administration's Policies on the Detention of Terrorist Suspects at Guantanamo Bay Represent a Departure from the Previous Administration's Policies?* Unpublished Paper, 2010.

15 It is noticeable, in this context, that the US approach – which privileges US citizens and US territory, in terms of protection while allowing almost unrestrained scope of official action, subject to legal sanction, regarding aliens – contrasts sharply with the situation in the European Union. There, in the case of the UK, anti-terrorist provisions passed by Parliament, which meant the detention as a security provision (not as criminal suspects) of ten non-citizens at the Belmarsh high security prison, were ruled to be contrary to the European Convention on Human Rights on the grounds that such discrimination in terms of human rights between citizens and non-citizens was not tenable. As a result, the ten were released but immediately detained once more under a new law that affected both citizens and non-citizens equally, but could not result in incarceration, merely restrictions on movement and monitoring – including the application of electronic tagging.

16 Philippe Sands, *Lawless World: America and the Making and Breaking of Global Rules*, London: Penguin, 2005.

17 *Getting Away With Torture?* Human Rights Watch, Washington DC, 2005.

18 *The Wall Street Journal*, 18 May 2009.

19 Milena Michalski and James Gow, *War, Image and Legitimacy: Viewing Contemporary Conflict*, London: Routledge, 2007, Chapter 6.

20 While the abuse incidents were probably not part of any formal policy, there were suspicions that an informal regime intended to 'soften' prisoners for interrogation, at least, had been in effect, with its tone set by General Geoffrey Miller. General Janice Karpinsky, the officer commanding the Abu Ghraib prison, has alleged that there was such a regime, although she was party to it, but suspended when the abuse was revealed, and that the personnel serving under her were being used as scapegoats to protect more senior figures. It is possible that she has General Miller in mind, who ironically, given the suspicions, was the senior officer placed in charge of removing abuse.

21 *The Washington Post*, 2 November 2005.

22 The six were: attention grab, attention slap, belly slap, long time standing, cold cell and water boarding. *ABC World News Tonight*, 18 November 2005, available via http://abcnews.go.com/WNT at 1 December 2005.

23 *ABC Good Morning America*, 29 November 2005 available via http://www.abcnews.go.com/GMA at 1 December 2005.

24 Uniform Extradition and Rendition Act (1980).

25 *Convention Against Torture and Other Cruel, Inhuman Or Degrading Treatment or Punishment* (1975) Art. 2.

26 Croser, *The Obama Administration's Policies*.

27 Darius Rejali, *Torture and Democracy*, Princeton: Princeton University Press, 2005.

28 Much of Chapters 5 and 7 of the official investigation into the September 11 attacks was based on intelligence analysis derived from interrogations of Sheikh Khalid Mohammed (KSM), *The 9/11 Commission Report: Final Report of the National Commission on Terrorist Attacks Upon the United States*, Authorized Edition, New York: Norton, 2004. KSM was subjected to waterboarding 183 times in five sessions. *The Daily Telegraph*, 20 April 2009; *Fox News*, 28 April 2009.

29 *ABC World News Tonight*, 18 November 2005, available via http://abcnews.go.com/WNT at 1 December 2005.

30 Elspeth Guild, 'The Judicialisation of Armed Conflict: Transforming the Twenty-first Century', in Jef Huysmans, Andrew Dobson and Raia Prokhovnik, *The Politics of Protection: Sites of Insecurity and Political Agency*, Abingdon: Routledge, 2006, pp. 122–35.

31 Gerry Simpson, *War, Law and Crime: War Crimes Trials and the Reinvention of International Law*, Cambridge: Polity, 2007.

32 Gow, *Defending the West*.

33 Adam Roberts, 'The End of Occupation'; Lawrence Freedman, *The Transformation of Strategic Affairs*, Adelphi Paper 379, Oxford: OUP and IISS, 2006.

34 In 1993, Scots Guardsmen James Fisher and Mark Wright were sentenced to life for the murder of an 18-year-old in Belfast. In 1990, paratrooper Lee Clegg was convicted of murder after shooting two teenage joyriders in Belfast. 'Solder charged with murder of Iraqi: Trooper to be tried in a civilian court after CO dismissed charge', *The Guardian*, 8 September 2004.

35 Rachel Kerr, *The Military on Trial: The British Army in Iraq*, Nijmegen: Wolf Legal Publishers, 2008.

36 For a fuller exposition of these cases, see ibid.

37 'Accused officer is just a "scapegoat" say colleagues', *The Independent*, 21 July 2005.

38 Presiding Judge, Mr Justice McKinnon, Transcript, 13 February 2007.

39 Opening statement, Mr. Julian Bevan for the prosecution, R v. Payne and others, Transcript, 19 September 2007, pp. 97–8.

40 Ibid., p. 100.

41 Ibid., p. 112.

42 Ibid., p. 91.

43 Ibid., pp. 91–2.

44 Ibid., p. 91.

45 Transcript, 23 October 2006, cited in REDRESS, 'UK Army in Iraq', p. 6.

46 Opening statement, Mr. Julian Bevan, p. 91.

47 Transcript, 2 February 2007, cited in REDRESS, 'UK Army in Iraq', p. 6.

48 Opening statement, Mr. Julian Bevan, p. 46.

49 Payne was the only convict in the case, in all probability, because he had no alternative to pleading guilty, as he was captured on film abusing the detainees. The film was also shown at the inquiry into Baha Mousa's death. The Baha Mousa Public Inquiry Day 103, 10 June 2010, Afternoon Session.

50 R. v. Payne, Transcript, 13 February 2007, p. 4958.

51 Brig Anthony Paphiti, Head of Army Prosecutions, 2003–5, *Panorama*, BBC1, 27 September 2010.

52 R. v. Payne, p. 4964.

53 Ibid., p. 4964.

54 Ibid., p. 4965.

55 Ibid., p. 4966.

56 Opening statement, Mr. Julian Bevan, pp. 21–2.

57 R. v. Payne, p. 4975.

58 Philip Shiner, Public Interest Lawyers, *Panorama*, BBC1, 27 September 2010.

59 Focus group research with senior military professionals explored the tensions involved in situations such as this and the merits of Court Martial and civilian trials, including the sense that media coverage of related material revealed the media 'hang the military out to dry', but that the changing social and political context of armed conflicts makes it increasingly in the interest of the armed forces to be seen as being purer than pure. FG 13 (in particular) and FGs 4,5, and 11 Strand C Shifting Securities www.mediatingsecurity.com.

60 'A bloody epitaph to Blair's war', *The Independent*, 17 June 2007.

61 R. v. Payne, p. 4964.

62 REDRESS, 'UK Army in Iraq'; Phil Shiner, 'A cover-up of torture, racism and complicity in war crimes', *The Guardian*, 23 April 2007.

63 *Panorama*, BBC1, 27 September 2010.

64 General Andrew Ritchie, cited in Forster, 'Breaking the Covenant', p. 1046.

65 Paul Kennedy and George J. Andreopoulos, 'The Laws of War: Some Concluding Reflections', in Michael Howard, George J. Andreopoulos and Mark R. Shulman, *The*

Laws of War: Constraints on Warfare in the Western World, New Haven: Yale University Press, 1994, p. 215.

6 Security, discretion and international law

1 M. Smith, 'Humanitarian Intervention: An Overview of Ethical Issues', *Ethics and International Affairs* 12/1, 1998, 66.
2 Independent International Commission on Kosovo, *Kosovo Report*, Oxford: Oxford University Press, 2000, p. 196.
3 N. White, 'The Will and Authority of the Security Council after Iraq', *Leiden Journal of International Law* 17/4, 2004, pp. 645–72. Also see Danish Institute of International Affairs, *Humanitarian Intervention: Legal and Political Aspects*, Copenhagen: Danish Institute of International Affairs, 1999, 62; and D. Armstrong, T. Farrell and H. Lambert, *International Law and International Relations*, Cambridge: Cambridge University Press, 2007, pp. 132–33.
4 S. Chesterman, *Just War of Just Peace?* Oxford: Oxford University Press, 2002, p. 5.
5 Ibid., p. 165.
6 A. Cassese, *International Law*, Oxford: Oxford University Press, 2005, p. 347.
7 T. Landman, *Studying Human Rights*, London: Routledge, 2005, p. 14.
8 M. Fitzmaurice, 'The Practical Working of the Law of Treaties' in M. Evans (ed.) *International Law*, Oxford: Oxford University Press, 2006, pp. 205–06.
9 L. Henkin, 'Compliance with International Law in an Inter-State System', *Academie de droit international, Recueil des cours 1989*, Dordrecht: Martinus Nijhoff, 1990, p. 250.
10 A. Hurrell, 'Legitimacy and the Use of Force: Can the Circle be Squared?' in D. Armstrong, T. Farrell and B. Maiguashca (eds.) *Force and Legitimacy in World Politics*, Cambridge: Cambridge University Press, 2005, pp. 20–21.
11 A. Bellamy, *Just Wars: From Cicero to Iraq*, London: Polity, 2006, p. 93.
12 Hurrell, 'Legitimacy and the Use of Force', p. 18
13 G. Simpson, *Great Powers and Outlaw States*, Cambridge: Cambridge University Press, 2004, p. 68.
14 H. Bull, *The Anarchical Society: A Study of Order in World Politics*, Basingstoke: Palgrave Macmillan and New York: Columbia University Press, 2002, p. 53.
15 White, 'The Will and Authority of the Security Council after Iraq', p. 666.
16 H. Briggs, 'Power Politics and International Organization', *American Journal of International Law* 39/4, 1945, p. 670.
17 D. Bourantonis, *The History and Politics of Security Council Reform*, London: Routledge, 2007, p. 6
18 J. Mertus, *The United Nations and Human Rights*, London: Routledge, 2009, p. 98.
19 Bourantonis, *The History and Politics of Security Council Reform*, p. 7.
20 White, 'The Will and Authority of the Security Council after Iraq', p. 646.
21 V. Gowlland-Debbas, 'Functions of the United Nations Security Council in the International Legal System' in M. Byers (ed.) *The Role of International Law in International Politics*, Oxford: Oxford University Press, 2000, p. 304.
22 *Prosecutor v. Tadic* (1996) Judgement, ICTY Case No. IT-94-1-AR72 (Jurisdiction), Appeals Chamber, 1995, 35 ILM 35, p. 43.
23 T. Franck, 'Interpretation and Change in the Law of Humanitarian Intervention' in J.L. Holzgrefe and R.O. Keohane (ed.) *Humanitarian Intervention: Ethical, Legal and Political Dilemmas,* Cambridge: Cambridge University Press, 2005, p. 206.
24 United States Department of State, 'The Crisis in Darfur: Secretary Colin Powell, Testimony before the Senate Foreign Relations Committee', 9 September 2004. http://www.state.gov/secretary/former/powell/remarks/36042.htm, date accessed 11 October 2007.

25 Y. Dinstein, *War, Aggression and Self-Defence*, Cambridge: Cambridge University Press, 2005, pp. 72–73.
26 W. Schabas, *Genocide in International Law: The Crimes of Crimes,* Cambridge: Cambridge University Press, 2000, p. 495.
27 Bourantonis, *The History and Politics of Security Council Reform*, p. 35.
28 International Commission on Intervention and State Sovereignty, *The Responsibility to Protect*, Ottawa: International Development Research Centre, 2001, p. 49.
29 Ibid., p. 51.
30 J. Welsh, 'Taking Consequences Seriously: Objections to Humanitarian Intervention' in J. Welsh (ed.) *Humanitarian Intervention and International Relations*, Oxford: Oxford University Press, 2006, pp. 185 & 210.
31 A. Bellamy, 'Whither the Responsibility to Protect? Humanitarian Intervention and the 2005 World Summit', *Ethics and International Affairs* 20/2, 2006, p. 155.
32 J. Bolton, 'Letter to President Ping', 30 August 2005. http://www.responsibilitytoprotect.org/files/US_Boltonletter_R2P_30Aug05[1].pdf. [accessed June 2010].
33 UK (2009) 'Statement by the Permanent Representative of the United Kingdom to the UN', 23 July 2009. http://www.responsibilitytoprotect.org/UK_ENG(1).pdf [accessed June 2010], p. 3.
34 China (2009) 'Statement by the Permanent Representative of China to the UN', 23 July 2009, http://responsibilitytoprotect.org/Statement%20by%20Ambassador%20Liu%20Zhenmin.pdf [accessed June 2010], p. 2.
35 House of Commons (2000) Foreign Affairs – Fourth Report, No. HC 28-1 of 7 June 2000, para 1138, www.publications.parliament.uk/pa/cm199900/cmselect/cmfaff/28/2802.htm, [accessed 12 June 2010].
36 Independent International Commission on Kosovo, *Kosovo Report*, p. 4.
37 G. Robertson, *Crimes Against Humanity*, London: Penguin, 2002, p. 382.
38 A. Bellamy, *Kosovo and International Society*, Hampshire: Palgrave Macmillan, 2002, p. 212.
39 R. Cooper, 'The New Liberal Imperialism', *The Observer*, 7 April 2002; M. Glennon, 'The New Interventionism', *Foreign Affairs* 78/3, 1999, 2; A. Linklater, 'The Good International Citizen and the Crisis in Kosovo', in A. Schnabel and R. Thakur (ed.) *Kosovo and the Challenge of Humanitarian Intervention*, New York: United Nations University Press, 2000; T. Nardin, 'The Moral Basis for Humanitarian Intervention' in A. Lang (ed.) *Just Intervention,* Washington D.C: Georgetown University Press, 2003; Robertson, *Crimes Against Humanity*.
40 J. Pattison, 'Humanitarian Intervention and International Law: The Moral Importance of an Intervener's Legal Status', *Critical Review of International Social and Political Philosophy* 10/3, 2007, 307–08; M. Reisman, 'Unilateral Action and the Transformations of the World Constitutive Process: The Special Problem of Humanitarian Intervention', *European Journal of International Law* 11/1, 2000, pp. 13–15.
41 Glennon, 'The New Interventionism', p. 2.
42 White, 'The Will and Authority of the Security Council after Iraq', p. 646.
43 J.M. Coicaud, 'Iraq and the Social Logic of International Security', in R. Thakur and W.P.S. Sidhu (ed.) *The Iraq Crisis and World Order: Structural, Institutional and Normative Challenges*, New York: United Nations University Press, 2006, p. 426.
44 Ibid., pp. 427–28.
45 D. Malone, *The International Struggle Over Iraq: Politics in the UN Security Council 1980–2005*, Oxford: Oxford University Press, 2006, p. 192.
46 R. Thakur and W.P.S. Sidhu, 'Iraq's Challenge to World Order', in R. Thakur and W.P.S. Sidhu (ed.) *The Iraq Crisis and World Order: Structural, Institutional and Normative Challenges*, New York: United Nations University Press, 2006, pp. 3–4.
47 E. Voeten, 'Delegation and the Nature of Security Council Authority', in B. Cronin and I. Hurd (ed.) *The UN Security Council and the Politics of International Authority*, London: Routledge, 2008, p. 52.

48 R. Caplan, 'Humanitarian Intervention: Which Way Forward?', *Ethics and International Affairs*, 14, 2000, p. 31.

49 White, 'The Will and Authority of the Security Council after Iraq', p. 660.

50 A.M. Slaughter, 'Good Reasons for Going Around the UN', *The New York Times*, 18 March 2003.

51 T. Blair, 'Full Text – Tony Blair's Speech', *The Guardian*, 5 March 2004, http://www.guardian.co.uk/politics/2004/mar/05/iraq.iraq, [accessed 2 May 2009].

52 Caplan, 'Humanitarian Intervention', p. 34.

53 UN High Level Panel on Threats, Challenges and Change, *A More Secure World: Our Shared Responsibility*, 2 December 2004, http://www.un.org/secureworld/report.pdf, [accessed 2 May 2009], p. 63.

54 R. Falk, 'Legality and Legitimacy: The Quest for Principled Flexibility and Restraint' in D. Armstrong, T. Farrell and B. Maiguashca (ed.) *Force and Legitimacy in World Politics*, Cambridge: Cambridge University Press, 2005, p. 42.

55 Malone, *The International Struggle Over Iraq*, p. 247.

56 I. Hurd, *After Anarchy: Legitimacy and Power in the United Nations Security Council*, Princeton, NJ: Princeton University Press, 2007, p. 130.

57 N. Rodley and B. Cali, 'Kosovo Revisited: Humanitarian Intervention on the Fault Lines of International Law', *Human Rights Law Review* 7/2, 2007, p. 278.

58 C. Guicherd, 'International Law and the War in Kosovo', *Survival* 41/2, 1999, 19–34; B. Simma, 'NATO, the UN and the Use of Force', *European Journal of International Law* 10/1, 1999, pp. 1–22.

59 M. Burton, 'Legalising the Sublegal', *The Georgetown Law Journal* 85, 1996, p. 430.

60 UN High Level Panel on Threats, Challenges and Change, *A More Secure World: Our Shared Responsibility*, p. 63; J. Whitman, 'Humanitarian Intervention in an Era of Pre-emptive Self-defence', *Security Dialogue* 36/3, 2005, pp. 259–74.

61 M. Newman, *Humanitarian Intervention: Confronting the Contradictions*, Hurst & Co: London, 2009, p. 81.

62 International Commission on Intervention and State Sovereignty, *The Responsibility to Protect*, p. 3.

63 Independent International Commission on Kosovo, *Kosovo Report*, p. 186.

64 A. Watts, 'The Importance of International Law' in M. Byers (ed.) *The Role of International Law in International Politics*, Oxford: Oxford University Press, 2001, p. 10.

65 Cassese, *International Law*, p. 339.

66 Malone, *The International Struggle Over Iraq*, p. 204.

67 J. Mueller, 'Force, Legitimacy, Success, and Iraq' in D. Armstrong, T. Farrell and B. Maiguashca (ed.) *Force and Legitimacy in World Politics*, Cambridge: Cambridge University Press, 2005, p. 123.

68 M. Byers, 'Not Yet Havoc: Geopolitical Change and the International Rules on Military Force' in D. Armstrong, T. Farrell and B. Maiguashca (ed.) *Force and Legitimacy in World Politics*, Cambridge: Cambridge University Press, 2005, p. 51.

69 F. Berman, 'Moral Versus Legal Legitimacy' in C. Reed and D. Ryall (ed.) *The Price of Peace*, Cambridge: Cambridge University Press, 2007, p. 61.

7 The human security agenda after 9/11

1 Aidan Hehir, 'Humanitarian Intervention: Past, Present and Future', *Political Studies Review*, 6/3, September 2008, p. 355.

2 Roland Paris, 'Saving liberal peacebuilding', *Review of International Studies*, 36/2, April 2010, pp. 337–367.

3 David Held et al, *Global Transformations: Politics, Economics & Culture*, Cambridge: Polity Press, 1999.

4 *Charter of the United Nations*, Chapter I, Purposes and Principles, available at: http://www.un.org

5 Nicholas J. Wheeler, *Saving Strangers: Humanitarian Intervention in International Society*, Oxford: Oxford University Press, 2002, p. 187.

6 S. Neil MacFarlane, *Intervention in Contemporary World Politics*, Adelphi Paper 350, Oxford and New York: Oxford University Press for International Institute of Strategic Studies, 2002, p. 66.

7 See SCR 940; http://daccess-dds-ny.un.org/doc/UNDOC/GEN/N94/312/22/PDF/N9431222.pdf?OpenElement

8 Thomas Franck, 'The Emerging Right to Democratic Governance', *American Journal of International Law*, 86, 1992, p. 59.

9 Eirin Mobekk, 'The Missing Ingredient: Justice in the International Intervention in Haiti', *International Relations*, 15/1, April 2000, pp. 30–40.

10 Alex Bellamy, 'Motives, Outcomes, Intent and the Legitimacy of Humanitarian Intervention', *Journal of Military Ethics*, 3/3, 2004, pp. 216–232.

11 Tony Blair, Chicago speech, 1999; Available at: http://www.pbs.org/newshour/bb/international/jan-june99/blair_doctrine4-23.html, accessed 25.10.2010.

12 Ian Brownlie, *Principles of Public International Law*, Oxford: Oxford University Press, 2008, p. 743.

13 Michael Glennon, *Limits of Law, Prerogatives of Power: Interventionism after Kosovo*, New York and Basingstoke: Palgrave Macmillan, 2001, p. 166.

14 Brownlie, *Principles*, p. 744.

15 Interfax, Moscow, in English, 1200 GMT, 31 January 1992, *BBC Summary of World Broadcasts*, SU/1294 C1/2, 3 February 1992.

16 Robert Jackson, *The Global Covenant: Human Conduct in a World of States*, Oxford: Oxford University Press, 2000.

17 Genadii Syosiev, 'Rossiia i Kitai ne namereny sozdat' blok', *Segodnia*, 3 June 1999.

18 Thomas M. Franck, 'Legal Interpretation and Change', in: J.L. Holzgrefe and Robert O.Keohane, *Humanitarian Intervention: Ethical, Legal and Political Dilemmas*, Cambridge: Cambridge University Press, 2003, p. 225.

19 Franck, 'The Emerging Right', p. 59.

20 Allen Buchanan, *Justice, Legitimacy and Self-Determination: Moral Foundations for International Law*, Oxford: Oxford University Press, 2004, p. 55.

21 International Commission on Intervention and State Sovereignty (ICISS), *The Responsibility to Protect: Report of the International Commission on Intervention and State Sovereignty*, Ottawa: International Development Research Centre, 2001, p. XI.

22 ICISS, pp. XI–XII.

23 ICISS, pp. XII–XIII.

24 Fernando Teson cited in Wheeler, *Saving Strangers*, p. 41.

25 Mary Kaldor, *Human Security: Reflections on Globalization and Intervention*, Cambridge: Polity Press, 2007.

26 Cited in Ramesh Thakur, *The United Nations, Peace and Security: From Collective Security to Responsibility to Protect*, Cambridge: Cambridge University Press, 2008, p. 232.

27 Nicholas Kerton-Johnson 'Justifying the Use of Force in a Post-9/11 World: Striving for Hierarchy in International Society', *International Affairs*, 84/5, 2008.

28 Matthew Evangelista, *Law, Ethics and the War on Terror*, Cambridge: Polity Press, 2008, p. 21.

29 Kenneth Roth, 'Setting the Standard: Justifying Humanitarian Intervention', Interventionism', *Harvard International Review* 26/1, 2004, p. 2.

30 Lord Goldsmith, *Secret Memo: Legal Advice on Further Action Without UNSC Authorisation*, 7 March 2003 (emphasis added).

31 Fernando R.Teson, 'Of Tyrants and Empires', *Ethics and International Affairs* 19/2, 2005.

32 Wheeler, *Saving Strangers*, p. 40.

33 Ken Roth, *War in Iraq: Not a Humanitarian Intervention*, available at: http://hrw.org/wr2k4/3.htm, accessed 05/02/2006.

34 Richard Falk, 'Legality and Legitimacy: The Quest for Principled Flexibility and Restraint', *Review of International Studies* 31, 2005, pp. 41–42.

35 Gareth Evans, 'When is it Right to Fight?', *Survival* 46/3, 2004, p. 71.

36 For example, James Kurth, 2006.

37 'Blair terror speech in full', 05.03.2004; available at: http://news.bbc.co.uk/1/hi/3536131.stm, accessed 20.10.2010.

38 Simon Chesterman, *You, the People: the UN, Transitional Administration, and Statebuilding*, Oxford: Oxford University Press, 2005, p. 5.

39 Kaldor, *New and Old Wars*, p. 191.

40 Michael Walzer, *Just and Unjust Wars: A Moral Argument with Historical Illustrations*, New York: Basic Books, 2000, pp. 121–122.

41 Alex Bellamy, 'The Responsibilities of Victory', *Review of International Studies*, 34/4, October 2010, pp. 601–627.

42 Franck, 'The Emerging Right'.

43 Richard Ponzio and Christopher Freeman, 'Conclusion: Rethinking Statebuilding in Afghanistan', *International Peacekeeping*, 14/1, 2007, p. 183.

44 http://www.un.org/peace/peacebuilding

45 Andrew Rathmell, 'Planning post-conflict reconstruction in Iraq: what can we learn?' *International Affairs* 81/5, October 2005, p. 1015.

46 Edward Newman, 'Critical Human Security Studies', *Review of International Studies*, 36/1, January 2010, p. 92.

47 Robert O, Keohane,'Political Authority after Intervention: Gradations in Sovereignty', in J.L. Holzgrefe and Robert O.Keohane (eds.), *Humanitarian Intervention: Ethical, Legal and Political Dilemmas*, Cambridge: Cambridge University Press, 2003, p. 279.

48 Nicholas J. Wheeler, 'Humanitarian Intervention after September 11 2001', in Anthony F. Lang Jr. (ed.), *Just Intervention*, Washington D.C.: Georgetown University Press, 2003, pp. 192–216.

49 High Level Panel Report, 2004, p. 4.

50 *A More Secure World: our Shared Responsibility, Report of the United Nations Secretary General High-Level Panel on Threats, Challenges and Change* (Foreign and Commonwealth Office, February 2005).

51 Kaldor, *Human Security*, p. 183.

52 Louise Arbour, 'The Responsibility to Protect as a Duty of Care and Practice', *Review of International Studies* 34/3, July 2008, p. 448.

53 Bellamy, 'The Responsibilities', p. 623.

54 Newman, 'Critical Human Security Studies', p. 79.

55 Paul Roe, 'The "Value" of Positive Security', *Review of International Studies*, 34/4, October 2008, p. 793.

56 Georg Nolte, 'Limits of the Security Council's Powers', *The Role of Law in International Politics: Essays in International Relations and International Law*, Oxford: Oxford University Press, 2000, p. 326.

8 Principles of pre-emption

1 I am grateful to those connected with the International Peace and Security Programme and the War Crimes Research Group at King's College London for discussion and comment on this piece, particularly Rein Mullerson and Rachel Kerr.

2 *The National Security Strategy of the United States* (2002), http://www.whitehouse. gov/nsc/nss.html (accessed 18 February 2008).

3 The US air action against Libya in April 1986 provoked some criticism, reflected in discussion of this issue, *inter alia*, by M. N. Leich, 'Contemporary Practice of the United States Relating to International Law', *American Journal of International Law* 80/3, 1986, pp. 612–44, especially pp. 631–36 and pp. 641–44 (the latter in the context of US domestic constraints on the use of force).

4 J. Gow, *Defending the West*, Cambridge: Polity, 2005.

5 I regard the failure to address the 'armed attack' question as a key weakness in my own work, just cited.

6 E. Wilmshurst, *Principles of International Law on the Use of Force by States in Self-Defence*, ILP WP 05/01, Chatham House, 2005, www.chathamhouse.org.uk/law

7 I am grateful to Elizabeth Wilmshurst for allowing my use of the scenarios, which she drew originally.

8 The present section draws on Gow, *Defending the West*, pp. 126–9.

9 'Statement of the Heads of State and Government of the United Nations Security Council', UN doc. S/23500, 31 January 1992.

10 M. Byers, *War Law*, London: Atlantic Books, 2005.

11 R. Müllerson, '*Jus ad Bellum*: Plus ça Change (le Monde) Plus C'est La Même Chose (Le Droit)?', *Journal of Conflict and Security Law* 7/2, 2002.

12 *Case Concerning Oil Platforms*, Merits, 6 November 2003, www.icj-cij.org (accessed 18 February 2008).

13 For example, the distinction between military and non-military enforcement measures in Articles 41 and 42 of the UN Charter marks this distinction in conventional thought.

14 This issue is discussed, for example, by T. Gazzini, *The Changing Rules on the Use of Force in International Law*, Manchester: Manchester University Press, 2005, p. 129 n.71.

15 'Letter to the Security Council', UN Doc. S/1998/789, 21 August 1998.

16 UN Security Council Resolution 1193, 28 August 1998.

17 I am grateful to Vesselin Popovski of the United Nations University in Tokyo for prompting awareness, in this respect originally and for sharing a draft manuscript; see also David Armstrong, Theo Farrell and Helene Lambert, *International Law and International Relations*, Cambridge: Cambridge University Press, 2007, pp. 180–1.

18 Müllerson, '*Jus ad Bellum*'; T. Franck, 'Terrorism and the Right to Self-Defense', *American Journal of International Law* 95, 2001; and R. Wedgwood, 'Responding to Terrorism: the Strikes Against Bin Laden', *Yale Journal of International Law* 24, 1999. It should be noted also that the verb in the clause is present conditional – if it occurs – and not, as I have heard many people falsely declare, a past tense conditionality, where an action must have occurred before action in self-defence is permissible. The distinction here is that hostile action, constitutive of causing destruction or damage, need not be completed before the right to self-defence is available. It is particularly important to note this in the context, for example, of anticipatory, or pre-emptive, self-defence.

19 Antonio Cassese suggests the need for a 'consistent pattern' of hostile action before the right to self-defence can be invoked, regarding non-state actors; 'The International Community's "Legal" Response to Terrorism', *International and Comparative Law Quarterly* 38, 1989, p. 596.

20 For discussion of constructing weapons, see M. Michalski and J. Gow, *War, Image and Legitimacy: Viewing Contemporary Conflict*, London: Routledge, 2007, pp. 7–9.

21 In this sense, non-military forceful measures are treated in Article 41 of the UN Charter, while military force is treated in Article 42, confirming a clear distinction between categories, in that context. Until 1973, economic measures were never regarded as constituting an 'armed attack'. However, the US interpreted the 1973 oil embargo as

'tantamount' to an 'armed attack', setting a precedent that has not, as yet, been followed. I am grateful, in particular, to Rein Mullerson for information and clarification on this point.

22 Article 1, *Convention on the Prohibition of the Development, Production, Stockpiling and Use Of Chemical Weapons and on Their Destruction.*

23 Article 8 xvii and xviii, *Rome Statute of the International Criminal Court.*

24 'Legality of the Threat or Use of Nuclear Weapons', Advisory Opinion, International Court of Justice, 8 July 1996.

9 Who killed the right to self-defence?

1 T.M. Franck, 'Who Killed Article 2(4)? Or: Changing Norms Governing the Use of Force by States', *The American Journal of International Law* 64/4, 1970, p. 810.

2 Report of the Secretary-General's High-level Panel on Threats, Challenges and Change (2004) accessed at http://www.un.org/secureworld, 10 July 2008. The Charter of the United Nations will be referred to herein as the 'Charter'.

3 Franck, 'Who Killed Article 2(4)?'.

4 See L. Henkin, *How Nations Behave: Law and Foreign Policy* (2nd ed), New York: Columbia University Press, 1979, Chapter 7.

5 There are other exceptions within the Charter, but self-defence is by far the most widely used exception to the illegality of the use of armed force.

6 The International Court of Justice will also be referred to herein as either the 'ICJ' or 'the Court'.

7 A.C. Arend and R.J. Beck, *International Law and the Use of Force*, London: Routledge, 1993, p. 29.

8 Ibid.

9 Ibid., p. 34.

10 Ibid.

11 Franck, 'Who Killed Article 2(4)?', p. 812.

12 Ibid.

13 United States Department of State, *Foreign Relations of the United States Diplomatic Papers, 1944. General*, Volume I (1944), 718,725, accessed at http://digital.library.wisc.edu/1711.dl/FRUS.FRUS1944v01, 24 July 2008.

14 T.M. Franck, *Recourse to Force: State Action against Threats and Armed Attacks*, Cambridge: Cambridge University Press, 2002, p. 45.

15 Ibid.

16 Franck, 'Who Killed Article 2(4)?'

17 I. Brownlie, *International Law and the Use of Force by States*, Oxford: Oxford University Press, 1963, p. 270.

18 Ibid. Originally, it was even placed in Chapter VIII of the Charter dealing with regional arrangements until a Soviet proposal to move it to Chapter VII was accepted on the basis that otherwise it might be construed too narrowly. Ibid., p. 274.

19 Ibid.

20 Y. Dinstein, *War, Aggression and Self-Defence* (4th ed.), Cambridge: Cambridge University Press, 2005, p. 180.

21 Ibid.

22 This is the approach taken by the Court in the *Case Concerning Military Activities and Paramilitary Activities in and Against Nicaragua (Nicaragua v. United States of America)*, I.C.J. Reports 14 (1986).

23 This requirement has generally been considered to be procedural in scope, and non-compliance would otherwise not affect the legal right to self-defence. C. Gray, *International Law and the Use of Force* (2nd ed.), Oxford: Oxford University Press,

2004, pp. 101–4. Also see D.W. Grieg, 'Self-Defence and the Security Council: What Does Article 51 Require? *International and Comparative Law Quarterly* 40/2, 1991, pp. 366–402. In *Nicaragua* the Court suggested that compliance with this requirement would be indicative as to whether a state actually believed it was acting in self-defence.

24 Gray, *International Law and the Use of Force*, pp. 98–9.
25 Ibid.
26 See J. Kammerhofer, 'Uncertainties of the Law on Self-Defence in the United States Charter', *Netherlands Yearbook of International Law*, 35, 2004, pp. 149–53.
27 S.A. Alexandrov, *Self-Defence against the Use of Force in International Law*, The Hague: Kluwer Law International, 1996, pp. 96–7.
28 United States Department of State, *Foreign Relations of the United States: Diplomatic Papers, 1945. Genera: the United Nations*, Volume I (1945), 665–670, accessed at http://digital.library.wisc.edu/1711.dl/FRUS.FRUS1945v01.
29 Ibid.
30 Ibid.
31 A. Randelzhofer, 'Article 51' in B. Simma, H. Mosler, A. Paulus and E. Chaitidou (eds), *The Charter of the United Nations: A Commentary*, Oxford: Oxford University Press, 2002, p. 790. Kammerhofer (2004) has an extensive discussion on this and other elements of the 'black-hole theory' at pp. 149–53.
32 A. Cassese, *International Law* (2nd ed.), Oxford: Oxford University Press, 2005, pp. 357–63.
33 Brownlie, *International Law and the Use of Force by States*, pp. 239–50.
34 Note that both the Covenant of the League of Nations and the Kellogg-Briand Pact only attempted to restrict recourse to war. They were both silent on the lawfulness of uses of force that were less than war, such as reprisals (Arend and Beck, *International Law and the Use of Force*, pp. 20–4). Uses of force that were less than war would presumably still have been covered by the *Caroline* principles. They are also largely silent on the matter of self-defence.
35 Cassese, *International Law*, pp. 357–63.
36 See Arend and Beck, *International Law and the Use of Force*, Chapter 5; and Rachel Bzostek, *Why Not Preempt? Security, Law, Norms and Anticipatory Military Activities*, Hampshire: Ashgate, 2008, chapter 6.
37 Brownlie, *International Law and the Use of Force by States*, pp. 239–50.
38 Ibid.
39 Gray, *International Law and the Use of Force*; Dinstein, *War, Aggression and Self-Defence*.
40 See supra note 14.
41 Gray, *International Law and the Use of Force*, p. 121.
42 R. Ago, 'Addendum to Eighth Report on State Responsibility', *International Law Commission*, 1980, para 106.
43 O. Schachter, *International Law in Theory and Practice*, Dordrecht: Kluwer Academic Publishers, 1991, p. 152.
44 See supra note 15.
45 Schachter, *International Law in Theory and Practice*, p. 153.
46 Ago, 'Addendum to Eighth Report on State Responsibility', para 120. This overlaps with the requirement of proportionality.
47 Schachter, *International Law in Theory and Practice*, pp. 153–54.
48 Ago, 'Addendum to Eighth Report on State Responsibility', para 120.
49 M. Byers, *War Law*, London: Atlantic Books, 2005, pp. 53–60.
50 Ibid.
51 Schachter, *International Law in Theory and Practice*, p. 153.
52 Ago, 'Addendum to Eighth Report on State Responsibility', p. 121.
53 Ibid.

54 Dinstein, *War, Aggression and Self-Defence*.
55 Ago, 'Addendum to Eighth Report on State Responsibility', para 122; Cassese, *International Law*, p. 373.
56 Gray, *International Law and the Use of Force*. This is also the approach taken by the ICJ.
57 Ago, 'Addendum to Eighth Report on State Responsibility', para 123.
58 Dinstein, *War, Aggression and Self-Defence*, p. 243.
59 *Nicaragua*, para 15.
60 Ibid., para 292.
61 Ibid., para 172.
62 Ibid., para 175.
63 Ibid., para 176.
64 Ibid.,paras 195 and 229.
65 Ibid., paras 195 and 230.
66 Ibid.
67 Ibid., para 249. See also J.L. Hargrove, 'The Nicaragua Judgment and the Future of the Law of Force and Self-Defence', *The American Journal of International Law* 81/1, 1987, p. 138.
68 Hargrove, 'The Nicaragua Judgment', p. 141.
69 *Nicaragua*, para 176.
70 Ibid., para 237. The Court found that, '[e]ven if the United States activities in question had been carried on in strict compliance with the canons of necessity and proportionality, they would not thereby become lawful'.
71 Ibid.
72 A. D'Amato, 'Trashing Customary International Law', *The American Journal of International Law* 81/1, 1987, pp. 101–05; T.M. Franck, 'Some Observations on the ICJ's Procedural and Substantive Innovations', *The American Journal of International Law* 81/1, 1987, pp. 116–21; Hargrove, 'The Nicaragua Judgment'; John Norton Moore, 'The Nicaragua Case and the Deterioration of World Order', *The American Journal of International Law* 81/1, 1987, pp. 151–59. It should be noted however that at least as many scholars agree with the Court's approach and consider it to reflect both the practice and statements of states. See for example Gray, *International Law and the Use of Force*, chapters 4 and 5.
73 *Nicaragua*, para 191.
74 Ibid.
75 Ibid. The actual phrase used in the Declaration is 'war of aggression' which itself seems to imply an even higher standard, i.e. that the action be the equivalent of a 'war'.
76 Ibid., para 192.
77 Ibid., para 195.
78 Ibid.
79 *Definition of Aggression*, Article 3, para (g) (emphasis added) accessed on 14 July 2008 at http://www.un-documents.net/a29r3314.htm. Referred to hereafter as *Definition*.
80 Ibid., Article 3. See also *Nicaragua, Schwebel dissent*, para 166.
81 Hargrove, 'The Nicaragua Judgment', p. 139, note 15.
82 *Definition*, Article 1. Article 4 of the Definition also makes it clear that the acts enumerated as aggression within the Definition are not an exhaustive list.
83 Judge Schwebel's discussion of the drafting history of the Definition adds further support to this point. *Nicaragua, Schwebel dissent*, para 162–167.
84 *Definition*, Article 3, paragraph (g).
85 *Declaration on Principles of International Law Concerning Friendly Relations and Cooperation among States*, Article 1, accessed on July15 at http://www1.umn.edu/humanrts/instree/principles1970.html.
86 *Nicaragua*, para 191.
87 *Definition*, Article 3.

88 *Nicaragua*, paras 186 and 202. Franck, 'Some Observations on the ICJ's Procedural and Substantive Innovations', 119; D'Amato, 'Trashing Customary International Law'. For a rule to constitute customary international law, it must be evidenced by state practice (states must usually behave the way as they say the law requires them to) and *opinio juris* (states must believe that the rule represents a legal obligation). Statements alone are not sufficient; evidence of state practice is required for a rule to be customary international law.

89 *Nicaragua*, para 195.

90 *Nicaragua, Schwebel dissent*, para 158–161.

91 J.A. Green, 'The Oil Platforms Case: An Error in Judgment?' *Journal of Conflict & Security Law* 9/3, 2004, p. 379.

92 Ibid.

93 Legality of the Threat or Use of Nuclear Weapons, Advisory Opinion, I.C.J. Reports 1996 226 (1996). (Referred to hereafter as *Nuclear Weapons*), para 1.

94 *Nuclear Weapons*, paras 38–41.

95 Ibid., paras 42 and 105.

96 Ibid., para 46.

97 However, the question of self-defence ended up not being relevant to the outcome of the case and the Court's language is largely *obiter dicta*. The real question in the case is whether the US violated a clause in a bilateral treaty with Iran.

98 Gray, *International Law and the Use of Force*, pp. 117–18.

99 Ibid.

100 Oil Platforms (Islamic Republic of Iran v. United States of America), I.C.J. Reports 2003 161 (2003) (referred to hereafter as *Oil Platforms*), paras 50 and 69.

101 Ibid., paras 46 and 65.s

102 Ibid., paras 77–78.

103 Ibid., para 51. It is not completely clear whether the Court is analysing self-defence as a matter of customary international law or as part of Article 51. It seems to be equating the two in more than in *Nicaragua*.

104 Ibid., para 43.

105 W.H. Taft IV, 'Self-Defence and the Oil Platforms Decision', *Yale Journal of International Law* 29, 2004, pp. 295–306.

106 *Oil Platforms*, para 72. It also was not clear whether this was an evidentiary issue regarding identification of Iran as the attacker or some other part of the circumstances that made it inconclusive.

107 Green, 'The Oil Platforms Case', pp. 381–82.

108 N. Ochoa-Ruiz and E. Salamanca-Aguado, 'Exploring the Limits of International Law Relating to the Use of Force in Self-Defence', *The European Journal of International Law* 16/3, 2005, p. 514.

109 Legal Consequences of the Construction of a Wall in the Occupied Palestinian Territory, Advisory Opinion, I.C.J. Reports 2004 136 (2004) (referred to hereafter as *Wall opinion*), para 1.

110 Ibid., para 139.

111 Ibid.

112 *Wall opinion, Higgins dissent*, para 33; Security Council Resolution 1368 (2001) and Security Council Resolution 1373 (2001). See also C.J. Tams, 'Light Treatment of a Complex Problem: The Law of Self-Defence in the Wall Case', *The European Journal of International Law* 16/5, 2005, pp. 963–78.

113 Case Concerning Armed Activities on the Territory of the Congo (Democratic Republic of the Congo V. Uganda), No. 116 General List (2005) (referred to hereafter as *DRC v. Uganda*), paras 142, 144.

114 Ibid., para 147.

115 Ibid., para 146.

116 Ibid., para 143.

117 Ibid., para 145.
118 *DRC v. Uganda, Kooijmans separate opinion*, paras 26–28; *DRC v. Uganda, Simma separate opinion*, paras 10–12.
119 *Kooijmans separate opinion*, paras 26–29. See also K.N. Trapp, 'Back to Basics: Necessity, Proportionality, and The Right of Self-Defence against Non-State Terrorist Actors', *International and Comparative Law Quarterly* 56, 2007, pp. 141–56.
120 Ibid., para 31.

10 Computer network attacks, self-defence and international law

1 M. Landler & J. Markoff, 'Digital Fears Emerge after Data Siege in Estonia', New York Times, 29 May 2007 available at http://www.nytimes.com/2007/05/29/technology/29estonia.html, accessed 10 July 2010.
2 Ibid.
3 C. Joyner and C. Lotrionte, 'Information Warfare as International Coercion: Elements of a Legal Framework', *European Journal of International Law* 12(5), 2001, p. 826.
4 D. Kuehl, 'Information Operations, Information Warfare, and Computer Network Attacks. Their Relationship to National Security in the Information Age', in M. Schmitt and B. O'Donnell (eds) *Computer Network Attack and International Law*, Newport, Rhode Island: Naval War College, 2002, p. 41.
5 For a definition of cyberspace see Kuehl, 'Information Operations', in Schmitt and O'Donnell, op. cit., p. 39. Alternatively the term information environment (IE) has been used by D. Tubbs, P. Luzwick and W. Sharp Sr., 'Technology and Law: The Evolution of Digital Warfare', in M. Schmitt and B. O'Donnell (eds) *Computer Network Attack and International Law*, Newport, Rhode Island: Naval War College, 2002, p. 18.
6 D. Hollis, 'Why States Need an International Law for Information Operations', *Lewis & Clark Law Review* 11, 2007, p. 1030 and Kuehl, 'Information Operations', in Schmitt and O'Donnell, op. cit., p. 42.
7 S. Kanuck, 'Information Warfare: New Challenges for Public International Law', *Harvard International Law Journal* 37, 1996, pp. 281–282.
8 Ibid., p. 282.
9 R. Hanseman, 'The Realities and Legalities of Information Warfare', *The Air Force Law Review* 42, 1997, p. 177. For a detailed overview see B. O'Donnell and J. Kraska, 'Humanitarian Law: Developing International Rules for the Digital Battlefield', *Journal of Conflict and Security Law* 8(1), 2003, p. 135. Other authors, however, caution that the impact of technology and information on warfare might be overstated. See D. Betz, 'The More You Know, the Less You Understand: The Problem with Information Warfare', *The Journal of Strategic Studies* 29(3), 2006, pp. 506–508.
10 R. Hughes, 'A Treaty for Cyberspace', *International Affairs* 86(2), 2010, pp. 530–533.
11 J. Kelly III & L. Almann, 'eWMDs', *Policy Review* 152, 2008/2009, p. 39.
12 R. Barnett, 'A Different Kettle of Fish: Computer Network Attacks', in M. Schmitt and B. O'Donnell (eds) *Computer Network Attack and International Law*, Newport, Rhode Island: Naval War College, 2002, p. 22.
13 S. Brenner, '"At Light Speed": Attribution and Response to Cybercrime/Terrorism/Warfare', *Journal of Criminal Law & Criminology* 97(2), 2006/2007, p. 404.
14 E. Haslam, 'Information Warfare: Technological Changes and International Law', *Journal of Conflict and Security Law* 5(2), 2000, p. 157 as well as S. Shackelford, 'From Nuclear War to Net War: Analogizing Cyber Attacks in International Law', *Berkeley Journal of International Law* 27, 2009, p. 199. For a good overview see Kuehl, 'Information Operations', in Schmitt and O'Donnell, op. cit., pp. 36–47 and M. Schmitt, 'Computer Network Attack and the Use of Force in International Law:

Thoughts on a Normative Framework', *Columbia Journal of Transnational Law* 37, 1998/1999, pp. 890–893.

15 See for example the frequently cited US Joint Doctrine for Information Operations. Joint Chiefs of Staff, Joint Publication 3-13, Information Operations (2006), available at http://www.dtic.mil/doctrine/jel/new_pubs/jp3_13.pdf, accessed 24 August 2009.

16 Haslam (2000), p. 162.

17 This is the case with network-centric warfare. See Betz (2006), p. 508.

18 Kanuck (1996), p. 283.

19 Joint Chiefs of Staff, Joint Publication 3-13, Information Operations (2006), p. II–5.

20 Kuehl (2002), p. 44.

21 L. Greenberg, S. Goodman and K. Hoo, *Information Warfare and International Law*, Washington, D.C.: National Defense University Press, 1998, p. 1.

22 V. Antolin-Jenkins, 'Defining the Parameters of Cyberwar Operations: Looking for Law in all the Wrong Places ?', *Naval Law Review* 51, 2005, pp. 139–140.

23 Kelly III & Almann (2008/2009), p. 40.

24 Ibid.

25 Ibid.

26 M. Landler & J. Markoff, 'Digital Fears Emerge after Data Siege in Estonia', New York Times, 29 May 2007 available at http://www.nytimes.com/2007/05/29/technology/29estonia.html, accessed 30 August 2009.

27 Antolin-Jenkins (2005), p. 140.

28 Ibid.

29 Ibid., p. 141.

30 Brenner (2006/2007), p. 409.

31 Ibid.

32 Antolin-Jenkins (2005), p. 136. For a general overview of how the internet works see Antolin-Jenkins (2005), pp. 135–138 as well as Tubbs, Luzwick & Sharp Sr. (2002), pp. 9–12.

33 This possibility should not be excluded due to possibilities created by technological advancements.

34 Shackelford (2009), pp. 200–201.

35 Barnett (2002), p. 26.

36 Article 2(4) United Nations Charter.

37 A. Randelzhofer, 'Article 2(4)', in B. Simma et al (eds) *The Charter of the United Nations. A Commentary*, Oxford: Oxford University Press, 2002, pp. 117–118.

38 Joyner & Lotrionte (2001), p. 845.

39 D. Silver, 'Computer Network Attack as a Use of Force under Article 2(4) of the United Nations Charter', in M. Schmitt and B. O'Donnell (eds) *Computer Network Attack and International Law*, Newport, Rhode Island: Naval War College, 2002, p. 82.

40 Ibid.

41 Ibid. See also Antolin-Jenkins (2005), p. 155.

42 Quoted in Silver (2002), p. 86.

43 Silver (2002), p. 86.

44 Ibid., p. 82.

45 Joyner & Lotrionte (2001), p. 845.

46 Silver (2002), p. 84.

47 Ibid., pp. 92–93.

48 Joyner & Lotrionte (2001), p. 850.

49 Silver (2002), p. 91.

50 See for example Joyner & Lotrionte (2001), pp. 847–850.

51 Silver (2002), p. 85.

52 See generally Y. Dinstein, 'Computer Network Attacks and Self-Defence', in M. Schmitt and B. O'Donnell (eds) *Computer Network Attack and International*

Law, Newport, Rhode Island: Naval War College, 2002, pp. 99–119 and Joyner and Lotrionte, op. cit.

53 This also applies to other terms used in the UN Charter such as aggression and use of force. See Antolin-Jenkins (2005), pp. 150–151.

54 Controversy over this gravity requirement, however, continues. See C. Gray, *International Law and the Use of Force*, 3rd edn., Oxford: Oxford University Press, 2008, pp. 147–148.

55 Dinstein (2002), p. 100.

56 *Military and Paramilitary Activities in and against Nicaragua (Nicaragua v United States of America)*, ICJ Reports (1986) 14, para 191.

57 Joyner & Lotrionte (2001), p. 845.

58 Schmitt (1998/1999), p. 935.

59 Joyner & Lotrionte (2001), p. 855.

60 Ibid., p. 856.

61 Dinstein (2002), p. 105.

62 Joyner & Lotrionte (2001), p. 851.

63 Schmitt (1998/1999), p. 935, emphasis added.

64 Silver (2002), pp. 92–93.

65 Schmitt (1998/1999), p. 911.

66 Ibid.

67 Ibid., p. 912.

68 Ibid., p. 911.

69 In order to solve these problems, Schmitt advanced six criteria that are supposed to help determine whether a particular form of CNA resembles armed force or falls into the economic and political coercion category. See Schmitt (1998/1999), pp. 914–917.

70 *Military and Paramilitary Activities in and against Nicaragua (Nicaragua v United States of America)*, ICJ Reports (1986) 14, para 195. See also discussion in Gray (2008), pp. 130–132.

71 Gray (2008), p. 130.

72 Ibid.

73 The International Court of Justice avoided answering the question whether there could be an armed attack by non-state actors in the absence of state involvement. See *Armed Activities on the Territory of the Congo (DRC v Uganda)*, ICJ Reports (2005) 168 para 147. See also Gray (2008), p. 134.

74 Shackelford (2009), p. 208.

75 Dinstein (2002), p. 112.

76 Shackelford (2009), p. 208.

77 Brenner (2006/2007), p. 424.

78 Ibid., p. 425.

79 Ibid., p. 423.

80 See generally M. Schmitt, "Wired Warfare: Computer Network Attack and the Jus in Bello', in M. Schmitt and B. O'Donnell (eds) *Computer Network Attack and International Law*, Newport, Rhode Island: Naval War College, 2002, pp. 187–218; L. Doswald-Beck, 'Some Thoughts on Computer Network Attack and the International Law of Armed Conflict', in M. Schmitt and B. O'Donnell (eds) *Computer Network Attack and International Law*, Newport, Rhode Island: Naval War College, 2002, pp. 163–185; and Haslam, op. cit.

81 Situations in which conventional weapons and computer network attacks are used do not pose a definitional problem. See Doswald-Beck (2002), p. 165.

82 Article 2 of the Geneva Convention for the Amelioration of the Condition of the Wounded and Sick in Armed Forces in the Field.

83 Schmitt (2002), p. 190.

84 The ICRC commentary to the Geneva Conventions provides that an 'armed conflict' involves, 'any differences arising between two States and leading to the intervention

of members of the armed forces is an armed conflict within the meaning of article 2, even if one of the parties denies the existence of a state of war. It makes no difference how long the conflicts lasts, or how much slaughter takes place.' Quoted in Haslam (2000), p. 169.

85 Schmitt (2002), p. 192, emphasis in original.
86 Doswald-Beck (2002), p. 165.
87 Article 49 (1) of the Protocol Additional to the Geneva Conventions of 12 August 1949, and relating to the Protection of Victims of International Armed Conflicts (AP 1).
88 Schmitt (2002), p. 194.
89 Ibid.
90 Hollis (2007), p. 1043.
91 Schmitt (2002), p. 195.
92 Ibid., pp. 196–197.
93 Ibid., p. 195.
94 Hollis (2007), p. 1043.
95 Ibid., pp. 1043–1044.
96 Ibid. p. 1044.
97 O'Donnell & Kraska (2003), p. 134, 140.
98 A. Cebrowski, 'CNE and CNA in the Network-Centric Battlespace: Challenges for Operators and Lawyers', in M. Schmitt and B. O'Donnell (eds) *Computer Network Attack and International Law*, Newport, Rhode Island: Naval War College, 2002, . 6.
99 Haslam (2000), pp. 159–160.
100 Article 31 of the Vienna Convention on the Law of Treaties.
101 Antolin-Jenkins (2005), p. 173.
102 Hollis (2007), pp. 1045–1046.
103 O'Donnell & Kraska (2003), p. 134.
104 Antolin-Jenkins (2005), pp. 134–135.
105 Silver (2002), p. 78.
106 Greenberg, Goodman & Hoo (1998), p. 4.
107 Hollis (2007), pp. 1046–1047.
108 Greenberg, Goodman & Hoo (1998), p. 4.
109 See generally Hollis, op. cit. and D. Brown, 'A Proposal for an International Convention To Regulate the Use of Information Systems in Armed Conflict', *Harvard International Law Journal* 47(1), 2006, pp. 179–221.
110 One such attempt was made by Russia in June 2009 advancing proposals for a treaty to ban states from secretly embedding malicious codes. See J. Markoff & A. Kramer, 'U.S. and Russia Differ on a Treaty for Cyberspace', New York Times, 28 June, 2009, www. nytimes.com/2009/06/28/world/28cyber.html, accessed 28 June 2009. Since then, however, the US, who has been rejecting discussions on the matter, has somewhat relaxed its position by agreeing to talks in the UN framework. See J. Markoff & A. Kramer, 'In Shift, U.S. Talks to Russia on Internet Security', *New York Times*, 13 December 2009, http://www.nytimes.com/2009/12/13/science/13cyber.html, accessed 10 July 2010.
111 Hollis (2007), p. 1055.
112 Schmitt (1998/1999), p. 897.
113 Ibid.
114 O'Donnell & Kraska (2003), p. 147.
115 Hollis (2007), p. 1046.

11 Conclusion

1 P. Rogers, *Why We're Losing the War on Terror*, London: Polity, 2008, p. viii.
2 C. Coker, *Ethics and War in the 21st Century*, Abingdon: Routledge, 2008, p. 81.

3 M. Byers, 'The Shifting Foundations of International Law', *European Journal of International Law* 13/1, 2002, p. 35.

4 Sir A. Watts, 'The Importance of International Law' in M. Byers (ed.) *The Role of International Law in International Politics*, Oxford: Oxford University Press, 2001, p. 7.

5 B. Bowring, *The Degradation of the International Legal Order?: The Rehabilitation of Law and the Possibility of Politics*, Oxon: Routledge-Cavendish, 2008.

6 D. Armstrong & T. Farrell, 'Introduction', in D. Armstrong, T. Farrell & B. Maiguashca (eds) *Force and Legitimacy in World Politics*, Cambridge, Cambridge University Press, 2005, p. 10.

7 H. Charlesworth and D. Kennedy, 'Afterword', in A. Orford (ed.) *International Law and its Others*, Cambridge: Cambridge University Press, 2009, p. 405.

8 T. Blair, 'Speech to the Labour Party Conference', 28 September 2004 http://www.labour.org.uk/ac2004news?ux_news_id=ac04tb, date accessed 2 May 2009.

9 Coker, *Ethics and War in the 21st Century*, p. 174.

Bibliography

S. A. Alexandrov, *Self-Defence against the Use of Force in International Law*, The Hague: Kluwer Law International, 1996

A. C. Arend and R. J. Beck, *International Law and the Use of Force*, London: Routledge, 1993

D. Armstrong, T. Farrell and H. Lambert, *International Law and International Relations*, Cambridge: Cambridge University Press, 2007

D. Armstrong, T. Farrell and B. Maiguashca (eds), *Force and Legitimacy in World Politics*, Cambridge, Cambridge University Press, 2005

I. Beckett, *Modern Insurgencies and Counter-Insurgencies: Guerrillas and Their Opponents Since 1750*, London: Routledge, 2001

A. Bellamy, *Kosovo and International Society*, Hampshire: Palgrave Macmillan, 2002

A. Bellamy, *Just Wars: From Cicero to Iraq*, London: Polity, 2006

P. Bobbitt, *Terror and Consent*, New York: Knopff, 2009

D. Bourantonis, *The History and Politics of Security Council Reform*, London: Routledge, 2007

B. Bowring, *The Degradation of the International Legal Order?: The Rehabilitation of Law and the Possibility of Politics*, Oxon: Routledge-Cavendish, 2008

I. Brownlie, *International Law and the Use of Force by States*, Oxford: Oxford University Press, 1963

I. Brownlie, *Principles of Public International Law*, Oxford: Oxford University Press, 2008

A. Buchanan, *Justice, Legitimacy and Self-Determination: Moral Foundations for International Law*, Oxford: Oxford University Press, 2004

H. Bull, *The Anarchical Society: A Study of Order in World Politics*, Basingstoke and New York: Palgrave Macmillan, 2002

R. J. Bunker (ed.), *Networks, Terrorism and Global Insurgency*, Abingdon: Routledge, 2005

M. Byers (ed.), *The Role of International Law in International Politics*, Oxford: Oxford University Press, 2001

M. Byers, *War Law*, London: Atlantic Books, 2005

R. Bzostek, *Why Not Preempt? Security, Law, Norms and Anticipatory Military Activities*, Hampshire: Ashgate, 2008

A. Cassese, *International Law*, Oxford: Oxford University Press, 2005

R. M. Cassidy, *Counter-Insurgency and the Global War on Terror: Military Culture and Irregular War*, Westport, CT: Praeger, 2006

S. Chesterman, *Just War of Just Peace?* Oxford: Oxford University Press, 2002

S. Chesterman, *You, the People: the UN, Transitional Administration, and Statebuilding*, Oxford: Oxford University Press, 2005

C. Coker, *Ethics and War in the 21st Century*, Oxon: Routledge, 2008

B. Cronin and I. Hurd (eds), *The UN Security Council and the Politics of International Authority*, Abingdon: Routledge, 2008

Danish Institute of International Affairs, *Humanitarian Intervention: Legal and Political Aspects*, Copenhagen: Danish Institute of International Affairs, 1999

Y. Dinstein, *War, Aggression and Self-Defence*, Cambridge: Cambridge University Press, 2005

M. Evangelista, *Law, Ethics and the War on Terror*, Cambridge: Polity Press, 2008

T. M. Franck, *Recourse to Force: State Action against Threats and Armed Attacks*, Cambridge: Cambridge University Press, 2002

P. Galbraith, *The End of Iraq: How American Incompetence Created a War Without End*, London: Pocket Books, 2006

D. Galula, *Counter-Insurgency Warfare: Theory and Practice*, Westport, CT: Praeger, 2006

T. Gazzini, *The Changing Rules on the Use of Force in International Law*, Manchester: Manchester University Press, 2005

F. Gerges, *The Far Enemy: Why Jihad Went Global*, Cambridge: Cambridge University Press, 2005

M. Glennon, *Limits of Law, Prerogatives of Power: Interventionism after Kosovo*, New York and Basingstoke: Palgrave Macmillan, 2001

J. Gow, *Defending the West*, Cambridge: Polity, 2005

C. Gray, *International Law and the Use of Force*, Oxford: Oxford University Press, 2004

R. Gunaratna, *Inside Al Qaeda: Global Network of Terror*, New York: Columbia University Press, 2002

F. Halliday, *Two Hours That Shook the World – September 11, 2001: Causes and Consequences*, London: Saqi Books, 2002

D. Held, A. McGrew, D. Goldblatt and J. Perraton, *Global Transformations: Politics, Economics & Culture*, Cambridge: Polity Press, 1999

L. Henkin, *How Nations Behave: Law and Foreign Policy*, New York: Columbia University Press, 1979

J. L. Holzgrefe and R. O. Keohane (eds), *Humanitarian Intervention: Ethical, Legal and Political Dilemmas*, Cambridge: Cambridge University Press, 2005

M. Howard, G. J. Andreopoulos and M. R. Shulman, *The Laws of War: Constraints on Warfare in the Western World*, New Haven: Yale University Press, 1994

I. Hurd, *After Anarchy: Legitimacy and Power in the United Nations Security Council*, Princeton, NJ: Princeton University Press, 2007

Independent International Commission on Kosovo, *Kosovo Report*, Oxford: Oxford University Press, 2000

International Bar Association, *International Terrorism: Legal Challenges and Responses*, New York: Transnational Publishers, 2003

International Commission on Intervention and State Sovereignty, *The Responsibility to Protect*, Ottawa: International Development Research Centre, 2001

R. Jackson, *The Global Covenant: Human Conduct in a World of States*, Oxford: Oxford University Press, 2000

J. T. Johnson, *The Quest for Peace: Three Moral Traditions in Western Cultural History*, Princeton: Princeton University Press, 1987

M. Kaldor, *Human Security: Reflections on Globalization and Intervention*, Cambridge: Polity Press, 2007

D. Kennedy, *Of War and Law*, Princeton: Princeton University Press, 2006

R. Kerr and E. Mobekk, *Peace and Justice: Seeking Accountability After* War, Cambridge: Polity, 2007

P. J. van Krieken, *Terrorism and the International Legal Order*, The Hague: TMC Asser Press, 2002

T. Landman, *Studying Human Rights*, London: Routledge, 2005

A. Lang (ed.) *Just Intervention*, Washington, DC: Georgetown University Press, 2002

K. N. Llwelleyn, *The Common Law Tradition*, Boston: Little, Brown, 1960

D. Malone, *The International Struggle Over Iraq: Politics in the UN Security Council 1980–2005*, Oxford: Oxford University Press, 2006

J. Mertus, *The United Nations and Human Rights*, London: Routledge, 2009

M. Michalski and J. Gow, *War, Image and Legitimacy: Viewing Contemporary Conflict*, London: Routledge, 2007

D. Moeckli, *Human Rights and Non-Discrimination in the 'War on Terror'*, Oxford: Oxford University Press, 2008

P. Neumann, *Old and New Terrorism*, Cambridge: Polity, 2009

M. Newman, *Humanitarian Intervention: Confronting the Contradictions*, Hurst & Co: London, 2009

A. Orford (ed.), *International Law and its Others*, Cambridge: Cambridge University Press, 2009

B. Orend, *The Morality of War*, Peterborough, Ontario: Broadview Press, 2006

D. L. Phillips, *Losing Iraq: Inside the Post-War Reconstruction Fiasco*, New York: Basic Books, 2006

C. Reed and D. Ryall (eds), *The Price of Peace*, Cambridge: Cambridge University Press, 2007

G. M. Reichberg, H. Syse and E. Begbe (eds), *The Ethics of War: Classical and Contemporary Readings*, Malden, MA: Blackwell, 2006

D. Rejali, *Torture and Democracy*, Princeton: Princeton University Press, 2005

G. Robertson, *Crimes Against Humanity*, London: Penguin, 2002

P. Rogers, *Why We're Losing the War on Terror*, London: Polity, 2008

M. Sageman, *Understanding Terror Networks*, Philadelphia, PA: University of Pennsylvania Press, 2004

P. Sands, *Lawless World: America and the Making and Breaking of Global Rules*, London: Penguin, 2005

B. Saul, *Defining Terrorism in International Law*, Oxford: Oxford University Press, 2006

W. Schabas, *Genocide in International Law: The Crimes of Crimes*, Cambridge: Cambridge University Press, 2000

O. Schachter, *International Law in Theory and Practice*, Dordrecht: Kluwer Academic Publishers, 1991

M. Schmitt and B. O'Donnell (eds), *Computer Network Attack and International Law*, Newport, Rhode Island: Naval War College, 2002

R. Scruton, *The West and the Rest: Globalization and the Terrorist Threat*, London: Continuum, 2002

B. Simma, H. Mosler, A. Paulus, E. Chatidou and M. Giuliano (eds), *The Charter of the United Nations. A Commentary*, Oxford: Oxford University Press, 2002

G. Simpson, *Great Powers and Outlaw States*, Cambridge: Cambridge University Press, 2004

G. Simpson, *War, Law and Crime: War Crimes Trials and the Reinvention of International Law*, Cambridge: Polity, 2007

R. Smith, *The Utility of Force: The Art of War in the Modern World*, London: Penguin, 2006

R. Thakur, *The United Nations, Peace and Security: From Collective Security to Responsibility to Protect*, Cambridge: Cambridge University Press, 2008

R. Thakur and W. P. S. Sidhu (eds), *The Iraq Crisis and World Order: Structural, Institutional and Normative Challenges*, New York: United Nations University Press, 2006

R. Thompson, *Defeating Communist Insurgency*, St Petersburg, FL: Hailer Publishing, 2005

L. Vidino, *Al Qaeda in Europe: The New Battleground of International Jihad*, New York: Prometheus Books, 2006

M. Walzer, *Just and Unjust Wars*, New York: Basic Books, 1991

J. Welsh (ed.), *Humanitarian Intervention and International Relations*, Oxford: Oxford University Press, 2006

R. Wertheimer (ed.), *Empowering our Military Conscience*, Farnham: Ashgate, 2010

N. J. Wheeler, *Saving Strangers*, Oxford: Oxford University Press, 2002

P. Wilkinson, *Terrorism Versus Democracy*, Abingdon: Routledge, 2006

J. Yoo, *The Powers Of War And Peace: The Constitution And Foreign Affairs After 9/11*, Chicago: University of Chicago Press, 2005

J. Yoo, *War by Other Means: An Insider's Account of the War on Terror*, New York: Atlantic Monthly Press, 2006

J. Yoo, *Crisis and Command: The History of Executive Power From George Washington to George W. Bush*, New York: Kaplan, 2009

Index

For Product Safety Concerns and Information please contact our EU
representative GPSR@taylorandfrancis.com
Taylor & Francis Verlag GmbH, Kaufingerstraße 24, 80331 München, Germany

www.ingramcontent.com/pod-product-compliance
Lightning Source LLC
Chambersburg PA
CBHW070417270326
41926CB00014B/2827

9 780415 724104